See Australia

National Parks

See Australia

National Parks

Ron & Viv Moon

Enjoying the beauty of
Australia's natural heritage

Publisher	Gordon Cheers
Associate Publisher	Margaret Olds
Art Director	Stan Lamond
Managing Editor	Kate Etherington
Senior Editor	Dannielle Doggett
Editor	Denise Imwold
Captions	Margaret McPhee Susan Page
Cover Design	Stan Lamond
Cartographer	John Frith
Map Editors	Louise Buchanan Heather McNamara Dee Rogers
Picture Research	Gordon Cheers
Photo Library	Alan Edwards
Typesetting	Dee Rogers
Index	Heather McNamara
Publishing Assistant	Erin King
Production	Rosemary Barry Bernard Roberts

Photographers

Fred Adler, Chris Bell, Rob Blakers, Lorraine Blyth, Ken Brass, Claver Carroll, Anna Cheifetz, Kevin Deacon, Grant Dixon, Mike Edmondson, Bruce Elder, Stuart Owen Fox, Peter Gill, Denise Greig, Ivy Hansen, Richard I'Anson, Ionas Kaltenbach, Judith Kempen, Colin Kerr, Stan Lamond, Mike Langford, Gary Lewis, John McCann, David McGonigal, Richard McKenna, Shane Mensforth, Ron Moon, Peter O'Reilly, Nick Rains, Jamie Robertson, Tony Rodd, Don Skirrow, Raoul Slater, Steve Starling, Ken Stepnell, Oliver Strewe, Glenn Tempest, Sharyn Vanderhorst, Colleen Vigar, Neil Wehlack, Murray White, Vic Widman, Geoff Woods, Grant Young, James Young

Captions for preliminary pages and state opening spreads

Page 1: Cascades of water in a mossy creekbed in Franklin–Gordon Wild Rivers National Park, Tasmania.
Page 2: Porcupine grass and ghost gums in Karijini National Park, Northern Territory.
Page 3: Red-winged parrot in Sundown National Park, Queensland.
Page 4: Kangaroo in Cape Range National Park, Western Australia.
Page 6: Walls of Jerusalem National Park, Tasmania.
Pages 12–13: Mount Mooloolong, in the KaKa Mundi Section of Queensland's Carnarvon National Park, at sunset.
Pages 52–53: Seven Mile Beach National Park, on the New South Wales south coast.
Pages 96–97: Looking towards Buffalo Plateau, Alpine National Park, Victoria.
Pages 140–141: Walls of Jerusalem National Park, Tasmania.
Pages 162–163: Aerial view of Lake Eyre, Lake Eyre National Park, South Australia.
Pages 192–193: The Pinnacles at Nambung National Park, Western Australia.
Pages 228–229: View of Kata Tjuta (the Olgas) from the top of Uluru (Ayers Rock), Northern Territory.

Published by
Gregory's Publishing Company
(A division of Universal Press Pty Ltd)
ACN 000 087 132

Marketed and distributed by Universal Press Pty Ltd
New South Wales: 1 Waterloo Road, Macquarie Park 2113
Ph: (02) 9857 3700 Fax: (02) 9888 9850
Queensland: 1 Manning Street, South Brisbane 4101
Ph: (07) 3844 1051 Fax: (07) 3844 4637
South Australia: Freecall: 1800 021 987
Victoria: 585 Burwood Road, Hawthorn 3122
Ph: (03) 9818 4455 Fax: (03) 9818 6123
Western Australia: 38a Walters Drive, Osborne Park 6017
Ph: (08) 9244 2488 Fax: (08) 9244 2554

Produced by Global Book Publishing Pty Ltd
1/181 High Street, Willoughby, NSW Australia 2068
Phone 61 2 9967 3100 fax 61 2 9967 5891

ISBN 0 7319 1448 1

National Library of Australia Cataloguing-in-Publication

Moon, Ron.
    See Australia : national parks.

    ISBN 0 7319 1448 1.

    1. National parks and reserves - Australia - Guidebooks. 2. Australia - Guidebooks. I. Moon, Viv. II. Title.
    (Series : See Australia (Sydney)).

    919.4047

Printed in Hong Kong by Sing Cheong Printing Co. Ltd, Film separation Pica Digital Pte Ltd, Singapore

Disclaimer

The authors and publisher disclaim any responsibility to any person for loss or damage suffered from any use of this guide for any purpose. While considerable care has been taken by the authors and the publisher in researching and compiling the guide, the authors and the publisher accept no responsibility for errors or omissions. No person should rely upon this guide for the purpose of making any business, investment or real estate decision.
The representation on any maps of any road or track is not necessarily evidence of public right of way. Third parties who have provided information to the author and publisher concerning the roads and other matters did not warrant to the author and publisher that the information was complete, accurate or current or that any of the proposals of any body will eventuate and, accordingly, the author and publisher provide no such warranty.

Photographers

Global Book Publishing would be pleased to hear from photographers interested in supplying photographs.

Key to Road Maps

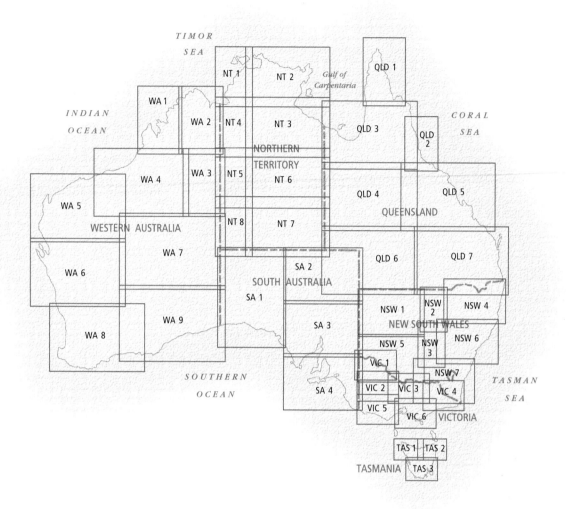

TIMOR
SEA

NT 1   NT 2   Gulf of
Carpentaria

QLD 1

WA 1

INDIAN
OCEAN

WA 2   NT 4   NT 3

QLD 3

QLD
2

CORAL
SEA

NORTHERN
TERRITORY

WA 3   NT 5

WA 4

NT 6

QLD 4

QLD 5

WA 5

WESTERN AUSTRALIA

NT 8   NT 7

QUEENSLAND

WA 7

SA 2

QLD 6

QLD 7

WA 6

SOUTH AUSTRALIA

SA 1

WA 9

SA 3

NSW 1   NSW
2

NSW 4

NEW SOUTH WALES

WA 8

NSW 5   NSW
3

NSW 6

VIC 1

SOUTHERN

OCEAN

SA 4

VIC 2   VIC 3

NSW 7

VIC 4

TASMAN
SEA

VIC 5

VIC 6   VICTORIA

TASMANIA   TAS 1   TAS 2

TAS 3

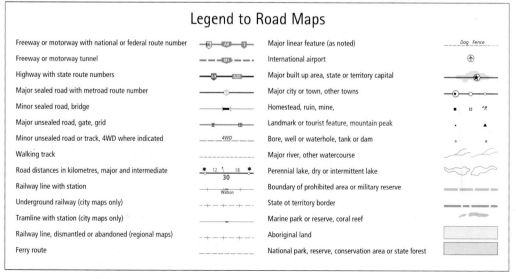

Legend to Road Maps

Freeway or motorway with national or federal route number		Major linear feature (as noted)	Dog Fence
Freeway or motorway tunnel		International airport	
Highway with state route numbers		Major built up area, state or territory capital	
Major sealed road with metroad route number		Major city or town, other towns	
Minor sealed road, bridge		Homestead, ruin, mine,	
Major unsealed road, gate, grid		Landmark or tourist feature, mountain peak	
Minor unsealed road or track, 4WD where indicated	4WD	Bore, well or waterhole, tank or dam	
Walking track		Major river, other watercourse	
Road distances in kilometres, major and intermediate	12 18 30	Perennial lake, dry or intermittent lake	
Railway line with station	Watson	Boundary of prohibited area or military reserve	
Underground railway (city maps only)		State ot territory border	
Tramline with station (city maps only)		Marine park or reserve, coral reef	
Railway line, dismantled or abandoned (regional maps)		Aboriginal land	
Ferry route		National park, reserve, conservation area or state forest	

Contents

See and Experience Australia's National Parks

Australia is an ancient land. The country we see today, and the plants and animals that inhabit it, are the result of eons of upheavals, weathering and dramatic climatic change. Some of the most ancient rocks on earth, dated to about 4500 million years old, are found in Western Australia. More recently, the invasion of the continent by humans has shaped the landscape.

It was, however, when Australia separated from the supercontinent of Gondwanaland, which started to break up about 180 million years ago, that the chain of events that really shaped this continent began. By around 55 million years ago, Australia was a single landmass floating north through the Indian Ocean. The animals that remained on this great, isolated raft began to develop into the monotremes and marsupials we know so well today.

Right: The mist-shrouded valleys of Lamington National Park are a refuge for many different species of plants, birds and animals in south-east Queensland.

Over the last 40 million years our continent has seen waves of invaders come and settle. First on the scene were probably bats flying in from the ever-closer continent of Asia and the island of Papua New Guinea.

Rodents followed and as the ice ages waxed and waned more and more animals made it to our shores.

Finally, some 50 000 to 100 000 years ago, humans floated on primitive rafts across the relatively narrow watery gaps that remained in the island chain that linked Australia with Asia. These settlers came via Indonesia and Papua New Guinea in a number of waves and, as traditional hunters and gatherers, spread out right across the continent.

The last group of settlers came from a faraway shore just a couple of hundred years ago and today their descendants, and those of the plants and animals

Twenty million years ago the ancestors of today's lizards were crawling along the rainforest floor. Today's lizards have adapted to a wide range of habitats.

they introduced, dominate much of the land and its flora and fauna.

A Rich Tapestry of Parks

This rich and varied heritage of our continent—its plants, animals and human history—is protected in the parks and reserves dotted across the vast Australian landscape, so that it can be seen and experienced.

Alpine meadows in the high country of New South Wales and Victoria; rich verdant rainforests in Queensland; the floodplains and escarpments of the Northern Territory; impenetrable temperate forests and untouched rivers in Tasmania; towering gums in the south-west of Western Australia; and the untracked desert country and outback

Below: *Nigli Gap in Keep River National Park in the Northern Territory. The rugged cliffs are a legacy of volcanic and glacial activity that shaped the landforms in this area.*

mountain ranges in South Australia: these are just some of the landscapes in our parks. All offer not only a safe habitat for our unique flora and fauna, but also places where we can seek solace, enjoyment and adventure as we get back to nature.

Australia is fortunate that it has the landmass and the lack of population pressure to incorporate much of its natural treasures in parks and reserves of significant size. In the last 25 years, with a growing awareness of our natural heritage, each state and territory has vastly increased the amount of land protected in national parks and reserves, with some of those parks in excess of one million hectares. Some parks are bigger than European countries!

Picturesque Cephissus Falls, in Tasmania's Cradle Mountain–Lake St Clair National Park is one of many scenic spots that reward bushwalkers prepared to spend some time trekking through the park.

Experiencing Our Wonderland of Parks and Reserves

Many national parks, forest scenic reserves, state parks and conservation parks have easy access and facilities such as developed camping grounds, picnic areas, toilets, and walking tracks with wheelchair access; other parks can only be reached by 4WD, and have remote area camping with few, if any, facilities.

Right: Litchfield National Park is an easy 2 hours' drive from Darwin, in the Northern Territory. The park has bush camping areas as well as areas with BBQ and toilet facilities, but visitors must be totally self-sufficient.

While bushwalking is permitted in most of our parks, with many parks having designated tracks and day walking trails, other activities may have restrictions placed on them. Wheeled transport such as mountain-bike riding, trail-bike riding and four-wheel driving are limited, or banned completely, in some of our parks.

A few parks and reserves in Australia have no access and no facilities at all, closed for very strong and compelling environmental reasons, the exception being for scientific research.

The Whitsunday Islands National Park, off Queensland's coast. Whitsunday Island is the largest island in the group, and has the best camping facilities.

Parklands are costly to maintain and most charge an entry fee. Charges vary from state to state and from park to park. Some have an entrance fee and others just a camping fee, while some parks have no fees at all.

Most states have a pass system of some sort where for the payment of an annual fee, you can camp in many of the parks and reserves in that state, or in certain areas of the state, for a considerable saving over the daily rate. Then there is the matter of rules and regulations. These too vary from state to state and from park to park, and especially between a state's national parks, state parks, conservation parks and forest reserves.

It is worth contacting each state's national parks' organisation for information on facilities, access, charges, regulations, and to find out if they operate any park pass systems. A good place to start is on the web, at each state's national park site.

Left: *A cross-country skier in Victoria's Alpine National Park. Although the northern half of Australia is tropical, there are plenty of opportunities for snow sports in parks in New South Wales, Tasmania and Victoria.*

Far left: *Visitors to Drovers Cave National Park in Western Australia. This park caters mainly to experienced cavers, but bushwalkers will also find the area of interest.*

Where to Go, What to See

The choice is endless and really only limited by your imagination and your experience. The lists that follow are just to get you started—they are by no means comprehensive.

Bushwalkers can stretch their legs in so many parks around the country it is almost impossible to name them all. For starters there's Blue Mountains National Park in New South Wales; Alpine National Park in Victoria; Flinders Ranges National Park in South Australia; Cradle Mountain–Lake St Clair National Park in Tasmania; Stirling Ranges National Park in Western Australia; Lamington National Park in Queensland; and West MacDonnell National Park in the Northern Territory. Each offers a unique and vastly different walking experience.

For skiers the choice might not be so great, but there are the vast Kosciuszko and Alpine National Parks along with the smaller but no less unique Baw Baw National Park and Mount Buffalo National Park, both in Victoria, while

Tasmania has Ben Lomond and Mount Field National Parks.

For those who love to spend their days afloat there are the waters around Wilsons Promontory National Park in Victoria; Myall Lakes National Park in New South Wales; Whitsunday Islands National Park in Queensland; Gurig National Park in the Northern Territory; Cape Range National Park in Western Australia; Coorong National Park in South Australia; and Franklin–Gordon Wild Rivers National Park in Tasmania.

Rock climbers, four-wheel drivers, history lovers, photographers and nature watchers all can claim their piece of paradise in Australia's national parks. There are adventures and experiences to last (and to take) a lifetime. You'd better start now!

Bird-watching is a popular activity in many national parks. Australia has about 700 bird species, with many, such as the emu (Dromaius novaehollandiae) unique to this country.

on the net

QUEENSLAND
Environmental Protection
  Agency
www.epa.qld.gov.au

NEW SOUTH WALES
National Parks and Wildlife
  Service
www.npws.nsw.gov.au/parks

VICTORIA
Parks Victoria
www.parkweb.vic.gov.au

TASMANIA
Department of Primary
  Industries, Water and
  Environment
Parks and Wildlife
www.dpiwe.tas.gov.au

NORTHERN TERRITORY
Commonwealth Parks and
  Reserves
Parks Australia–Environment
  Australia Parks and Reserves
www.ea.gov.au/parks

NORTHERN TERRITORY
Government Parks and Wildlife
Parks and Wildlife Commission
  of the Northern Territory
www.nt.gov.au/paw/parks/parks.
  htm

SOUTH AUSTRALIA
Department of Environment
  and Heritage
www.dehaa.sa.gov.au/parks

WESTERN AUSTRALIA
Department of Conservation
  and Land Management
www.calm.wa.gov.au

Queensland

Queensland's national parks system is the most diverse in the nation, encompassing tropical rainforests, deserts, melaleuca heathland, granite country, mangrove-lined estuaries, eucalypt forests and beautiful islands bordered by coral reefs. The state's 220 national parks provide homes and protection for many varieties of wildlife, including some of Australia's rarest and most endangered creatures and plants, as well as Australian Aboriginal artworks and artefacts. Apart from providing a protected habitat for wildlife, Queensland's national parks offer visitors numerous opportunities to enjoy the great outdoors. The coastal and island parks are the most popular, but the inland parks also offer visitors a variety of experiences and delights.

Daintree National Park

Stretching along the coast from the Daintree River in the south to the Bloomfield River in the north, the Daintree National Park is divided into two parts, the larger centred around the Mossman River and Gorge, and the other spread along the coast between the Daintree River and the Bloomfield River, further north.

fact file

WHERE: The Mossman Gorge section is located 80 km north of Cairns; the Cape Tribulation section starts another 25 km further north Map: Qld 3 N3

WHEN: End of April until October

WHY: Bushwalking, bird-watching, 4WD

SIZE: 73 600 ha

RANGER: Cape Tribulation (07) 4098 0052; Mossman Gorge (07) 4098 2188; Mission Beach (07) 4068 7183

The park is a spectacular wilderness of rugged mountain ranges, fast-flowing streams, towering rainforest trees and lush, tangled undergrowth in myriad shades of green. At Cape Tribulation the visitor can experience the splendour of north Queensland's tropical rain-forests while being only a stone's throw from the World Heritage listed Great Barrier Reef.

In the Past

The 56 500 hectare Mossman Gorge section of the Daintree National Park is 80 km north of Cairns, while the 17 100 hectare Cape Tribulation section is 104 km north of the city. These two sections of park were combined in 1988 to become an important component in the Wet Tropics World Heritage Area that takes in much of the surrounding range country.

Captain James Cook named Cape Tribulation itself when his ship, the *Endeavour*, was holed on a reef just north of the cape in 1770. The Aboriginal word for the cape—'Kurranji', which means casso-wary—was the name used by the Kuku Yalanji people who had lived in this piece of coastal paradise for thousands of years.

Wildlife

Because of its wide range in elevation from sea level to more than 1300 metres above that, the Cape Tribulation area is home to some of Australia's rarest types of mammals. The largest and most spec-tacular of these is the Bennett's tree-

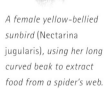

A female yellow-bellied sunbird (Nectarina jugularis), using her long curved beak to extract food from a spider's web.

kangaroo. Confined almost entirely to the rainforests of Cape Tribulation and nearby Cedar Bay to the north, this little-known marsupial is more often heard than seen as it crashes through the forest canopy.

The smallest member of the kangaroo family, the musky rat-kangaroo, is also only found here. In many ways it is more particularly like a possum, not only in looks, but also in its ability to climb trees.

Another rarely encountered rainforest resident is the Herbert River ringtail possum. Found only at altitudes of 300 metres above sea level, this beautiful black and white possum is sometimes seen at night with the aid of a torch.

QLD

Bird life in both the Mossman Gorge and Cape Tribulation sections is varied and prolific. The large flightless cassowary, which often stands up to 2 metres tall, is occasionally sighted by bush-walkers on rainforest tracks. Never try and get too close to these stocky, helmeted birds as they can inflict serious injuries with their powerful legs.

Unfortunately, cassowaries have become rare due to land clearing, and even in protected places like the Daintree they are threatened by feral pigs that destroy their nests.

Light scratching sounds in the leaf litter on the forest floor usually indicate the presence of chowchillas nearby. These conspicuous 28 cm long birds,

with their dark brown backs and white and orange neck and chest markings, are confined to the Wet Tropics region. The large brush-turkey and the slightly smaller orange-footed scrubfowl are other ground dwellers regularly seen in the park.

Above: *The coastal lowland rainforest of Cape Tribulation reaches right to the shoreline, giving the cape the label of 'where the rainforest meets the reef'.*

Left: *The southern cassowary (Casuorius casuorius) has a bony 'helmet' to protect its head. This flightless bird lives in the dense undergrowth of the rainforest.*

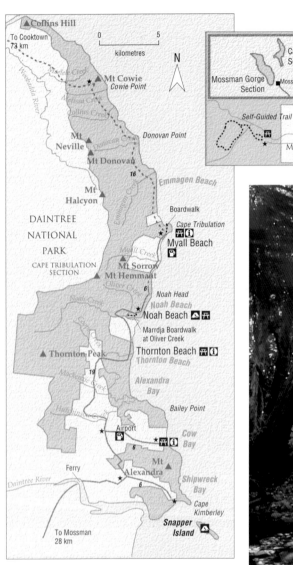

Below: *The dense canopy of the tropical rainforest trees blocks out much of the sunlight, but there are still plenty of plants growing alongside the creeks.*

The white-lipped tree frog (Litoria infrafrenata), like all Australia's tree frogs, is a descendant of ancestors existing before the Australian continent separated from Gondwana. It is about 13 cm long, one of the largest frogs in the world.

At least six species of rainforest pigeons inhabit the Daintree. The largest and most impressive of these is the colourful wompoo fruit-dove which spends most of its time in the upper canopy. Other pigeons include the superb fruit dove and the Torresian imperial pigeon.

Another impressive bird of this area is the brilliantly plumed buff-breasted paradise kingfisher, which breeds in this region but migrates to New Guinea for the cooler months of the year.

Activities

A short track from the car park leads along the edge of the Mossman River to a popular swimming and cooling-off spot. But beware, the fast current flow can be dangerous and the slippery rocks can trap the unwary. The river is also subject to flash flooding and a number of drownings have occurred here.

A walking track continues over the swinging bridge across Rex Creek and takes you along a self-guided walk through the rainforest. This 2.7 km loop trail follows Rex Creek for a section and brings you back to the swing bridge.

There are no easily accessible waterfalls, despite some maps showing them. In fact, most of the Mossman Gorge section of the Daintree is wilderness that is virtually inaccessible. Anyone trying to hike in this beautiful region should be a fully

experienced and equipped bushwalker. Those intending to hike in the park need to discuss their plans with park staff and complete a bushwalking registration form. Bushwalkers also require a permit if they plan to camp overnight in the remote areas of the park. Permits can be obtained before setting out from the Queensland Parks and Wildlife Service office in Mossman.

Roaring Meg Falls are in the north of the park, on the upper Bloomfield River. These falls can only be reached by 4WD vehicles; the 2-hour drive goes past some spectacular scenery.

There are some beautiful walks in the Cape Tribulation section, including the 4 hour return trip from Myall Beach, just south of Cape Tribulation, to Emmagen Creek. Walkers should start this hike on the outgoing tide so they can skirt around the rocks at Emmagen Beach.

At the Kulki picnic area at Cape Tribulation, a 400 m boardwalk leads from the car park to a viewing platform overlooking the sea and the beach. From Dubuji there is a 1200 m boardwalk through rainforest, swamp and mangrove areas.

At Oliver Creek, near Noah Beach, the very interesting Marrdja Boardwalk winds its way for 800 metres through mangroves and rainforest.

South of Cow Bay village, the Jindalba picnic area is the starting point for two walking trails, a short one providing good views over the rainforest and a longer hiking trail.

did you know?

Many of the rainforest plants in this park are relict species that have grown in these forests for tens of millions of years. This area has the highest concentration of primitive flowering plants in the world.

The rock orchid (Dendro-bium speciosum) is one of many epiphytic plants growing on the rainforest trees, which may play host to ferns, fungi and mosses as well as orchids.

The beautiful beaches north and south of Cape Tribulation are great for swimming from late April until the end of September when bluebottles and other marine stingers are absent. Never swim anywhere near the mouth of a saltwater creek or in the Daintree and Bloomfield Rivers, as estuarine crocodiles inhabit these places.

You can also enjoy snorkelling and sea kayaking along this coast.

The beach, reefs and coastal waters are protected in the Great Barrier Reef Marine Park and fishing and spearfishing, as well as any collecting, are prohibited within the designated National Park zone north of, and including Cape Tribulation. South of Cape Tribulation limited line fishing and bait netting are allowed.

The drive north from Cape Tribulation to the Bloomfield River is only suitable for 4WD vehicles but is a highlight of a trip to this park. Numerous steep, slippery climbs mean that this trip is generally reserved for the dry season, and it is closed after heavy rain. Check with the RACQ by phoning 1300 130 595 or (07) 4033 6433, for current road conditions.

Access

The best way to the Mossman Gorge section of the park is to drive north along the Cook Highway for 76 km until you reach Mossman. A 5 km bitumen road connects the town to the picnic ground at Mossman Gorge.

To reach Cape Tribulation, go north from Mossman for 28 km until you reach the Daintree River ferry, which operates 6 am to midnight, 7 days a week except Good Friday and Christmas Day. It is free to use!

From the northern side of the Daintree River the bitumen road winds

for about 40 km through private land and segments of the national park until it reaches Cape Tribulation.

Motorists who want to continue on to the Bloomfield River from Cape Tribulation must do so in a 4WD vehicle. This road is graded dirt, and is often impassable after heavy rain. Drive slowly to avoid hitting wildlife. It makes an enjoyable way to go to Cooktown.

Camping

Apart from bush camping, there are no facilities for camping in the Mossman Gorge section of the park.

The main camping ground in the Cape Tribulation section is at Noah Beach, 8 km south of Cape Tribulation. Toilets, showers and drinking water are provided. Camp fires are prohibited in the park, and only fuel stoves should be used. The camping area is closed during the wet season.

Snapper Island, south of Cape Kimberley, has four camping sites with toilet and barbecue facilities. A permit from the Queensland Parks and Wildlife Service in Cairns or Mossman is essential.

Private camping areas, hostels, resorts and holiday units can be found adjacent to the Cape Tribulation section of the park and there is some accommodation in Mossman township.

Although most of the Mossman Gorge Section is undeveloped, part of the gorge itself is easily accessible. In some places there are quiet pools; in others the water swirls through rocks.

Below: *Perhaps the most luxurious of the accommodation options for Daintree visitors, Silky Oaks Lodge is surrounded by trees and overlooks a natural lagoon.*

dingoes

The dingoes on Fraser are the purest strain of dingoes in Australia and in many ways the island is probably the best place to see the wild dogs at close quarters.

However, because people have fed the dogs, many attacks on humans, especially young children, have occurred. Feeding the dingoes is now completely banned and fines apply for people found doing so. Children should not be left alone.

are crystal clear with white sandy bottoms, others have a reddish colour which comes from tea-trees growing near the lake. The water is so pure in the lakes that only three species of small fish live in them.

Apart from the dune lakes the island has a number of freshwater streams which flow consistently throughout the year. Eli Creek is the biggest of these.

The biggest stream on the island is Eli Creek, which flows onto the eastern beach a few kilometres south of the *Maheno* shipwreck. At numerous other places along the beach fresh water bubbles out of the sand, providing easy access to good drinking water. None of this water has to be boiled as the sand filters out any impurities.

Activities

For more than 70 years visitors have been travelling to Fraser Island to enjoy its fantastic fishing. At the height of the season, between July and October, hundreds of anglers from around Australia gather on the surf beaches of the island's east coast to try their luck and skills against the huge schools of taylor which migrate up the coast.

Other fish found on the east coast beaches include silver bream, jewfish and golden trevally. In the calm waters on the western side of the island flathead, whiting, bream and a few other species of fish can be caught throughout the year. Mud crabs are also present in

good numbers around the mangrove-lined estuaries on the western side of the island, although you will probably need a small boat to get to the places where you can drop your crab pots.

Since there are no formed roads on Fraser Island, a 4WD vehicle is necessary if you want to explore the island. Some of the inland tracks are difficult to negotiate due to the soft sand; you should try to keep your beach driving within 2 hours either side of low tide. It is best to keep tyres deflated to around 140 kPa (20 psi).

As visitor numbers increase, accidents on the inland sandy tracks are becoming all too common, so take care.

Apart from walks along Fraser Island's beautiful coastline, there are numerous forest hiking trails in the central and southern parts of the island. One excellent track to start out on is the 6 km Lake Birrabeen to Central Station walk, which would take about 2 hours one way. Birdwatchers will love this track as it meanders through a wide variety of the park's vegetation. A short walking track at Central Station (25 minutes one way) follows the crystal clear Wanggoolba Creek past towering brush box, hoop pine, white beech, ribbon wood and strangler figs.

Access

Fraser Island is approximately 190 km north of Brisbane. The island can be reached by a number of methods including vehicular barges, passenger launches, aircraft or private boats.

A 4WD vehicle is essential for driving on the island. If you don't have your own, they can be hired at Hervey Bay, Rainbow Beach, the Sunshine Coast and Brisbane.

People bringing a vehicle to Fraser Island must get a RAM vehicle permit

The beach at Waddy Point is a good launching spot for the fantastic reef fishing on the Gardner Banks east of Waddy Point and Indian Head.

An aerial view of Fraser Island shows the blanket of sand-adapted vegetation that covers most of the inland area. The plant types include grasses, eucalypt and banksia woodland and sub-tropical rainforest.

did you know?

Fraser Island is the largest sand island in the world. It is 123 km from north to south and 25 km across at its widest point. It was formed from the sediments carried by rivers to the coast over hundreds of thousands of years.

and attach it to their car windscreen. The permit is valid for one month. Normal road rules apply for beach driving.

There are five vehicular barges that service Fraser Island. On the southern end of the island two barges operate between Hook Point and Inskip Point just north of Rainbow Beach, phone (07) 5486 3227.

From Hervey Bay, barges to Wanggoolba Creek and Kingfisher Bay depart from River Heads. The barge to Moon Point leaves from Urangan boat harbour. Bookings are required for the three Hervey Bay barges, phone (07) 4125 4444.

Visitors who arrive by light aircraft will land either at Toby's Gap, which is managed by the Queensland Parks and Wildlife Service, or at Wanggoolba Creek, which is managed by the Eurong Beach Resort. Landing permission and entry permits are needed for private aircraft before arrival. Contact airstrip managers or Queensland Parks and Wildlife Service, Maryborough, phone (07) 4121 1800.

Camping and Accommodation

The Queensland Parks and Wildlife Service has camping grounds at Lake Boomanjin, Central Station, Lake Allom, Waddy Point, Wathumba, Dundubara and Lake McKenzie. Facilities in these places include toilets, picnic tables, barbecues and showers (except for Lake Allom). Lake McKenzie and Dundubara are the only places that are suitable for camper trailers.

Beach camping is permitted at undeveloped sites along the east coast and at some spots on the west coast. Always select existing formed beach camp sites.

Private camp grounds, suitable for caravans, exist at Cathedral Beach Resort, phone (07) 4127 9177 and Dilli Village, phone (07) 4127 9130.

Motel type accommodation is available at Eurong, phone (07) 4127 9122; Dilli Village, phone (07) 4127 9130; Happy Valley, phone (07) 4127 9144; and Kingfisher Bay Resort, phone 1800 072 555.

The Australian pelican (Pelecanus conspicillatus) is found near the water (seasides, lakes and rivers) throughout most of Australia, as well as on islands like Fraser.

Cooloola

The Cooloola section of the Great Sandy National Park protects the largest tract of natural land on Queensland's southern coast. Spectacular sand dunes and the tranquil headwaters of the Noosa River are the main highlights.

Lakes are also a major feature of this section of the park and Poona, nestled high in the dunes, is one of the five main perched lakes found in Cooloola. Apart from a few little grebes and musk ducks, Poona is almost devoid of waterfowl. In contrast, other larger lakes such as Cootharaba are slightly brackish and teem with marine life that provide food for many species of birds such as pelicans and sea-eagles.

One of the many other features of Cooloola is its rainforests. An excellent way to experience the tranquillity of these forests is to do the 4.4 km, 2 hour return walk to Lake Poona.

In the Past

The Kabi people were the original inhabitants of this area, but, as on Fraser Island, when the timber-getters arrived in the 1840s the local people were almost wiped out by the diseases that came with the new arrivals.

Activities

Surf fishing is a favourite pastime at Cooloola, with whiting, bream and flathead among the frequent catches. River fishing is also popular, as is swimming, though marine stingers can be a problem when northeasterlies blow.

Canoeing is the best way to explore the Noosa River. Canoes can be hired from Elanda Point. The park has a number of 4WD tracks leading through it or onto the beach. There are many walks in the area to enjoy.

Access and Camping

There are two approaches to the park. Coming from the south you turn off the Bruce Highway near Eumundi and continue to Tewantin and catch the ferry across the Noosa River. From there a gravel track a few kilometres long brings you to the track which leads to the beach. The second approach is from the north: take the Tin Can Bay turn-off at Gympie and continue for about 47 km until the turn-off to Rainbow Beach. Five km before you reach this small town you will see a national parks sign to the Freshwater camping area.

The Freshwater camping area is the most developed, but there are other sites on the banks of Noosa River, at Poverty Point and on the Cooloola Wilderness Trail. You can also camp on the beach between the Noosa Shire boundary and Little Freshwater Creek. Sites should be booked in advance with the ranger.

Flaked stone tools like these ones found in Cooloola were used by Australian Aboriginals in many areas of Queensland. Tools made from bone, teeth and wood were also used.

Opposite page: Tall rainforest trees near Lake Poona grow in sand. Open forests of blackbutt and tallowwood as well as coastal heaths are also found in Cooloola.

---

tourist info

Kinaba Information Centre, Elanda Point
(07) 5449 7364

Carnarvon National Park

The area comprising Carnarvon National Park is only a part of the massive Consuelo Tableland. This predominantly sandstone region rises to 900 metres and is home to four of eastern Australia's major river systems.

fact file

WHERE: 720 km north-west of Brisbane
Map: Qld 7 D1

WHEN: June to November (summer can be very hot)

WHY: Breathtaking scenery, good walking tracks, 4WD

SIZE: 298 000 ha

RANGER: (07) 4984 4505

The park is made up of a number of different sections: Carnarvon Gorge, Buckland Tableland, Ka Ka Mundi, Goodliffe, Salvator Rosa, Mount Moffat and Moolayember. Although Carnarvon Gorge occupies only a fraction of the park, it is by far the most scenic and easily accessible section.

The main 30 km long gorge was created by Carnarvon Creek. Vertical sandstone cliffs, some up to 200 metres high, rise up from the gorge floor, their colours varying from brilliant whites through to yellow, orange and brown.

A wide variety of wildlife can be observed while walking through the gorge. The diversity of plant life found in the park provides many ideal habitats for the area's numerous bird species.

Australian Aboriginal rock art at the 'Art Gallery' which is one of the largest and most interesting of the fifty-odd rock art sites in the park.

Magnificent Aboriginal Rock Art

The original Australian Aboriginals have long since vanished from the area, leaving only their unique artistry behind them. For thousands of years they depicted their way of life on the undersides of many of the large rock overhangs found throughout the gorge.

Cathedral Cave, one of the largest rock art sites so far discovered, is about 10 km from the

day-use area. Boomerangs, spears, emus' feet and goannas are pictured on one side of this large sandstone wall, while on another section human hands, which signify a person's relationship to one particular place, are found.

The 'Art Gallery' is another stone-age masterpiece—which has been carbon-dated at over 4000 years—and is found 500 metres off the main track.

Activities

At least 3 or 4 days should be set aside to visit Carnarvon just to explore the beauty of the main gorge.

The best way to do this is to follow the well-defined trail which begins near the ranger's headquarters at Carnarvon Gorge, tracing the contours of Carnarvon Creek until it reaches Cathedral Cave 10 km upstream. This will take about 8 hours for the return walk.

Access and Camping

The park is generally accessible to conventional vehicles, except perhaps after heavy rain. From Brisbane, the best route is probably via Roma and Injune. The road is good bitumen except for the last 43 km or so, which is dirt.

The main camping area has been closed, and only a day-use area is located near the ranger base and visitor information centre at Carnarvon Gorge Section. Bushwalkers can pitch their tent at Big Bend camping area, which is 10 km into the gorge. The only facility is a toilet.

Campers and those looking for accommodation are catered for at the Carnarvon Gorge Wilderness Lodge, phone (07) 4984 4503, and the Takarakka Bush Resort, phone (07) 4984 4535, both located just outside the park. Both facilities also have convenience stores.

Bush camping is allowed in the sections of Ka Ka Mundi, Mount Moffat and Salvator Rosa.

Adventurous hikers can travel a further 15 km into the more remote parts of the gorge. There are also a number of side gorges to be explored such as Hellhole Gorge and Violet Gorge.

Left: *Cabbage tree palms, fine-needled casuarinas and weeping bottlebrush grow along Carnarvon Creek; up higher, iron-bark, flooded gums and swamp mahogany pre-dominate.*

don't miss

The clear shallow waters of Carnarvon Creek are home to the elusive platypus. Sightings of this intriguing creature can occasionally be made from some of the higher banks along the creek.

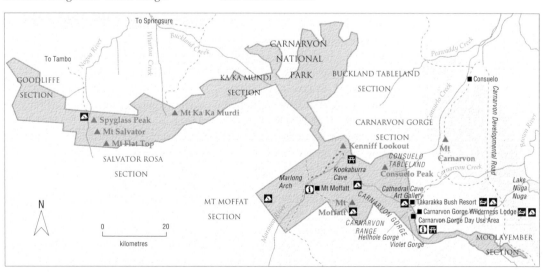

Lamington National Park

The lush rainforest-covered ridges and misty valleys of Lamington National Park have been silently beckoning nature-lovers and travellers for nearly 90 years. Apart from being the most popular national park in Queensland, Lamington is also one of the oldest, gazetted in 1915.

fact file

WHERE: 85 km south-west of Surfers Paradise
Map: Qld 7 N8

WHEN: All year

WHY: Rainforest walks, wildlife, waterfalls

SIZE: 20 600 ha

RANGER: Green Mountains (07) 5544 0634; Binna Burra (07) 5533 3584

The park owes much of its existence to the dedication of Robert Collins, who campaigned tirelessly throughout the early 1900s to have the area protected from logging. When Collins died it was Romeo Lahey, whose family owned one of Queensland's largest timber mills at the time, who led the final push to have the 20 600 hectare wilderness declared a national park.

Rich Flora, Abundant Wildlife

A wide range of vegetation can be found within the park. Huge brush box, tulip oak, giant stinging trees and buttress-rooted Moreton Bay figs are just a few of the many plant species which thrive here.

Gnarled Antarctic beech trees thrive in the higher parts of the park that are more than 1000 metres above sea level. Eucalypt woodlands, grass-trees and other dry vegetation dominate the lower sections of the park.

The male regent bower-bird (Sericulus chryso-cephalus) builds his bower on the ground like other bowerbirds, but otherwise lives in the trees.

Having such a wide range of vegetation, it is little wonder that Lamington is regarded as one of the most important refuges for wildlife in south-east Queensland. Red-necked wallabies and whiptail wallabies are often seen while other common mammals found include the brush-tail possum, sugar glider, greater glider, the rare brush-tailed phascogale, the red-necked pademelon, mountain brush-tail possum, ringtail possum, both the short- and long-nosed bandicoots and the endangered tiger quoll. Reptiles are also abundant, among them large rainforest skinks and beautifully patterned snakes such as the carpet python.

Lamington is renowned as a bird-watcher's paradise. Some of Australia's rarest and most colourful species are found here, including the noisy pitta, crimson rosella, king parrot, Albert's lyrebird and regent bowerbird.

Wonderful Walks

The well-marked system of trails in Lamington provides hikers with some of the best walks in Australia. These can vary from pleasant, 2 hour jaunts

Gold Coast and can be accessed by conventional vehicles. The park is made up of two sections, Binna Burra and Green Mountains—Binna Burra is 35 km by bitumen road from Nerang, while Green Mountain is 115 km from Brisbane and can be accessed via Canungra. Caravans are not recommended.

Camping in the Binna Burra section is only available in the private camping area, part of Binna Burra Lodge, while a national park camp ground is situated near the ranger station at Green Mountain. Showers, toilets, picnic tables and drinking water are provided. Fires are banned within the park. Camping permits need to be booked well in advance, phone the ranger on (07) 5544 0634.

Accommodation is available at O'Reilly's Rainforest Guesthouse (Green Mountain), phone (07) 5544 0644, or Binna Burra Mountain Lodge, phone (07) 5533 3622.

Left: *The tall straight hoop pine* (Araucaria cunninghamii) *thrives on this exposed slope. The park's rich volcanic soils allow a wide range of vegetation to flourish.*

did you know?

Lamington National Park was named for Lord Lamington, Governor of Queensland from 1896–1902. Unfortunately, he will not be remembered as one of Queensland's early nature-lovers; he marked his only visit to the region by shooting a koala.

to 3 day hikes over parts of Queensland's roughest terrain.

One interesting way of viewing the park's many wonders from above is via the rainforest canopy walk. Here visitors can stroll across a suspension bridge dangling 15 metres above the forest floor.

Access and Camping

Lamington is situated 120 km south of Brisbane and 85 km southwest of Southport on the

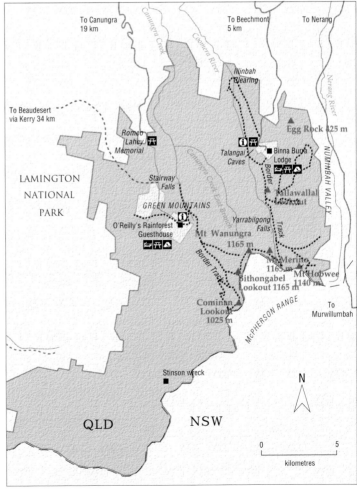

Lawn Hill National Park

Located 400 km northwest of Mount Isa, Lawn Hill National Park is becoming a favoured spot for nature-lovers from all over Australia. The dominant feature of this sprawling 262 000 hectare wilderness is Lawn Hill Gorge, which cuts its way through the rugged sandstone plateaus of the Constance Range. The 60 metre walls of the gorge, which rise up almost vertically, protect the warm, emerald green waters of one of Australia's most pristine waterways.

fact file

WHERE: 400 km north-west of Mount Isa, on the Queensland/Northern Territory border
Map: Qld 3 A8

WHEN: June to September

WHY: Wildlife, canoeing, bushwalks, 4WD

SIZE: 262 000 ha

RANGER: (07) 4748 5572

Above right: Lawn Hill Creek is a permanent watercourse, fed from many springs.

Although freshwater crocodiles (Crocodylus johnstoni) look danger-ous, they are not a threat to people.

Australian Aboriginal habitation at Lawn Hill goes back some 17 000 years. The Waanyi people hunted and fished there until the 1930s when missionaries 'removed them' to Mornington Island. Their ancient art can be seen at the Rainbow Dreaming and Wild Dog Dreaming art sites.

The more remote Riversleigh section of the park, which the Gregory River flows through, has a World Heritage listed fossil deposit of the remains of prehistoric mammals and reptiles.

North-west of Lawn Hill Gorge is the Highlands Plains area. This is a designated wilderness region with no access to vehicles.

Wildlife

Besides harmless freshwater crocodiles, the park is a haven for an amazing variety of wildlife, including more than 135 species of birds and 36 different types of mammals. Snakes and lizards are also plentiful.

Early mornings in Lawn Hill are particularly beautiful, with the calls of countless parrots, kookaburras and magpies filling the air.

Nights in Lawn Hill often have a magical touch—the sound of croaking frogs mingling with the high-pitched shrills of little bats. Dingoes are common throughout the park as well, and their long, drawn-out howling can provide that extra-special touch to a night in the great outdoors.

Activities

At least 3 or 4 days should be spent in Lawn Hill to fully appreciate it.

There are 20 km of walking tracks in the park. The 7 km return walk (about 3 hours) to the upper gorge is a good one as it passes through a wide variety of diverse habitats.

Take your canoe or inflatable boat (or hire one from the camping ground or from Adels Grove), as many peaceful hours can be spent paddling along the creek.

Access

Reaching Lawn Hill is an adventure in itself. The gravel roads in this region can be hard on conventional vehicles and a 4WD is recommended.

Visitors should be self-sufficient in food, fuel, camping supplies and vehicle spare parts. The nearest place to buy fuel is Gregory Downs Hotel, phone (07) 4748 5566, 100 km east of the park. Mount Isa,

400 km to the south-east, is the best spot to buy food and other essentials.

During the wet season, access can be cut for weeks at a time and the roads closed. Contact the RACQ, phone 1300 130 595, for the latest reports.

Camping

The camp sites have toilets, showers and fireplaces, but collecting firewood within the park is strictly prohibited. Gas fires are preferred. There is also a private and popular camp site 10 km away at Adels Grove, phone (07) 4748 5502.

For more information and permits, contact the ranger.

While much of the park is grassland and open forest, the red cliffs around Lawn Hill Gorge are covered by rainforest plants.

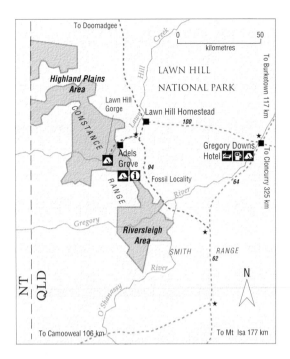

Whitsunday Islands National Park

White sandy beaches, azure blue seas, forest-covered slopes, abundant wildlife and isolated camping spots are just some of the more inviting aspects of a trip to the Whitsunday Islands National Park. These sparkling isles are part of the Cumberland and Northumberland Island groups that lie off the Queensland coast between Bowen and Mackay.

There are 70-odd islands in the Whitsundays, and all are protected by various national parks. The Whitsunday Islands National Park covers 32 islands, including Whitsunday Island, the largest in the group.

Australian Aboriginals lived on many of the larger islands, such as Lindeman, Whitsunday and Hook, and traded with other tribes on the mainland.

The islands visible today were once the peaks of a large coastal mountain range. About 6000 years ago the valleys were flooded when sea levels rose.

Captain James Cook sailed through the islands in 1770, noting that they abounded in good, safe anchorages and naming them the 'Whitsundays' after the day on which they were first sighted.

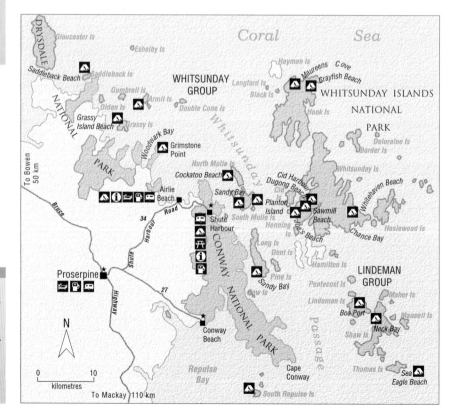

The Great Barrier Reef is made up of approximately 2900 individual reefs. Thousands of tropical fish, coral, mollusc, seaweed and bird species live in this beautiful habitat.

Diving and Snorkelling

The lure of swimming among the colourful coral and fish in the Great Barrier Reef Marine Park is one of the main attractions that entice thousands of people every year to the Whitsundays. Visitors can either go out with one of the many professional diving outfits based at Airlie Beach (ProDive Whitsundays, phone 07 4948 1888), or bring their own snorkel, mask and fins.

Access and Camping

Unless you arrive in your own boat, the best way to visit the Whitsunday Islands is to book with one of the many travel agencies operating in the region. Various types of power and sail boats operating out of Airlie Beach transport visitors to and from the different island camp sites. Contact the Airlie Beach Tourist Information Centre, phone (07) 4946 6255.

Visitors to the Whitsundays have a wide choice of islands to camp on, although many of them are isolated and difficult to reach.

Covering an area of 10 930 hectares, Whitsunday Island is by far the largest, and offers the best camping facilities in the Whitsunday group. Whitehaven Beach on the east of the island is a spectacular white, sandy beach stretching for 6 km along the coast. The largest camping ground on Whitsunday Island is located at Dugong Beach, on the western side, where up to 40 people can stay at any one time.

Other islands with facilities include North Molle (Cockatoo Beach) and Thomas Island (Sea Eagle Beach).

If you prefer solitude and wilderness, you could try Crayfish Beach on Hook Island. This camping spot is for a maximum of two people. Other great places for bush camping include Geographers Beach on Henning Island—great for views and forest walks—and Princess Alexandria Bay on Lindeman Island.

Apart from Whitsunday Island and North Molle, drinking water must be taken with you. Adequate food supplies for your stay, plus 2 extra days' emergency rations in case the weather delays your departure, should also be taken.

A medical kit that has vinegar to treat marine stings should be included with your camping gear.

Camping permits and more information can be obtained from the Queensland Parks and Wildlife Service Whitsunday Information Centre, Airlie Beach, on (07) 4946 7022.

Rainbow lorikeets (Trichoglossus haematodus) *are very sociable birds, flying and feeding in groups of up to fifty, and gathering in even larger groups to roost at night.*

Lakefield National Park

Lakefield is Queensland's second-largest national park, covering 537 000 hectares north of Laura and taking in much of the Normanby, Bizant, Morehead, Hann, North Kennedy and Kennedy Rivers.

The carefully restored Old Laura homestead is one of a few historic sites in the park.

fact file

WHERE: 300 km north-west of Cairns
Map: Qld 1 E10, Qld 3 L1

WHEN: May to October

WHY: Great fishing, camping, nature watching

SIZE: 537 000 ha

RANGER: New Laura (07) 4060 3260; Lakefield (07) 4060 3271; Bizant (07) 4060 3258

This rich region of flat grassy plains and flood plains attracts thousands of birds, making the area a birdwatcher's delight. As well as the 180-odd species of birds recorded, there are 18 species of mammals and 38 species of reptiles. Lakefield is one of the few parks in Queensland where fishing is allowed, and the prize fish is the mighty barramundi. There are some top spots to catch fish, with a number of places suitable to launch a boat. No fishing is allowed between 1 November and 31 January; at other times a bag limit applies.

Access and Camping

Access is restricted to the dry season, with the best access via Laura on the main road north from Cairns. Contact the RACQ, phone 1300 130 595, for the latest road reports.

The main route through the park runs north from Laura past the ranger stations of New Laura and Lakefield, and then west to the small tourist stop of Musgrave. All the roads and the country here demand a 4WD vehicle.

There are many camp sites available in Lakefield with most of them located on the larger waterholes. An excellent camp with toilets, fireplaces and tables is located at Kalpowar.

The Hann River Crossing is a popular camping spot for 4WD enthusiasts during the dry season, but the low-lying area becomes flooded in the wet season.

More National Parks of Importance

Currawinya National Park

SIZE: 151 300 ha
MAP: Qld 6 L9

Currawinya, in the south-west of the state, was gazetted a national park in 1991. The semi-arid park was established to protect the area's freshwater lakes, which are an important refuge for inland birds in times of drought. Lake Wyara abounds with black swans, pelicans and many duck species, while Lake Numalla, in the north-west of the park, is a 2200 hectare body of fresh water.

There are no designated walking tracks in the park but birdwatching is popular. Fishing is allowed (no permit required) in the Paroo River but not in the freshwater lakes.

Access to the park is via Cunnamulla and Eulo, Bourke or Thargomindah. 4WD vehicles are recommended. You should check road conditions with the ranger before setting out.

Because it is such a remote park with no real facilities, visitors should come well supplied with food and water. There are numerous bush camping sites, and camping permits and fees apply.

For more details, contact the ranger on (07) 4655 4001.

Eungella National Park

SIZE: 51 700 ha
MAP: Qld 5 F3

Towering mountain peaks, deep gorges, tumbling waterfalls and crystal clear streams all combine to make Eungella one of the treasures of Queensland. Much of the park is trackless wilderness

but the southern part is easily accessible and popular.

A number of reasonably easy walking trails have been constructed around Broken River but the main drawcard for many people is the plentiful number of platypus that can be seen here. Early morning or sunset is best. The 2 hours after dusk are the best time to see the nocturnal animals of the rainforest (ringtail possums, short-nosed bandicoots, bush rats are some), as this is when they move to new feeding areas.

This brown tree snake (Boiga irregularis) in Eungella National Park is mildly venomous to humans. It is found in tropical northern Australia and down along the eastern coast to Sydney.

The park is also a paradise for birdwatchers, with over 100 species being recorded.

From Mackay, a good bitumen road leads all the way to the park, with the park's camping ground located at Fern Flat. It can be popular with visitors, so book ahead for a site.

Camping permits are required. Contact the ranger, phone (07) 4958 4552.

Above: *The black swan (Cygnus atratus) is Australia's only native swan. Currawinya provides a refuge for these birds in the dry season.*

The lotusbird (Irediparra gallinacea) can be found along Australia's north and north-east coasts. It is one of the many bird species in Eungella.

Girraween National Park

SIZE: 11 700 ha
MAP: Qld 7 L9

Girraween National Park, situated in rugged granite country 260 km south-west of Brisbane on the Queensland–New South Wales border, is a spectacular paradise for wildlife, wildflowers, and wilderness seekers.

There are some easy-to-follow walking tracks, ranging from the 900 metre link circuit to the 10.4 km trail that weaves its way through the forest to Mount Norman.

A large waterhole in Bald Rock Creek near the picnic area is a great place to go swimming.

The park is accessible to conventional vehicles throughout the year. There are two large camping grounds, one at Bald Rock Creek, the other across the road at Castle Rock Camping Area. Both are well equipped. Due to the park's popularity, visitors should book with the ranger, phone (07) 4684 5157.

The granite landscape of Girraween has eroded over millions of years to form enormous granite boulders and domes.

Green Island National Park

SIZE: 12 ha
MAP: Qld 2 B2

Situated 27 km north-east of Cairns in the waters of the Great Barrier Reef Marine Park, Green Island is a coral cay with its own surrounding reef.

This tiny island is almost covered by rainforest, courtesy of the wind and birds that carried seeds there. Hikers can enjoy walking through the lush vegetation, but the island's small size

Right: The waters around Green Island are paradise for snorkellers, with starfish, sea urchins, turtles and giant clams as well as beautifully coloured fish and coral to be seen.

(300 metres by 650 metres) ensures the walks are brief.

The main attraction is the reef: the clear waters around the island make conditions excellent for diving and snorkelling, as the reef abounds with countless varieties of colourful fish and other sea life.

Camping is not permitted on Green Island, although visitors can stay at the small luxury resort. Many visitors come just for the day, to swim and snorkel. There is an underwater observatory too.

For further information, contact Queensland Parks and Wildlife Service, Cairns, on (07) 4046 6600, or Green Island Resort, on (07) 4052 7855.

Hinchinbrook Island National Park

SIZE: 39 000 ha
MAP: Qld 2 C6

Nature lovers and wilderness seekers are drawn to the pristine rainforests, isolated sandy coves, mountain peaks and mangrove-lined estuaries which are just a few of the facets of Hinchinbrook Island, Australia's largest island national park and a refuge for many endangered plants and animals.

Hinchinbrook Island's picturesque eastern coast. The island was part of the Australian mainland until the end of the last ice age, when sea levels rose.

Below: *Cunninghams Gap in Main Range National Park is named for Allan Cunningham, who explored this area while searching for a pass across the mountains.*

The island has some of the best walking trails in Queensland, including the tough 32 km Thorsbone Trail that runs from Ramsay Bay to George Point.

Most visitors to the island travel by boat from the small town of Cardwell. Hinchinbrook Ferries runs a return service to the island for day visitors as well as campers; phone (07) 4066 8388.

Campers should be well prepared and bring everything they need. Only fuel stoves are permitted.

For camping permits, contact the ranger at the Rainforest and Reef Centre, Cardwell on (07) 4066 8601.

Main Range National Park

SIZE: 18 400 ha
MAP: Qld 7 M8

Main Range National Park has long been known as one of the finest bushwalking areas in south-east Queensland.

Situated 116 km west of Brisbane, the park straddles the Great Dividing Range from Kangaroo Mountain in the north to Wilsons Peak on the border. An extensive range of vegetation, including rainforest, eucalypts and grass-trees, can be found, while its fauna is also extremely varied.

One of the best places to take in the grandeur of Main Range is from Governors Chair lookout, a 150 metre walk up from the car park in the Spicers Gap section of the park.

The park headquarters is located just off the Cunningham Highway. The main camping area is at Cunninghams Gap on the banks of West Gap Creek, located near the ranger station. The quieter Spicers Gap camping area can be reached via the Moogerah Dam road.

For more details contact the ranger on (07) 4666 1133.

Cunningham's skink (Egernia cunninghami) grows to about 30 centimetres long. It usually lives in rock crevices or under large rock slabs, and can be seen in Main Range National Park.

Moreton Island National Park

SIZE: 17 000 ha
MAP: Qld 7 N6

Moreton Island National Park is only 40 km east of Brisbane and a short barge trip from the mainland. The island is made up almost entirely of sand, and there are several freshwater lakes, including beautiful Blue Lagoon.

Simpson Desert National Park

SIZE: 550 000 ha
MAP: Qld 6 A3

The Simpson Desert National Park is the biggest national park in the state. This remote desert country was one of the last areas in Australia to be explored by Europeans, with the route taken by travellers from Birdsville being established in the late 1950s. Glistening salt lakes are found in the park's west.

A 4WD vehicle is essential for this area. A permit is needed to enter and camp in the park, which is available from the Queensland Parks and Wildlife Service in Birdsville, phone (07) 4656 3249, or Longreach, phone (07) 4652 7333.

The rocky headland of Cape Moreton in the north of Moreton Island is the site of Queensland's oldest lighthouse, built in 1857.

Many visitors come to Moreton for the great fishing. Once on the ocean beach you can either head north to Cape Moreton or south to Reeders Point.

A number of barges cross to Moreton, including The Combie Trader, phone (07) 3203 6399, and the Moreton Venture, phone (07) 3895 1000.

The island is suitable for 4WD vehicles only. There is a fee for vehicles and passengers and also a landing fee, valid for one month. Contact the ranger on (07) 3408 2710, for details.

There are five Queensland Parks and Wildlife Service camping grounds on Moreton. You can also bush camp at most other places around the coast. Food, fuel and ice can be purchased at the small township of Bulwer and at Kooringal.

Access is only via the main road from Birdsville, then onto the QAA Line to the border and then south to Poeppel Corner.

Camping is only allowed beside the track. The most popular camp sites are at the eastern boundary of the park or at Poeppel Corner itself. Wood is scarce, so a gas stove is recommended.

Right: *Even the desolate sand dunes of the Simpson Desert support some plant life, and the plants give cover to a large number of small reptiles. Dingoes are also often seen.*

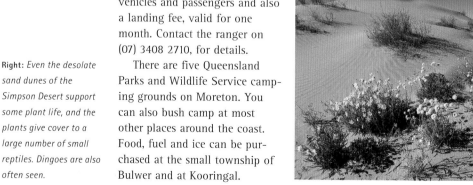

Popular Parks at a Glance

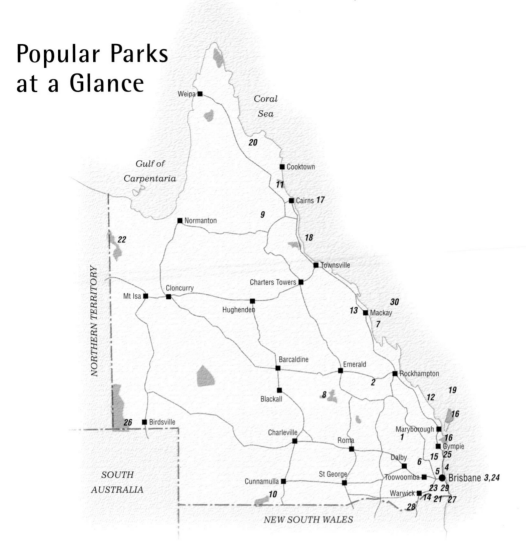

	Camping	Caravan Access	Disabled Access	4WD Access	Picnic Areas	Toilets	Walking Tracks	Kiosk	Information
1 Auburn River NP	●			●	●	●	●		
2 Blackdown Tableland NP	●		●		●	●	●		
3 Blue Lake NP (Stradbroke Is)							●		
4 Bribie Island NP	●			●	●				
5 Brisbane FP	●		●		●	●	●	●	●
6 Bunya Mountains NP	●			●	●	●	●		●
7 Cape Palmerston NP	●			●	●	●			
8 Carnarvon NP	●	●	●		●	●	●		●
9 Chillagoe–Mungana Caves NP					●	●	●		
10 Currawinya NP	●			●	●	●			●
11 Daintree NP	●		●		●	●	●		
12 Deepwater NP	●			●	●	●			
13 Eungella NP	●	●			●	●	●		●
14 Girraween NP	●		●		●	●	●		●
15 Glasshouse Mountains NP				●		●	●	●	
16 Great Sandy NP	●		●	●	●	●	●		●
17 Green Island NP				●			●	●	
18 Hinchinbrook NP	●				●	●	●		
19 Lady Musgrave Island NP	●						●	●	
20 Lakefield NP	●			●	●	●			●
21 Lamington NP	●				●	●	●		●
22 Lawn Hill NP	●	●			●	●	●		●
23 Main Range NP	●	●			●	●	●		●
24 Moreton Island NP	●			●	●	●			●
25 Noosa NP					●	●	●		●
26 Simpson Desert NP	●			●					
27 Springbrook NP	●				●	●	●		●
28 Sundown NP	●	●		●	●	●	●		●
29 Tamborine NP	●				●	●	●	●	●
30 Whitsunday Islands NP	●					●	●	●	●

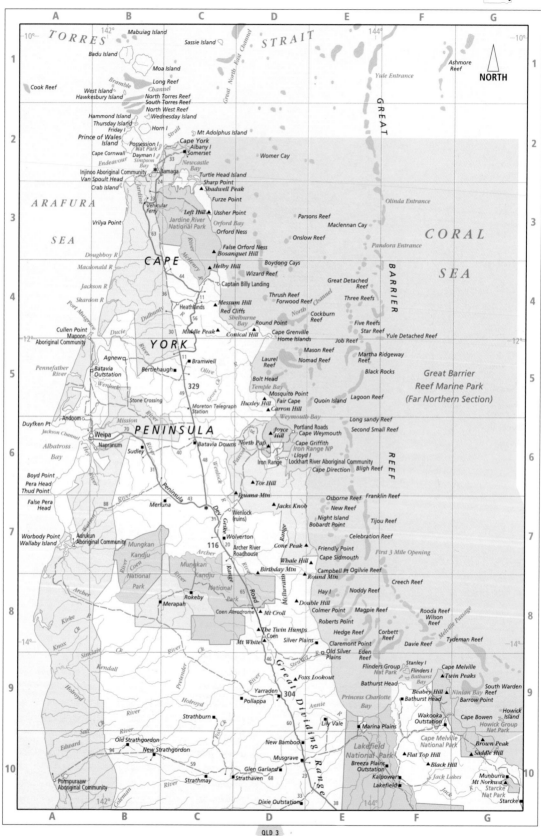

0 20 40 60 80
kilometres

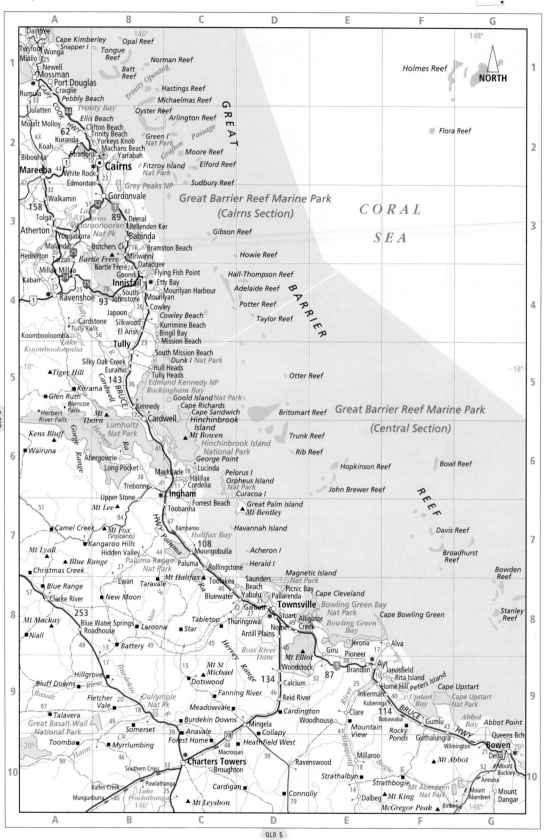

Daintree
Cape Kimberley
Snapper I
Twyford Wonga
Miallo 25
Newell
Mossman
Rumula
33
Craiglie
Port Douglas
Pebbly Beach
Julatten
Mount Molloy
Koah
Biboohra
Mareeba
Kuranda
Stratford
White Rock
Edmonton
Walkamin
Tolga
Atherton
Yungaburra
Malanda
Herberton
Tarzali
Millaa Millaa
Kaban
Ravenshoe
Koombooloomba
Lake
Koombooloomba
Tiger Hill
Kirrama
Glen Ruth
Herbert
River Falls
Kens Bluff
Wairuna
Camel Creek
Mt Lyall
Christmas Creek
Blue Range
Clarke River
Mt Mackay
Niall
Bluff Downs
(Basalt)
Talavera
Toomba
Mungunburra
Balfes Creek

Cape Kimberley
Opal Reef
Tongue Reef
Norman Reef
Batt Reef
Hastings Reef
Michaelmas Reef
Trinity Opening
Oyster Reef
Arlington Reef
Green I
Nat Park
Moore Reef
Elford Reef
Fitzroy Island
Nat Park
Sudbury Reef

GREAT

Holmes Reef

NORTH

Flora Reef

CORAL

SEA

BARRIER

Gibson Reef
Howie Reef
Hall-Thompson Reef
Adelaide Reef
Potter Reef
Taylor Reef

Great Barrier Reef Marine Park
(Cairns Section)

Otter Reef

Britomart Reef

Great Barrier Reef Marine Park
(Central Section)

Trunk Reef
Rib Reef
Hopkinson Reef
Bowl Reef
John Brewer Reef

REEF

Davis Reef
Broadhurst Reef
Bowden Reef
Stanley Reef

Cairns

Gordonvale
Deeral
Bellenden Ker
Babinda
Butchers Ck
Miriwinni
Datadgee
Bartle Frere
Goondi
Flying Fish Point
Innisfail
Etty Bay
South
Johnstone
Mourilyan
Mourilyan Harbour
Cowley
Japoon
Cowley Beach
Cardstone
Silkwood
Kurrimine Beach
Tully Falls
El Arish
Bingil Bay
Tully
Mission Beach
South Mission Beach
Dunk I Nat Park
Silky Oak Creek
Euramo
Hull Heads
Tully Heads
Edmund Kennedy NP
Rockingham Bay
Goold Island Nat Park
Kennedy
Cape Richards
Cape Sandwich
Cardwell
Hinchinbrook
Island
Mt Bowen
Hinchinbrook Island
National Park
George Point
Lumholtz
Nat Park
Abergowrie
Long Pocket
Mackade
Lucinda
Trebonne
Halifax
Cordelia
Upper Stone
Ingham
Forrest Beach
Toobanna
Great Palm Island
Mt Bentley
Bambaroo
Havannah Island
Halifax Bay
Moongobulla
Acheron I
Hidden Valley
Paluma
Herald I
Rollingstone
Magnetic Island
Mt Halifax
Nat Park
Ewan
Taravale
Toolakea
Saunders
Beach
Picnic Bay
New Moon
Bluewater
Yabulu
Pallarenda
Cape Cleveland
Garbutt
Townsville
Bowling Green Bay
Nat Park
Blue Water Springs
Roadhouse
Laroona
Star
Thuringowa
Stuart
Alligator
Creek
Nome
Battery
Tabletop
Antill Plains
Bowling Green
Bay
Cape Bowling Green
Hillgrove
Mt St
Michael
Dotswood
Ross River
Dam
Jerona
Giru
Pioneer
Alva
Mt Elliot
Woodstock
Brandon
Ayr
Jarvisfield
Rita Island
Cape Upstart
Fletcher
Vale
Fanning River
Calcium
Reid River
Home Hill
peters Island
Inkerman
Upstart
Bay
Cape Upstart
Nat Park
Meadowvale
Cardington
Woodhouse
Clare
Koberinga
Bobawaba
Abbot
Bay
Abbot Point
Burdekin Downs
Mingela
Somerset
Anavale
Collapy
Mountain
View
Rocky
Ponds
Gumlu
Guthalungra
Wilmington
Queens Bch
Bowen
Myrrlumbing
Forest Home
Heathfield West
Macrossan
Millaroo
Mt Abbot
Delta
Mount
Buckley
Southern Cross
Charters Towers
Broughton
Ravenswood
Strathalbyn
Strathbogie
Mt Aberdeen
Nat Park
Armunia
Mount
Aberdeen
Mount
Dangar
Powlathanga
Lake
Powlathanga
Cardigan
Connolly
Dalbeg
Mt King
Birbee
Mt Leysbon
McGregor Peak

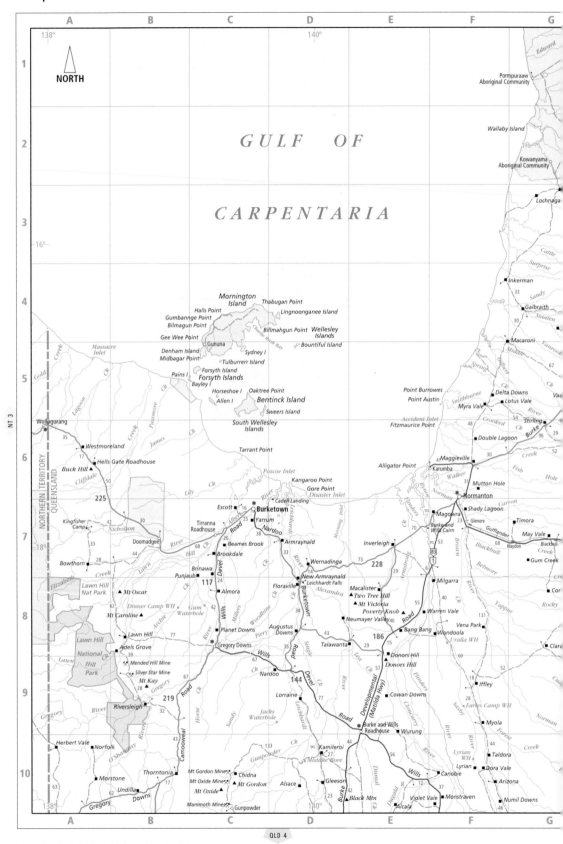

NORTH

GULF OF

CARPENTARIA

138°
140°

Pormpuraaw
Aboriginal Community

Wallaby Island

Kowanyama
Aboriginal Community

Lochnaga

Cattle
Surprise

Inkerman
33
Sandy
Galbraith
30
Maaten

Macaroni
Vanrook
Middle
Silver
67

Delta Downs
Lotus Vale
Va
Smithburne
Myra Vale
River

Crooked
54
Stirling
Ck
Burke
Double Lagoon
36 29
52

Creek
Fish
Hole

Mornington
Island
Thabugan Point
Halls Point
Lingnoonganee Island
Gumbannge Point
Bilmagun Point
Billmahgun Point
Wellesley
Islands
Gee Wee Point
Bountiful Island
Gununa
Denham Island
Sydney I
Midbagar Point
Tulburrerr Island
Forsyth Island
Pains I
Forsyth Islands
Bayley I
Horseshoe I
Oaktree Point
Allen I
Bentinck Island
Sweers Island
South Wellesley
Islands

Tarrant Point

Point Burrowes
Point Austin

Accident Inlet
Fitzmaurice Point
48

Maggieville
30
Alligator Point
Karumba
41
Mutton Hole
31

Wollogorang
35
Westmoreland
17
Hells Gate Roadhouse
Buck Hill
Cliffdale
50

Pascoe Inlet
Kangaroo Point
Gore Point
Disaster Inlet

Walker
Normanton
Carron
Shady Lagoon
23
Magowra
Glenore
Timora
70
Burke and
Wills Cairn
Guffander
70 53
68
May Vale
Haydon
Blackbull
Creek
Belmore
Gum Creek

Massacre
Inlet

225

Kingfisher
Camp
42
30
Nicholson
33
Doomadgee
44
River
68
Ck
Hill
Brookdale

Escott
16
Burketown
Tirranna
Roadhouse
25
Yarrum
26
Nardoo
38
Beames Brook
Armraynald
33

Cadell Landing
Leichhardt Falls

Inverleigh

73
228
29
Milgarra
Cor

Bowthorn
28

Brinawa
Punjaub
14
117
24
Almora

Wernadinga

New Armraynald

Floraville
Alexandra
34

Macalister
Two Tree Hill
Mt Victoria
Poverty Knob
Neumayer Valley
40
55
Warren Vale
131
Vena Park
Wondoola
Bang Bang
186
Uralla WH
Clara

Rocky

Lawn Hill
Nat Park
Mt Oscar
62
Dinner Camp WH
Gum
42
Waterhole
Mt Caroline

Planet Downs
Augustus
Downs
43
Talawanta
29

Donors Hill
Donors Hill
57
60
52
18
Iffley

Lawn Hill
National
39
Adels Grove
Mended Hill Mine
Silver Star Mine
Mt Kay
28
219
32
Riversleigh
Herbert Vale
Norfolk
O'Shanassy

Hill
Park
67
Gregory
Ck
Road

Gregory Downs
67
Nardoo
144
Lorraine
77

Jacks
Waterhole

Cowan Downs
28
Faires Camp WH
Myola

Burke and Wills
Roadhouse
Wurung
Developmental
(Matilda Hwy)
44
Lyrian
WH
44
Taldora

133
75
Kamileroi
27
Mistake Bore
56
Canobie
Dora Vale
Arizona

Thorntonia
Mt Gordon Mine
Chidna
Mt Oxide Mine
Mt Gordon
Alsace
Gleeson
Wills
12
Monstraven
Numil Downs
46

Morstone
63
62
Undilla
Downs
Mammoth Mines
Gunpowder
17
Mt Oxide
42
Black Mtn
23
Violet Vale
Alcala
37

Herbert Vale
Gregory

138°
140°

0 20 40 60 80
kilometres

Grid columns: H J K L M N P
Grid rows: 1 2 3 4 5 6 7 8 9 10

New Strathgordon
New Strathgordon
Musgrave
New Bamboo
Cape Melville National Park
Flat Top Hill
Murdoch Pt
Brown Peak
Saddle Hill
Lizard I Nat Park
Yonge Reef
Cooks Passage
146°
Cormorant Passage

Glen Garland
Strathaven 68
Strathmay
59
River
23
Kalpawar
Breeza Plains Outstation
Lakefield
Black Hill
Jack Lakes
Munburra
Mt Norkua
Starcke Nat Park
Starcke
Eagle I
Martin Reef
Lookout Point
Rocky Islets Nat Park
Ribbon Reef

Dixie Outstation
33
New Dixie
304
Lakefield National Park
Jack
River
Glenrock
Eldersile
Cape Flattery
Great Ribbon

Oroners Outstation
Killarney
Kalinga
Hann River Roadhouse
Mt Jack
Battle Camp
Hope Vale Aboriginal Community
Cape Bedford
Louisiana
Nob Point
Great Barrier Reef Marine Park (Cairns Section)

l and Alice Rivers national Park
8 Mile
Creek
Koolburra Outstation
Old Laura
Hazelmere
Endeavour
Marton
Endeavour River Nat Park
Cooktown
Osterland Reef

Kimba
Pinnacles
Fairview
Olive Vale
Laura
Mt Cook Nat Park
Walker Bay
Archer Point
Forsberg Pt Gill Patches
Cairns Reef

Koolatah
Strathleven
King Junction
Fairlight
Mt Emma
Crocodile
Springvale
Cooktown
Helenvale
Rossville
Cedar Bay Point
Rattlesnake Point
Ayton
Wujal Wujal
Weary Bay
Degarra
Agincourt Reefs
16°

Drumduff
Mt Daintree
Palmerville
Maiden Peak
Mt Hann
Maytown (ruins)
Mt Lukin
Lakeland
Mt McDowall
Palmer River Roadhouse
Daintree Nat Park
Cape Tribulation
Thornton Beach
Alexandra Bay
Mackay Reef
St Crispin Reef

Highbury
Mt Mulgrave
Mount Mulgrave
Groganville
Mt Hurford
Woods Peak
Maitland Downs
177
Daintree National Park
Mt Spurgeon
Mt Elephant
Daintree
Twyford
Wonga
Dayman Point
Newell
Mossman
Mossman Gorge
Cooya Beach
Port Douglas
Craiglie
Rudder Reef
Opal Reef
Snapper I
Tongue Reef
Norman Reef
Batt Reef

Staaten River National Park
Burke
Gamboola
Bellevue
Hurricane
Mount Carbine
Maryfarms
Rumula
Pebbly Beach
Julatten
Mount Molloy
Koah
Kuranda
Trinity Bay
Ellis Beach
Clifton Beach
Trinity Beach
Yorkeys Knob
Machans Beach
Yarrabah
62
Michaelmas Reef
Oyster Reef
Trinity Opening
Green I Nat Park

Bulimba
Nychum
Mount Mulligan
Kays Mtn
Kingsborough
Biboohra
Mareeba
White Rock
Edmonton
Stratford
Cairns
Fitzroy I Nat Park

Blackdown
Rookwood
Chillagoe
Thornborough
Wolfram
Mutchilba
Walkamin
Dimbulah
Tinaroo Falls
Tolga
158
Gordonvale
89
Deeral
Bellenden Ker
Grey Peaks NP

Mungana
Chillagoe Mungana Caves NP
Calcifer
Fluorspar
Verdure
Atherton
Yungaburra
Gordonvale
Malanda
Bartle Frere
Babinda
Bramston Beach
Miriwinni
Deeragun

Torwood
Jubilee Mtn
Almaden
Petford
Irvinebank
Herberton
Millaa Millaa
Goondi
Innisfail
Etty Bay

Bolwarra
Fischerton
Tate Tin Mines
Ootann
Koorboora
Gilmore Mine
Kaban
Ravenshoe
Japoon
Silkwood
Mourilyan
Cowley
Kurrimine Bch
El Arish

Mt May
Bullock Creek
Gingerella
Mount Garnet
Innot Hot Springs
Morecambe
Koombooloomba
Cardstone
Tully
Tully Falls
93
Silky Oak Creek
Dunk I
Mission Beach
Tully Heads

Abingdon Downs
Minnies Outstation
Mt Emu
Barney Knob
Burlington
Barwidgi
Lyndbrook
Sundown
Gunnawarra
Lake Koombool-oomba
Euramo
Kirrama
Edmund Kennedy NP
Goold I
Kennedy

Strathmore
Eden Vale
Campbell Mtn
Van Lee
Dagworth
O'Briens Creek Gemfields Cabana
Brooklands
Springfield
Frewhurst
Mt Poole
Forty Mile Scrub National Park
Tiger Hill
143
Blencoe Falls
Cardwell

Tabletop
Chadshunt
Gilbert River
Inorunie
Ironhurst
Hot Springs Talaroo
Mount Surprise
Undara Lava Tubes Guide Stn
Yarrabah
Minnamoolka
Glen Ruth
Herbert River Falls
Lumholtz Nat Park

149
Forest Home
Georgetown
Durham
Eveleigh
138
Undara Volcanic National Park
Yarramulla
Meadowbank
Glen Harding
Kens Bluff
Wairuna
Abergowrie
Long Pocket

Riverview
Donnyville
Lornvale
Einasleigh
Rosella Plains
Mt Webster
Mt Tabletop
92
Bowman Hill
Lake Lucy
Upper Stone
Trebonne
Ingham
Toobanna

Brennans Knob
Idalia
Forsayth
Wirra Wirra
Narrawa
Mt Misery
Spring Creek
Valley of Lagoons
Conjuboy
Mt Lee
Camel Creek
Mt Fox (Volcano)
Kangaroo Hills
Hidden Valley
Paluma
Paluma Rd NP

Esmeralda
Mt Helpman
Robinhood
Cobbold Gorge
The Oaks
Mywyn
Kidston
Carpentaria Downs
The Lynd Junction
Wyandotte
Greenvale
Mt Lyall
Christmas Creek
Blue Range
Ewan
Taravale

Victoria Vale
Bellfield
Pelham
Strathpark
Bairds Table Mtn
North Knob
Oak Park
Mt Lookout
Lyndhurst
Teddy Mtn
Pandanus Creek
Montgomery Range
Clarke River
Mt Mackay
Niall
Blue Water Springs Roadhouse
253
Laroona
Battery
New Moon

Middle Park
Blackbraes National Park
Blackbraes
Oak Valley
Big Ben
Clarke Hills
Maryvale
Mt Louisa
Bluff Downs
Hillgrove
146°

Map 4

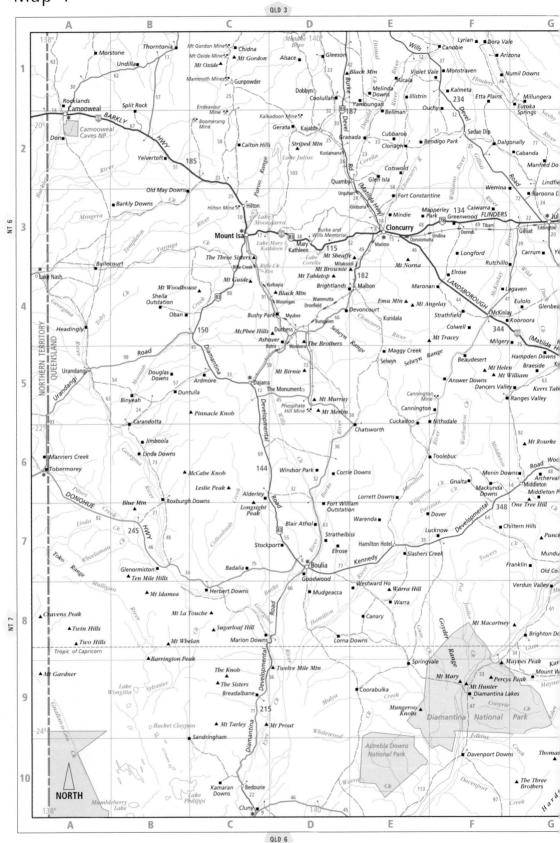

0 20 40 60 80
kilometres

Grid columns: H J K L M N P
Grid rows: 1 2 3 4 5 6 7 8 9 10

Pelham · Strathpark · Middle Park · Blackbraes National Park · Blackbraes · Montgomery Range · Big Ben · Oak Valley · North Gregory River · Niall · Battery · Maryvale · Hillgrove · Bluff Downs · Fletcher Vale · Dalrymple Nat Pk · Somerset

Etheldale · Chudleigh Park · Castle Hill · Clarke Hills · Mount Louisa · Nulla Nulla · Talavera · Toomba · Munjumburra · Myrrlumbing · Southern Cross

Glengalla · Elmore · Somerville · Bylong · Mount Norman · Maiden Springs · Kennedy · Reedy Spring · Kings Knob · Cuba Plains · Cargoon · Killarney · Lake Cargoon · Great Basalt Wall National Park

Kilterry · Rockvale · Runnymede · Burleigh · Hazelwood · Doncaster · Charlotte Plains · Pretty Plains · Mt Courtney · Mount Emu Plains · Mt Pleasant · Lolworth · Powlathanga · Lake Powlathanga

Nonda · Molesworth · Acton Downs · Silver Hills · Villa Dale · Spring Valley · Wongalee · Mt Emu · Mt Sturgeon · Boonderoo · Porcupine Gorge Nat Pk · Oak Vale · Homestead · Mt Windsor · Mt Redan

Maxwelton · Richmond · Killeen · Riverdale · Rokeby · Torver Valley · Blantyre · Burra · Kiora · Cape River · Pentland · River View · Lascelles · Corea Plains · Pajingo

FLINDERS Hughenden · Marathon · Mumu · Boree · Tindo · Prairie HWY · Warreah · Torrens Creek · Warrigal · Milray · GREAT DIVIDING RANGE

Minamere · Maxwelton · Merriula · Lucindale · Myuna · Wilfred Downs · Hillview · Mt Devlin · Penrice · Oakley · Oxenhope Outstation · Broadfeigh Downs · Longton · Egera · Natal Downs

Langdale · Essex Downs · Warianna · Afton Downs · Ashton · Webb Lake

Coleraine · Exmoor · Elton Downs · Eldorado · Stamford · Braemar · Mootinya Nat Pk · Ulva · Yarrowmere · White Cliffs

Dimora · Dundee · Glenlyon · Nottingham Downs · Chinbi · Ensay · Eyrie · Uanda · Atherfield · Mundoo Bluff · Thirlstone · Lake Buchanan · Darkies Ra

Wanora Downs · Clio · Sesbania · Elvira · Whitewood · Tarvano · Katandra · Barenya · Mt Hopwood · Tiree · Abertoyle · Bowie

Mt Etna · Brooklyn · Coorabelle · Woolfield · Broadford · Tangorin · Bannockburn · Rainsby · Carmichael

Bendemeer · Werna · Lana Downs · Corfield · Escombe · Olio · Burnside · Birricannia · Kyong

Berrifels · Enryb Downs · Thornville · Burslem · Thornton · Thistlebank National Park · Lake Galilee · Tomahawk · Shuttleworth

Hexham · Strathfillan · Daintree · Eskdale · Hardington · Thistlebank · Lou Lou Park · Eastmere

Leeson · Teviot · Oondooroo · Kywong · Aldingham · Mahrigong · Bangall · Llorac · Lilarea · Cornish · Hazelmere · Coorabah · Lake Dunn · Widgeman

Collingwood · Winton · Marita Downs · Mt Cobcroft · Mount Cornish · Muttaburra · Kingsborough · Fortuna · The Lake · Clare · Dunrobin

Kalkadoon · Jarvis Field · Vindex · Lorraine Station · Dillcar · Culladar · Prairie Peak · Rosebery Downs · Wilton · Stagmount · Ravenswood · Lennox · Boongoondra

Colston · Bladensburg Nat Park · Chorregon · Baratari · Rimbanda · Crossmoor · Aramac · Shandon Vale · Texas · Rosedale

Whyralla · Warnambool Downs · Mt Euston · Hereward · Morella · Dalmore · Dilulla · Auteuil · Taree · Garfield

Cork · Walters Knob · Evesham · Euston · Darr · Fairfield · Rodney Downs · Beaconsfield · Grant · Edwinstowe

Eildon Park · Mt Douglas · Yandilla · Fermoy · Jugiong · Mt McEvoy · Cramsie · Longreach · Ilfracombe · Brixton · Barcaldine · Tropic of Capricorn · Richmond Hills · Jordan Avon · Jericho

Opalton · Wammadoo · Manero · Strathmore · CAPRICORN · Westbourne · Geera · Lochnagar · Spring Vale · Wololla · Burgoyne

Georges Seat · The Ranch · Alroy · Clovelly · Devonshire · Mafeking · Joycedale

Mayneside · Vergemont · Mt Vergemont · Spring Plains · Arrilalah · Bandon Grove · Nereena · Amor Downs · Dandaraga · Urambie · Delta South · Lancevale · Mendip Hills

Withywine · Wellshot · Honan Downs · Trent · Boorara · Helen Vale · Yalleroi

Tonkoro · Wantagong · Bogewong · Westland · Hazelwood · Somerset · Greycroft · Mena Park · Evora · Elsie Hills

Westerton · Noonbah · Lochern Nat Park · Lochern · Gaza · Greenwoods · Portland Downs · Alice Downs · Glenusk · East Lynne

Onoto · Beatrice Downs · Bimerah · Isisford · Isis Downs · Gowan Hills · Erne

Mt Fairview · Mt Senex · Warbreccan · Evangy · Glenroy · Stonehenge · Pandora Park · Oma · Mons · Thornleigh · Barcoo · Blackall · Mt Northampton

Mt Affleck · Goon Goon · Glen Afton · Bilbah Downs · Rutland Park · Blairgowrie · Benlidi · Glenstuart

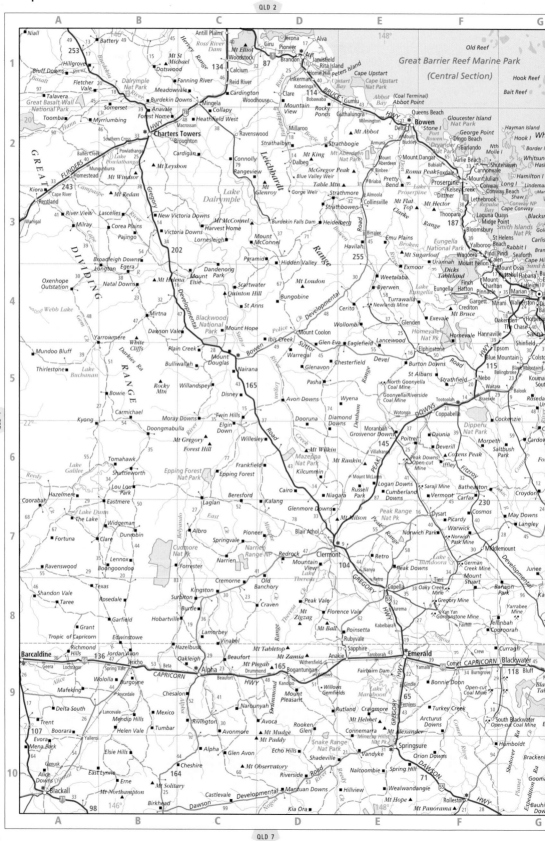

©Global Book Publishing Pty Ltd & Universal Press Pty Ltd

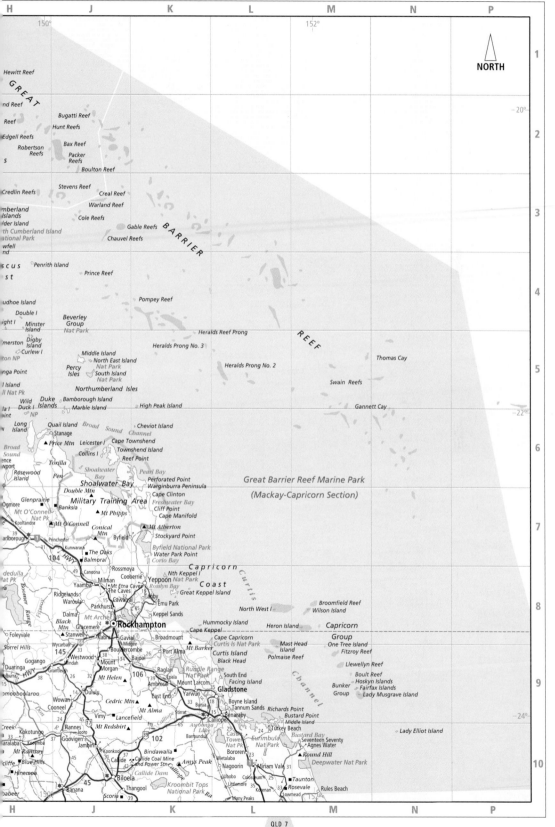

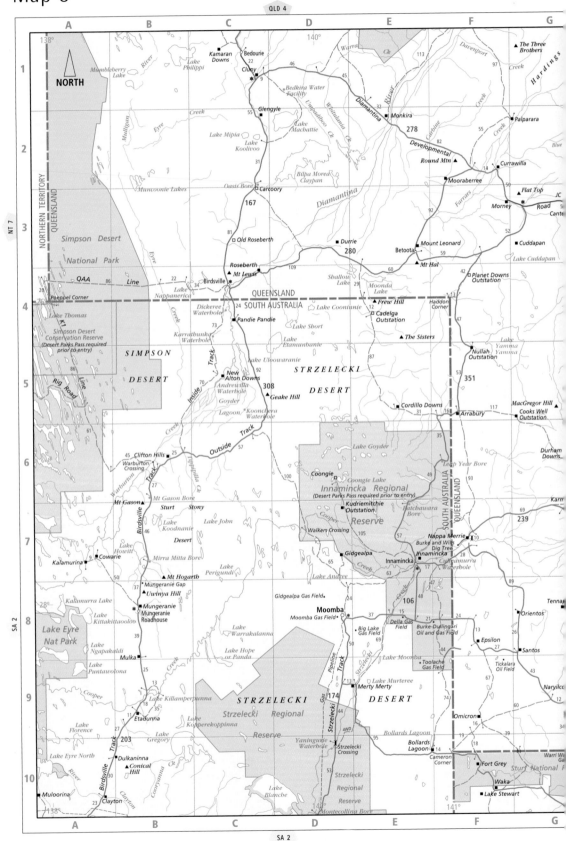

0 20 40 60 80
kilometres

H J K L M N P

Row 1
Connemara · Mt Fairview · Mt Senex · Warbreccan · Glenroy · Bimerah · Isisford · Mons · Gowan Hills · Glenusk · Alice Downs · East Lynne · Erne
Evangy · Stonehenge · Pandora Park · Oma · Thornleigh · Barcoo · Blackall · Mt Northampton
Mt Affleck · Goon Goon · 29 · 105 · Rutland Park · 33 · 98
64 · 66 · Rd · Glen Afton · Bilbah Downs · Blairgowrie · 33
Trewalla · Glenariff · Swan Vale · 50 · Benlidi · Milton Park · Bloomfield · 65
Dev · Needle Creek · New Deer · Mekaree · 25 · Emmet · Mt Sentinel · Terrick · Terrick · Eastwood · Innis Downs
Braidwood · Opal Hill · Arno · Ungo · Emmet Downs · 36 · Mount Harden · Lorne · Summervale
155 · Jundah · Mt Perrier · Yaraka · 53 · Observatory Hill · Idalia · Koondoo · Bonnie Doon · Prospect
Glenvalley · Mount Marlow · Highlands · 43 · National · Adavale · 33 · Alva · Kootchee
Longford 51 · Wandsworth · 46 · Park · Coolabara · Amaroo · Listowel Downs · Myall Creek
Thomson · 79 · Retreat · Trafalgar · Mt Welford · 48 · Warrego · Range · Tarrina
Galway Downs · Coniston · Advance · Budgerygar · Powell · Creek · Blackall · Listowel Valley · Glanworth · Bayrick
114 · Currareva · 57 · Oakham · Hell Hole Gorge · Gilmore · Hut · Caranna · Langlo Downs
Windorah · 6 · 17 · Hammond Downs · Alfred Bluff · National Park · Gooyer · Bulloo · Baykool · Noella
28 · Thunda · Moothandella · Trinidad · 75 · Bulloo Lakes Hut · Wakes Lagoon · 301 · Oakwood
Galway · Kyabra · Clifton · Lynwood 61 · Milo · 49 · Blackwater · Bronte
Tenham · 30 · Bulgroo Outstation · 85 · Gundary · Mariala · Mount Morris
Mt Poolpiree · 44 · Springfield · 49 · Canaway Downs · Arawee · 41 · Adavale · Hoomooloo Park · Nat Park · Ambathala · Oakleigh
Keeroongooloo · 226 · 53 · Bulls Gully · Wade Hill · 114 · Rosebank · Oakpark · 26°
48 · Thylungra · Ray · Goombie · 34 · Gumbardo · Langlo Crossing · Rocksville
Raymore · Kyabra · Warrabin · Emudilla · Mona Vale · Grenfield · Lake Dartmouth · 53
27 · 46 · 42 · Bull Creek Opal Field · Corona · 66 · Mt Gunnadorab · 81
Kyabra · Pinkilla · Como · 51 · Boothulla · 69 · Nimboy · 17
Mount Howitt · Diamantina · Naretha · Comongin · Moble Springs · Pingine · Tiranna
38 · 19 · 58 · Cooma · Mt Bellalie · 41 · 30 · Quilpie · 12 · 24 · Arranfield · Yalamurra · 57
Plevna Downs · Eromanga · Tebin · 63 · 209 · Cheeple · 27 · Cooladdi · 32 · Mayfield
Blue Hills · 36 · Bargo Bargo Mtns · 45 · Boolbanna · Developmental · 21 · Bierbank · 18 · Weaner Creek · 48
McGregor Range · 26 · Congie · Moble · 49 · 45 · 42 · Yarronvale · Dillalah · 68
Bellalie · Mount Margaret · 52 · Nerrigundah · South Comongin · 25 · Cowley · Armdobilla · Coolabah · 192
58 · RANGE · Ingeberry · 62 · Coparella · 28 · Doobibla · Kynnersley · Alpha
Mt Tabbatbcubbah · Bowalli · Toompine · Wareo · 17 · Cliffdale · Rosevale · Wyandra
70 · Tobermory · Tinderry · 37 · Duck Creek Opal Field · Big Creek · Mount Alfred · 45 · Warrego Park
Kihee · Bundeena · Ardoch · Prairie · Mt Anderson · Humeburn · Claverton
32 · Jackson Oil Field · 36 · 6 · Kiandra · 185 · Dundoo · Boobera · Cocklarina · Coongoola
18 · Bulloo · Nockatunga (Adventure · 111 · Norley · Soonah Crossing · 61 · Alroy · Tilboroo · 88 · Goora · 98 · Glendilla · Charlotte Vale · Nardoo
Noccundra · Way) · Developmental · 38 · The Three Pioneers · Yowah Opal Field · 23 · 48 · Baroona · Nulla · Horton Vale · 54 · Mayvale
Wilson · Kulki · Lake Toomaroo · Yowah · Bundoona · Cunnamulla · Charlotte Plains
Mt Lucas · Thargomindah · 51 · Lake Bindegolly National Park · Dynevor Downs · Carpet Springs · 200 · 15 · 5 · Burrenbilla · Weelamurra
Mt Shillinglaw · Nooyeah Downs · 37 · Lake Bindegolly · 55 · Mt Bingara · Eulo · 17 · 55
31 · Mt Koldonera · 68 · Gumahah · Tuen · Westlea
Bulloo Lake · Bulloo Downs · Yakara · Yenlora · Pisa · 117 · 25 · Noorama
Tickalara · 88 · Zenonie · 146 · 64 · Boorara · Tinnenburra · 22 · Thurulgoonia
Tallyboe · Kilcowera · Lake Wyara · Caiwarro · Beulah
Currawinya National Park · Lake Numalla · 36 · Lake Wombah · Barringun
Moombidary · Currawinya · 14 · 10 · Rostella · Eureka Plains
Wompah Gate · Adelaide Gate · QUEENSLAND · Hamilton Gate · Waverly Gate · Hungerford · Cuttaburra Basin · Wirrawarra · 38
Narcowla · NEW SOUTH WALES · Waverley Downs · Brindingabba · Comeroo · Enngonia · Beulah
Lake Wasby · Thurloo Downs · Ourimbah · Nungunyah · Thoura · Yantabulla · 146°
Narrierra · 144° · Mooleyarrah

Map 7

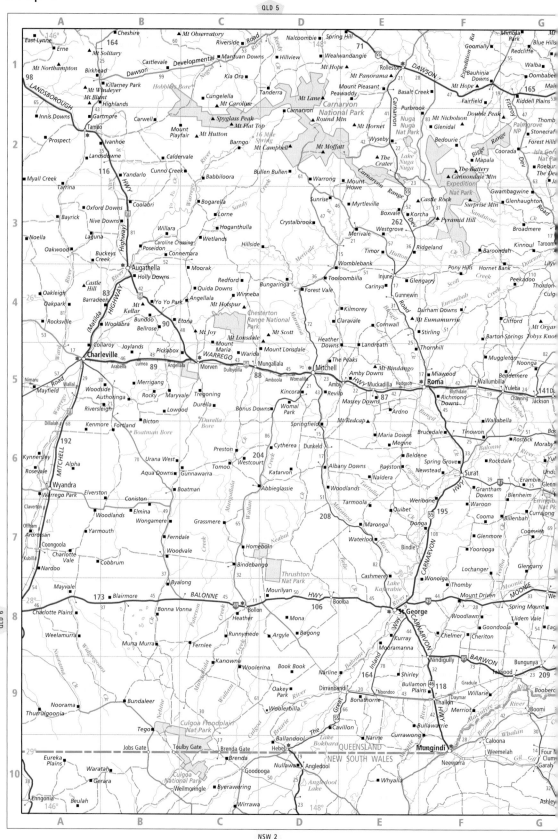

© Global Book Publishing Pty Ltd & Universal Press Pty Ltd

0   20   40   60   80
kilometres

NORTH

Great Barrier Reef Marine Park
(Mackay-Capricorn Section)

SOUTH

PACIFIC

OCEAN

Sunshine

Coast

Gold

Coast

New South Wales

Of all the states in Australia, New South Wales' national parks provide
the greatest variety of scenic wonders, diversity of vegetation and opportunities for recreational pursuits. There are coastal parks that include some
of the world's best beaches, and remote areas with breathtaking scenery.
The parks also link us to Australian Aboriginal heritage with excellent art
sites and middens to be found. Almost every park has access by conventional vehicles to superb picnic areas, camping grounds and walking
trails. Many of the parks also provide opportunities for 4WD devotees.
Like the 1994 bushfires, the fires of December 2001 and January 2002
left some parks blackened and temporarily closed. The Australian bush,
however, is resilient and quick to regain its natural beauty.

Blue Mountains National Park

Part of the Greater Blue Mountains World Heritage Area, the Blue Mountains National Park attracts over 3 million visitors a year. It's little wonder really, considering it is virtually in sight of Sydney, being only 100 km west of the Harbour Bridge, and it has some of the most spectacular scenery of any of the national parks in Australia.

The visitor to Blue Mountains National Park will be astounded at the raw beauty of the sandstone cliffs and the deep gorges. There is a variety of activities to pursue in the mountains, from sitting around a campfire listening to bird calls and watching a fiery sunset reflect off the giant cliff faces, to dangling precariously on the end of a rope as you abseil down a waterfall into a valley that dates from the Jurassic era.

In the Past

The sandstone, which forms the dramatic scenery, was originally deposited by river systems that drained into a coastal plain more than 275 million years ago. Then 50 million years ago the area was uplifted, forming the Great Dividing Range. Volcanoes added to the dramatic scene before the weathering process began to etch the landscape. The deep gorges and towering cliffs of today are the result of continual weathering.

Australian Aboriginals once inhabited this area and there is a great deal of evidence of their occupation, dating back 14 000 years, in the form of art sites and grinding-stone marks in the sandstone cliffs.

The mountains formed a natural barrier to the early settlers in Sydney. A route over the mountains was not found until 1813 when Blaxland, Wentworth and Lawson stumbled across the only possible route. The rich plains to the west ensured that a rough road was quickly cut, and the present-day Great

Western Highway follows closely the route of the first coach trail.

The mountains remained sparsely populated until 1868 when the Great Western Railway opened, which brought the scenic beauty of the mountains within reach of the growing Sydney population. In the 1890s reserves were established to protect the natural areas within the mountains, while Blue Mountains National Park itself was proclaimed in 1959.

Activities

Tourism is big in the mountains and there are plenty of places to stay, as well as unusual ways to enjoy the natural wonders. A good example is the Scenic Railway, with its near-vertical

Pulpit Rock Lookout is so-called because it stands out from the main cliff face. The lookout provides magnificent views of Mount Banks, the Grose Valley and the cliffs where Govetts Leap is situated.

Below left: *Katoomba Falls has two drops separated by a small ledge. The water falls 200 metres into the Jamison Valley below.*

Below: *The turpentine tree* (Syncarpia glomulifera) *was given this name because the smell of its sap reminded early explorers of turpentine.*

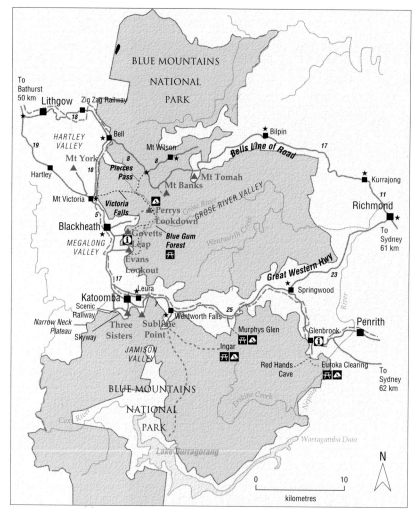

tourists that flock to the area. For something completely different you could try rock climbing or abseiling on one of the Three Sisters and there are plenty of adventure companies based in the mountains that can assist you in this pursuit.

Bushwalking is another great activity and the park has many wonderful trails. Some are quite easy and include the scenic lookouts, while others require a degree of fitness and an overnight camp, as they extend into deep river valleys. The National Parks and Wildlife Service has excellent publications detailing the many walks and giving their degree of difficulty and the time they take.

Around the major towns of Katoomba, Leura and Blackheath there are impressive lookouts accessible to everyone. The already mentioned Three Sisters has viewing platforms, walks to the base of the rock formations and a well-stocked information and souvenir shop.

From Katoomba it is possible to follow the cliff drive which passes several other lookouts over the Jamison Valley, as well as some great picnic locations both east and west of Katoomba. Along this route you will also find the Skyway and the Scenic Railway.

At Leura there are several splendid lookouts over Sublime Point. These are among the best in the park and are within an easy five minute walk from the car park.

In the Glenbrook area there are good walks with views over the Nepean River

drop, and the Skyway cable car that stretches across deep, fern-filled gullies.

The most famous attraction in the mountains is the Three Sisters rock formation. Situated within the confines of the town of Katoomba, there is very easy access, parking being the only problem due to the huge number of

Protected, moist gullies of the Blue Mountains National Park contain pockets of warm temperate rainforest in which plants such as tree ferns, epiphytes and coachwood and sassafras trees thrive.

as well as Aboriginal hand stencils to view at Red Hands Cave. Abseiling off the cliffs in this part of the park is also popular and every weekend you will find groups of people enjoying this exhilarating sport.

There are a number of adventure tour companies who can safely take you on abseiling trips off huge cliffs, rock-climbing expeditions, or canyoning through narrow gorges where waterfalls plunge into deep pools of icy cold water. Or you could try the Grand Canyon Track, which lets you have the thrill of canyoning without getting wet.

West of Katoomba, around Blackheath, there are several roads out to lookouts above the Grose Valley. This is one of the most spectacular regions as the rock faces of the cliffs are several hundred metres high. The better known lookouts include Evans, Govetts Leap, Perrys Lookdown and Victoria Falls. There are several easy walking trails along the top of the escarpment that will take no longer than 2 hours.

The most renowned walks in the Blue Mountains are those that descend into the Grose Valley from Govetts Leap and Perrys Lookdown. You will need to be fit to tackle the steep trails and you must always be prepared for dramatic changes in the weather. Because the mountains are at a high altitude, sudden temperature drops and even snowfalls are common. Heavy rain can cut tracks in the valleys and the area should be avoided in this type of weather.

There are several walks in the Grose Valley, with the famous Blue Gum Forest being one of the better known attractions. This beautiful forest was saved from destruction back in the 1930s by keen bushwalkers.

If you are planning a walking trip into the Grose Valley it is suggested that you contact the Heritage Centre at Blackheath to obtain maps and advice about your intended walk. It is very wise to let someone reliable know of

NSW

The striking, bright red, wax-like waratah (Telopea speciosissima) glows like a jewel in the shrub understorey of the Blue Mountains. The best time to see them is September to November.

The Three Sisters, hard sandstone rock pinnacles, are the most famous feature in the park and are best viewed from the lookout at Echo Point in Katoomba.

Dramatic Narrow Neck is best seen from Cahills Lookout off the western end of Cliff Drive in Katoomba. Spectacular views of Boars Head Rock and the Megalong Valley are also provided from this lookout.

Coachwood (Ceratopetalum apetalum) are tall slender trees noted for the mossy circles on their trunks. They are common in the park's rainforest areas.

your intended route and time of return in order to avoid unnecessary searching.

There are some good lookouts off the Bells Line of Road and these are found a few minutes off the main road at Pierces Pass, Mount Banks and Mount Tomah, where you'll find the excellent high country botanical gardens.

Access

The park takes in some 248 148 hectares of rugged country west of Sydney and is best accessed along the Great Western Highway. It stretches in the east from Glenbrook, almost at the foot of the mountains, to west of Katoomba near Mount Victoria where the road descends onto the western plains. Its northern boundary is the Bells Line of Road where the Wollemi National Park continues northwards and its southern section stretches all the way to Wombeyan Caves, west of Mittagong.

The park has three distinct regions: the Glenbrook section covering the lower Blue Mountains down to Lake Burragorang and west to Wentworth Falls; the southwestern section which includes the Jamison Valley and the Three Sisters, and is the most remote area extending south towards Kanangra-Boyd National Park and on to Wombeyan Caves; and the northern section between

the Great Western Highway and the Bells Line of Road, which includes the Grose Valley and contains some of the best lookouts and walking trails.

You can even visit the park by train or bus. Check out the CityRail website to plan your railway journey or the local bus network website for the town nearest the places you would like to visit.

Camping

Entry is free to all areas of the park except those areas south of Glenbrook. Camping fees apply throughout the park. You need to take drinking water with you to most areas.

In the Glenbrook section there is a camping ground at Euroka Clearing, however, unless you have a New South Wales Parks Annual Pass, you'll need to buy a vehicle day pass as well as pay a camping fee. It is necessary to book and pay for your site at the Glenbrook Tourist Information Centre, phone (02) 4739 6266.

There are also camping locations at Ingar and Murphys Glen, both south of Woodford, which are accessed off the highway at Wentworth Falls.

In the northern section, or the Grose Valley, there is one official camp site at Perrys Lookdown. This is accessed off the Great Western Highway at Black-heath. This section of the park is very popular with bushwalkers, however, bush camping is permitted in only two places in the Grose Valley: Acacia Flat and Burra Korain Flat. In other areas outside the Grose Valley it is possible to bush camp away from roads, walking trails and picnic areas.

The southern section is much more remote, and camping within 3 km of Lake Burragorang is not permitted as this is part of the catchment area for Sydney's water supply.

The agile, arboreal ring-tail possum (Pseudo-cheirus peregrinus) is so-called because the tip of its long prehensile tail can be coiled into a ring and acts as a fifth limb.

Kosciuszko National Park

Kosciuszko National Park is the leader in New South Wales in terms of size, attractions, activities and grandeur. At 690 000 hectares it is the largest park in the state, taking up nearly 1 per cent of the state's landmass. It stretches from the Victorian border all the way to the Brindabella Range west of Canberra and sprawls across the highest peaks of the Great Dividing Range. It protects Australia's tallest mountain, Mount Kosciuszko, which reaches a height of 2228 metres. The park includes more than 300 000 hectares of wilderness area.

Mount Kosciuszko National Park provides excellent winter skiing conditions for both downhill and cross-country skiers.

fact file

WHERE: About halfway between Melbourne and Sydney; 2 hours' drive from Canberra
Map: NSW 7 G8

WHEN: June to September for skiing; November to February for bushwalking and camping

WHY: Ski fields, excellent walks with mountain scenery, 4WD

SIZE: 690 000 ha

RANGER: National Parks and Wildlife Service, Jindabyne (02) 6450 5555

Right: Fishing, in season, is a major attraction in the park. Rivers and lakes are regularly stocked from trout hatcheries.

The Snowy Mountains, over which the park spreads its protective mantle, are the home of Australia's largest power generating scheme, the Snowy Mountains Hydro-Electric Scheme. Only in the far south and the north-east of the park are you totally free from the signs of this huge development, but the man-made lakes do add another dimension to the scene.

The park is known primarily for its sensational snow-skiing over the winter months. During summer it becomes an idyllic escape for many hundreds of visitors who savour the crisp mountain air and expansive mountain views. During this time many of the fabulous camp sites beside the rivers and lakes of the mountains are filled to over-flowing with campers enjoying the bright blue skies and fresh air. The walking tracks across the main range are visited by numerous walkers, awestruck by the uninterrupted views and carpets of wildflowers. Below, in the deep valleys, the lakes created by the hydro-electric scheme and the rivers are full of boats, canoes and anglers.

Bushwalkers can explore the wilderness areas, while historians will enjoy discovering the huts and homesteads of the high country left by the pioneers.

In the Past

It is known that the Australian Aboriginals visited the mountains at times during the year, the harsh winter making them unsuitable for permanent human habitation. Europeans ventured into the mountains in the early 1800s as graziers searched for better grasslands to feed their stock. The Polish explorer Count Strzelecki supposedly climbed the highest peak in 1840 and named it for Polish patriot Tadeusz Kosciuszko; however, some say that he was, in fact, on Mount Townsend.

In 1859 there was a minor gold rush at Kiandra and during the late 1800s and early 1900s timber-getters worked the giant stands of timber in the lower valleys.

In 1944 the Kosciuszko State Park was established and

five years later the Snowy Mountains Scheme began. This was indeed an engineering feat of epic proportions. Five rivers were diverted from an easterly flow to a westerly flow; 145 km of tunnels were bored through solid rock; 17 dams were constructed; 7 power stations established and over 1600 km of roads blazed through some of the most rugged country in the land. This brought enormous economic development to Australia in the form of power generation and irrigation for the Western Plains. However, some are now arguing that the changes to nature will ultimately wreak havoc over our land.

The Kosciuszko National Park was proclaimed in 1967 and more recently it has been recognised by UNESCO as an International Biosphere Reserve.

Carpets of cheerful alpine buttercups (Ranunculus anemoneus), *which are found in the wild only on the slopes of Mount Kosciuszko, are a feature of the park in spring and early summer.*

NSW

Activities

In winter there is primarily one pastime in the park: skiing. The whole of the mountains can be blanketed in metre-deep snow for up to 4 months. There are tremendous opportunities for down-hill and cross-country skiing as well as snowboarding, and thousands flock to the ski fields each winter to enjoy the slopes and the night life in the resorts.

At higher altitudes, some parts of the park are covered with snow for much of the year. Vegetated areas may be scattered or follow the contours of the slopes.

The park lends itself to a much greater variety of activities during the warmer months. Although the nights can still be extremely cold, the days are usually clear and sunny. The scenery at this time is excellent and many bush-walkers prefer this time of year to tackle the many hundreds of kilometres of walking trails that are available.

It would be impossible to list all of the tracks that can be walked—details of these trails can be obtained from the National Parks and Wildlife Service office in Jindabyne. The tracks vary from short walks of as little as one hour duration to overnight camp-outs which cover up to 20 km of the mountaintop ranges. If you are planning a long overnight walk ensure that you are totally self-sufficient and ready for the worst blizzard-style, weather conditions. You will also need to carry your own cooking stoves and fuel with you, as the lighting of fires in higher altitudes is severely restricted.

There are excellent opportunities for boating, canoeing and swimming in the rivers and lakes of the valleys during

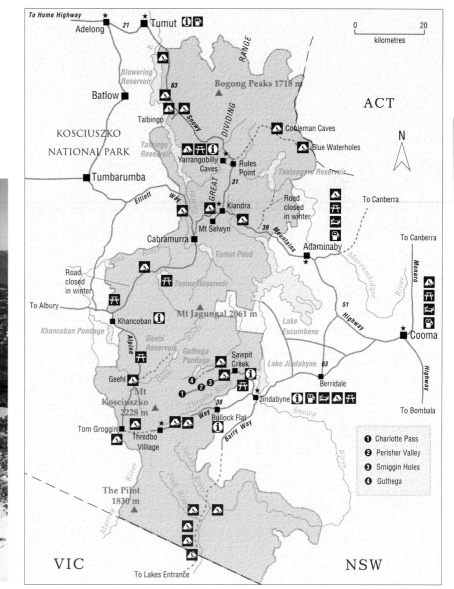

did you know?

Blue Lake in Mount Kosciuszko National Park is one of only four glacial lakes in mainland Australia. The lake was created by glaciation wearing down the granite bedrock, and is frozen over in winter.

summer. Trout fishing in season is another major attraction as the rivers and dams are regularly stocked from trout hatcheries. Make sure you are aware of any local regulations (many rivers are open only to fly fishing) and wherever you fish in New South Wales you require a fishing licence.

Horseriding is a popular activity but is only permitted in approved areas. Check before setting out or use an approved trail-riding operator. Mountain bike riding is allowed on management trails but not on designated walking

tracks, and the bikes are not to be taken off the trails. There are a number of bike hire and tour operators in the area.

Whitewater rafting on the Snowy River, the Geehi River and the Murray River, as well as other similar adventure sports, are readily catered for.

Other visitors to the park will have an interest in the mighty hydro-electric scheme that reshaped the mountains and there are tours conducted to the power stations and dams.

The Yarrangobilly and Cooleman Caves are another feature of the Snowy

Upper Pond Dam is one of the 17 dams built during the construction of the massive Snowy Mountains Hydro-Electric Scheme (1949–1972).

Mountains. The underground majesty of these caves is difficult to rival and there are self-guided tours as well as professional tours. There is even a natural hot spa at Yarrangobilly that can be enjoyed throughout the year.

The resort town of Thredbo, in the southern part of the park, offers a multitude of activities all year round.

The National Parks and Wildlife Service provides discovery tours and talks during the summer and there are commercial tour operators that can also meet your needs.

Access

It takes about 6 hours to drive to the park from Sydney or 2 hours from Canberra. The major entry into the park is via the Monaro Highway from Canberra, driving through Cooma and then on to Jindabyne.

You can also fly to Cooma and then drive to Jindabyne, but most people come by car or by coach.

There are alternative access routes into the park and each of them is spectacular. For those living in the western parts of the state it would be easiest to follow the Snowy Mountains Highway

through Tumut before climbing the mountains past Lake Blowering up to Kiandra. From there it's onto Adaminaby and Cooma, from where the major ski resorts of Perisher and Thredbo are easily accessed via Jindabyne.

As an alternative, from Kiandra follow the Alpine Way to Cabramurra and then along the mountains on their western side to Khancoban. This marks the third possible entry point into the Snowies. For those travelling from Albury or Melbourne this would be an ideal route to follow as it traces the shoreline of the Hume Weir. Khancoban nestles at the foot of the towering mountains and from here you can follow the Alpine Way past Geehi and Tom Groggin to Thredbo, eventually emerging at Jindabyne.

It is possible to virtually circumnavigate the Snowy Mountains on a good road. However, some sections are closed in winter as the road is subject to heavy snowfalls.

During winter (1 June to 10 October) all vehicles travelling to and through the park must carry properly fitting snow chains and fit them when advised.

Camping

There are many opportunities for camping within the park, but be aware that sudden and severe weather changes are always possible.

The snow gum (Eucalyptus pauciflora subsp. niphophila) is a small tree usually twisted and bent by wind, with beautiful bark.

Seaman's Hut is one of several old huts scattered across the high country that are ideal refuges for bushwalkers and cross-country skiers in bleak weather. The huts were built by the early graziers.

Even in midsummer there is the chance of heavy snowfalls and freezing conditions occurring.

There is a daily entry fee into Kosciuszko National Park, per vehicle, or you can purchase an annual pass that also provides access to all other parks in New South Wales. The pass is available from the National Park Centre, phone 1 300 361 967 or (02) 9253 4600, or from any national park in the state.

The major camping ground for tents and caravans in the park is at Sawpit Creek. Here you will find toilets, hot showers, fireplaces and even cabins for rent. However, bookings need to be made in advance.

It is possible to camp anywhere in the park provided you are not in sight of a road or near a watercourse. Some of the better camp sites for the car-based camper are found at Tom Groggin beside the Murray River, near Geehi on the Murray Flats, in the old town site of Ravine, or Lobbs Hole below the Yarrangobilly Caves, and at Cooleman Caves on the Long Plain east of Rules Point. In the north there are several short-term camp sites beside Blowering and Talbingo reservoirs.

There are commercial camping grounds in Jindabyne and Cooma and a huge number of ski chalets, motels and hotels in both these towns as well as in Thredbo and Perisher Valley, some providing on-snow accommodation.

For the avid bushwalker there are countless excellent bush camp sites along the many hundreds of kilometres of walking trails.

NSW

Barrington Tops National Park

A major attraction of the Barrington Tops is the clean, fresh air. But visitors are also rewarded with a vast array of walking tracks, magnificent scenery and lookouts, superb wildflowers, spectacular rainforest, snow gums and peat swamps. It is easy to say that Barrington offers everything. The park covers 73 884 hectares that vary from snowplains to impenetrable forests dissected by raging rivers with some wonderful waterfalls.

Right: Barrington Tops National Park provides a protected environment for this mountain brush-tail possum or bobuck (Trichosurus caninus) and her baby.

The many different species of flora and fauna are also a feature of the park. As well, the park is surrounded by vast areas of state forest which cater to the traveller with provision of trails, camping and picnic areas.

Activities

The Barrington Tops provide a wide variety of activities, the most popular ones being camping and bushwalking, and there is a very good network of walking trails throughout the park. Some are easy, short walks, while others are demanding and involve overnight camps in high altitude areas.

Anglers will find trout in the mountain streams, but check with local National Parks and Wildlife Service personnel regarding permits and seasons. You will need a New South Wales fishing licence.

The area has always been attractive to drivers with 4WD vehicles but track closures and wilderness declarations in recent years have greatly reduced these opportunities. Check with the National Parks and Wildlife Service and State Forests as to access and track availability.

In the lower reaches of the mountains, rafting and canoeing are favourite pastimes on the Barrington, Cobark and Gloucester Rivers.

Access

Good roads lead to most areas but during winter many of these can be slippery or covered with snow. Vehicle access from the south via Dungog or Gresford leads to the well-known Barrington Guest House and its surrounding superb walking trails. It also provides access to the state forest areas of Chichester Dam and Telegherry Forest Park where excellent picnic and camping facilities are available. From the east, access is via Gloucester to either the Gloucester Tops or further west into the area's highest peaks along the Scone–Gloucester road. If approaching from the west, travel via Scone and Moonan Flat before ascending the range

on the Scone–Gloucester road. This is the most direct route to the more remote camp sites around Careys Peak and the Big Hole.

Camping

If you are bushwalking, you can camp almost anywhere, as long as you are more than 300 metres from a trail or official camp site.

If you wish to camp with your vehicle there are well-maintained camping sites in the southern section, in the Chichester State Forest, at Telegherry Forest Park and Allyn River Forest Park. In the Gloucester Tops region is a well-kept but more restricted camping area.

The state forest camping area at Polblue Swamp is excellent. The camping sites at Junction Hole and the Big Hole are favoured by more adventurous bushwalkers.

It would be wise to check with the National Parks and Wildlife Service for availability and access to most of the camping sites.

Left: Superb World Heritage listed rainforests are a feature of the park, which also contains Antarctic beech forests, snow gum woods, wild rivers and wilderness areas.

NSW

This part of the Great Dividing Range is subject to dramatic weather changes—one of the forces which helped shape this natural rock sculpture.

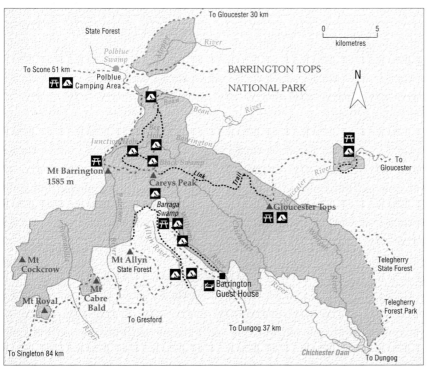

To Gloucester 30 km

State Forest

River

Polblue
Swamp

To Scone 51 km

Polblue
Camping Area

BARRINGTON TOPS
NATIONAL PARK

0   5
kilometres

N

Bean

Bean River

Junction Hole

Barrington

Mt Barrington
1585 m

Black Swamp

Careys Peak

Link

Trail

To
Gloucester

River

Barraga
Swamp

Gloucester Tops

Mt
Cockcrow

Mt Allyn
State Forest

Allyn River

Telegherry
State Forest

Mt Royal

Mt
Cabre
Bald

Barrington
Guest House

River

Telegherry
Forest Park

To Gresford

To Dungog 37 km

To Singleton 84 km

Chichester Dam

To Dungog

Deua National Park

The Deua National Park encompasses the mountains inland from the south coast towns of Moruya and Narooma. Although it is primarily a wilderness park, everyone can enjoy the wilderness areas. There are great camping spots beside clear rivers, 4WD trails, fabulous walks, caves, diverse flora and a huge range of wildlife. There have been 80-odd species of birds recorded from the park and a wide range of mammals, of which swamp wallabies are one of the most common.

Vegetation in Deua National Park changes markedly with altitude, providing a rich diversity of habitats for a variety of birds and other animals.

fact file

WHERE: 100 km south-east of Canberra
Map: NSW 7 K5

WHEN: September to May

WHY: Scenery, 4WD, camping, canoeing

SIZE: 82 926 ha

RANGER: National Parks and Wildlife Service, Narooma (02) 4476 2888

Activities

The park includes a number of challenging 4WD tracks from which drivers can enjoy superb views, and one of the best camp sites in New South Wales waiting at the end of the day in the Bendethera Valley. Although the roads are not particularly difficult, all visitors should know how to use their 4WD vehicles in rough terrain. Organised 4WD tag-along tours are conducted by Great Divide Tours, phone (02) 9913 1395.

Speleologists can explore the Bendethera and Wyanbene Caves, while remote country bushwalkers can venture into the rugged southern end of the park. Canoeists can paddle in the upper reaches of the Shoalhaven River, and mountain bike riders will also enjoy the 4WD trails.

Access and Camping

The Araluen–Moruya Road runs along the Deua River and gives access to the Bendethera–Merricumbene Fire Trail that gives the easiest access into the park from the north or from the coast.

The Braidwood–Nimmitabel Road, often referred to as the Krawarree Road, passes along the backbone of the Great Divide and the western boundary of the park. This provides access to the Big Hole, Wyanbene Caves and 4WD access onto the

Mount Dampier and Bendethera Trails that lead into the heart of the park.

From the coast there's also 4WD access via a network of forestry trails out of Moruya that eventually lead to the Bendethera Trail.

Once in the park the trails are the domain of the 4WD; the Bendethera, Merricumbene, Mount Dampier and Minuma Trails provide varying degrees of difficulty. 4WD tracks should not be used in wet conditions. The few trails that dissect the park have remained open thanks to appropriate management by the National Parks and Wildlife Service.

There are established camp sites with pit toilets and barbecues on the Araluen Road at the Deua River Camping Area, approximately halfway between Araluen and Moruya, and at Bakers Flat. This road is very narrow as it twists and follows the river, but it is accessible to conventional vehicles.

Right: *The tawny frogmouth owl (Podargus strigoides) is resident in Deua National Park. Unlike other owls it does not hide during the day but roosts, motionless and head erect, on branches.*

On the Krawarree Road from Braidwood, the Berlang Camping Area provides picnic and camping opportunities. The Shoalhaven River is nearby and it is a 30 minute walk to the Big Hole. The Big Hole is a result of the hillside collapsing into an underground limestone cavern, creating a hole 30 metres across and 90 metres deep.

The Bendethera Valley deep in the heart of the national park stretches for over 4 km, and it provides the best opportunity for camping for those with 4WD vehicles. There are pit toilets and fire pits provided. The valley can be reached from both east and west.

Entry and camping fees apply.

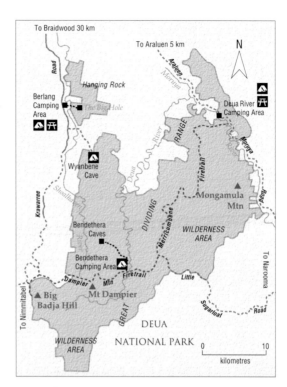

Deua National Park contains a number of rivers which have carved their way down the steep ridges to the valleys. In some places there are sparkling waterfalls, in others tranquil pools.

Kanangra–Boyd National Park

This spectacular park is only three hours' drive from Sydney and has some of the most inspiring scenery in Australia. In the heart of the park are the awesome Kanangra Walls and everyone should see them at least once in their lifetime. The Blue Mountains National Park joins its eastern and southern boundary, while state forests border much of the rest.

fact file

WHERE: 3 hours' drive west of Sydney via Jenolan Caves
Map: NSW 6 F8

WHEN: Spring and summer

WHY: Wilderness areas, lookouts, walks, 4WD

SIZE: 68 661 ha

RANGER: National Parks and Wildlife Service, Oberon (02) 6336 1972, or Blackheath (02) 4787 8877

Attractions

The scenery and the isolation of the area are the major interest points of the park. There are sheer cliffs of several hundred metres, magnificent waterfalls and superb walking trails. There are also some great camping spots and an abundance of wildlife. The park is primarily wilderness, covering 68 661 hectares stretching from Jenolan Caves to Colong Caves.

Activities

There are some brilliant walks and views in the park. At the end of the Kanangra Walls Road there are easy, level walking trails leading to several magnificent lookouts over the Walls. There is wheelchair access at this point.

Here you will also find the Waterfall Walk that takes only 30 minutes to the base of the Kalang Falls, while the Plateau Walk gives you some great views over the wilderness areas.

There are many longer walks that entail overnight camps and

There is limited four-wheel driving in the park, however, there is some exciting driving to be had crossing the Kowmung River.

you need to be experienced and very fit. These walks wind their way into deep gorges, passing mountains with such evocative names as Cloudmaker, Strongleg, Wild Dog, Stormbreaker and High and Mighty.

The walk out to the top of Morong Falls on the Boyd River is also worth the effort. Here you'll find impressive cascades and swimming holes; the walk will take at least one hour.

Cycling is only allowed on the public roads and trails. Bikes are not allowed on walking trails.

Caving is popular, and canyoning and abseiling are growing activities within the park.

Access

Although this is a wilderness area, access is quite reasonable. The major route from Sydney is via the Jenolan Caves Road from the Great Western Highway to the caves and then onto the Kanangra Walls Road. This road is 30 km of all-weather gravel but caution is needed in wet weather. You can also approach this road from Oberon or, if

The Morong Falls on the Boyd River have stunning cascades and some excellent swimming holes. The beauty and seclusion to be found here is worth the strenuous hour-long walk.

This abandoned slab hut in the rugged terrain of Kanangra–Boyd National Park was originally a bushman's home.

tourist info

CAVING: Permits for Tuglow and Colong Caves required in advance from the National Parks and Wildlife Service

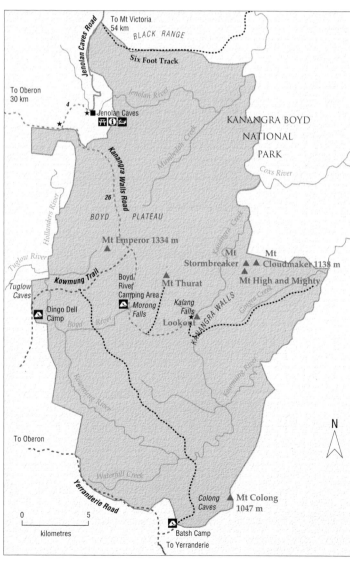

you have a 4WD vehicle, you would find the route through the Dingo Dell Camping Area and across the Kowmung River the most interesting.

All other access into the very heart of the park is by foot.

Camping

There is a vehicle-based camping area on the Kanangra Walls Road at the Boyd River crossing that has toilets and barbecues. Accessible by conventional vehicles, it is subject to extreme weather conditions and snow can fall at any time. The Dingo Dell Camping Area, with pit toilets but plenty of fresh water, is 4WD-accessible only and it is better protected from bad weather.

Sturt National Park

Here red kangaroos, emus and wedge-tail eagles reign supreme, the heat shimmers off the burnt red rock and the mulga bushes whistle in the breeze. This is the outback, and it is here where you'll find the driest and most remote of the New South Wales national parks. Established in 1972 and situated in the far north-west corner of the state, Sturt National Park covers an area of 310 634 hectares.

WHERE: 330 km north of Broken Hill
Map: NSW 1 B1

WHEN: March to November

WHY: Remote semi-desert landscape, wildlife, history, 4WD

SIZE: 310 634 ha

RANGER: National Parks and Wildlife Service, Tibooburra
(08) 8091 3308

In the Past
There is ample evidence of Australian Aboriginal occupation in the form of middens and stone relics throughout the area. Charles Sturt, after whom the park is named, spent a year in and around this region in 1844 on his central Australian expedition. In 1880 gold was discovered and pastoralists soon followed. The longest fence in the world, the Dog Fence, was constructed along the New South Wales borders with Queensland and South Australia.

Attractions
The vastness of the outback is the major attraction of this park, but there is much more of interest. The park has a huge kangaroo and emu population and there

The pink cockatoo (Cacatua leadbeateri) *is also known as the Major Mitchell cockatoo, after the explorer. It is becoming a rare sight in this park.*

is ample opportunity to see these magnificent animals at close range. Of equal appeal is the evidence of human endeavour, in the form of explorers' camps at Depot Glen and Fort Grey, and the sheep stations such as Olive Downs and Mount Wood.

Visitors who drive through the area after rain will be rewarded with brilliant displays of wildflowers.

Activities
There are a number of short walking trails including trails from Dead Horse

The world's longest fence goes through Sturt National Park. The Wild Dog Fence, or Great Dingo Fence, is 5614 km long, stretching from Jimbour in Queensland to the Great Australian Bight.

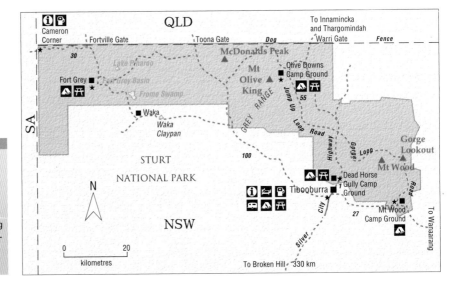

NSW

Gully, and at Mount Wood and Olive Downs. At Fort Grey you can walk to the old holding yard constructed by Sturt during his exploration as he searched for the inland sea.

For those interested in history there is also a reconstruction of gold mining techniques at Golden Gully.

The park also has a self-guided and well-mapped drive tour. The drive encompasses 110 km and takes travellers via Mount Wood and Olive Downs through what is the prettiest part of the park.

Access

Sturt National Park stretches from the state's northern and western borders at Cameron Corner east to the Silver City Highway and south to Tibooburra.

The park is very remote and travel in summer is best avoided. Autumn through to spring is a much better time to visit, but you can expect very cold nights in winter.

A mixture of bitumen and graded gravel road stretches for 330 km between Broken Hill and Tibooburra, or there is an unsealed route via Bourke and Wanaaring. Both routes can be impassable after rain so always check the condition of the roads with local police.

The roads within the park and to each of the camping sites and picnic areas are generally gravel with some sandy sections.

Camping

Sturt National Park caters for the tourist with three well-appointed camp sites. Just 1 km out of Tibooburra is the Dead Horse Gully Camp Ground, while further north, just outside the old homestead of Olive Downs, is another camp site which provides a beautiful setting among the mulga trees.

The other recognised camping area is at Fort Grey on the western fringe of the park, just 30 km before Cameron Corner on the state border.

Above: *Remote and semi-arid, the park has a diverse landscape, containing vast stony plains, rolling red sand dunes, remnant gidgee woodland, ancient granite tors and even some wetlands.*

Left: *Sturt's desert pea (Swainsona formosa), with its distinctive scarlet and black flowers, grows in the wild only in dry outback conditions.*

tourist info

4WD TOURS: Tri State Safaris (08) 8088 2389

Ku-ring-gai Chase National Park

The Ku-ring-gai Chase National Park lies just north of Sydney and protects some of the most fascinating and beautiful sandstone escarpment country and Australian Aboriginal art sites found in Australia. The rugged land-scape discouraged early settlers, and by 1894 its environ-mental importance was recognised by national park status.

Akuna Bay Marina in Ku-ring-gai Chase National Park is situated in the quiet, sheltered waters of Coal and Candle Creek.

Activities

Numerous walking trails throughout the park cater for all levels of fitness and ability. There are magnificent views over Broken Bay and from West Head Lookout. The Australian Aboriginal rock engravings and stencils are best seen along Resolute Track.

The park is a wonderful place to explore by boat, and in spring and summer wildflowers colour the scene.

Picnic facilities, including tables, fire-places and toilets, are available at Apple Tree Bay, Bobbin Head, The Basin, West Head, Cottage Point and Akuna Bay, and there are kiosks at Bobbin Head, Apple Tree Bay, Akuna Bay and Cottage Point.

Access

Access to the park is easy, as it's only a 40 minute drive along sealed roads from the centre of Sydney. Each of

these access routes passes through fee collection gates and a daily fee per vehicle applies.

If travelling by train you can reach the park from Mount Colah, Mount Ku-ring-gai, Berowra and Cowan stations.

Access by water is also possible to the camping and picnic area at The Basin, with ferries leaving from the Pittwater side of Palm Beach.

Camping

This park is primarily for day visitors. There is only one camping area—at The Basin on Pittwater. It is accessible by ferry from Palm Beach or is a 3 km walk from West Head Road.

The best way to see the wonders of Ku-ring-gai Chase National Park is to walk. There are marked tracks which vary from easy to difficult, taking in a range of environments.

South East Forest National Park

The South East Forest National Park has a continuous but convoluted border. It spreads over the rugged forested mountain country that stretches north from the Victorian border to join with the southern boundary of Wadbilliga National Park. The park, covering 115 372 hectares, straddles the spine of the Great Dividing Range.

fact file

WHERE: 450–550 km south of the centre of Sydney
Map: NSW 7 K8

WHEN: All year

WHY: Old-growth forest, scenic drives, 4WD

SIZE: 115 372 ha

RANGER: National Parks and Wildlife Service, Bombala (02) 6458 4080, Narooma (02) 4476 2888 or Merimbula (02) 6495 5000

The park protects outstanding old-growth forest, heathlands, swamps and fern-lined gullies. Over 110 species of birds have been recorded from the region and swamp wallabies are the most common large mammal seen. The old-growth forests are also home to a wide variety of possums and gliders along with bandicoots and potoroos.

Activities

Scenic drives provide access to picnic areas at Six-Mile Creek, Wolumla Peak, White Rock River, Myrtle Mountain, Big Jack and Myanba Creek.

A viewing platform with wheelchair access at Myanba Gorge gives great views over the Towamba Valley. Another viewing platform can be found at Pipers Lookout on the west side of the park, just off the Mountain High-way 60 km west of Bega.

Off the Pambula–Wyndham road you'll find parking and a barbecue area near the interesting and scenic Goodenia Rainforest Walk.

Horseriding, mountain bike touring and bush-walking are also enjoyed in this park.

Access and Camping

The Mountain Highway from Bega cuts through the park, along with a number of other bitumen roads.

Creeks and waterfalls, ferny gullies and superb old-growth forests are home to a diversity of native flora and fauna in this outstanding park.

Good gravel roads are accessible to conventional vehicles, while forestry trails that are suitable for a 4WD open up more of the park to keen travellers.

Car-based camping is available at Six Mile Creek and Postmans Track (accessible only by 4WD), with toilets and drinking water provided.

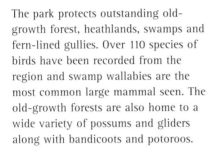

Around sunset is when you are most likely to see koalas (Phascolarctos cinereus) here, as this is the time they move around in search of food. Noted for their sleepy demeanour, they sleep 80 per cent of the time.

Warrumbungle National Park

The Warrumbungle National Park is situated 27 km west of Coonabarabran and it attracts over 80 000 people annually to experience the clear mountain air and enjoy the extensive range of walking trails that crisscross the Warrumbungle Ranges.

Right: *The Breadknife is a wall of rock with a serrated edge resembling a bread knife. The rock is the remnant of volcanic action, which took place some 13 to 18 million years ago.*

Activities

Bushwalking is the major attraction and there is a huge selection of excellent walking trails. The scenery of the Warrumbungles is a feature of most walks and the well-known Breadknife, a 90 metre wall of solid rock, is one of the renowned features of the park.

There are a number of easy, short walks including Whitegum Lookout and Gurianawa Track that are only 1 km long and wheelchair accessible.

Rock climbers may pursue this activity in selected areas but must obtain a permit from the ranger.

Access

The park is easily accessed by conventional vehicle from either Coonabarabran or Coonamble. The road through the range is gravel. The southern section of the park can be accessed via Gilgandra, again over a gravel road.

There are limited vehicle trails within the park. The track to Camp Burbie is open to 4WD vehicles only.

Camping

There are a number of delightful camp sites, including Camp Blackman, Camp Wambelong

Warrumbungle National Park is one of the country's best natural habitat havens for kangaroos and other wildlife.

and Camp Elongery. Camp Burbie is accessible only by 4WD. In the southern section of the park, accessed from Gilgandra, is Camp Guneemooroo.

For bushwalkers there are designated camp sites along the longer walking trails but you must register with the ranger to camp at these sites.

The lighting of wood fires is not permitted in the park.

More National Parks of Importance

Ben Boyd National Park

SIZE: 10 260 ha
MAP: NSW 7 L9

This park stretches along the southern coast of New South Wales in two sections separated by Twofold Bay and the town of Eden.

The southern section is of major historic interest with the ruins of the bygone whaling era, while the northern section contains interesting coastal flora and a unique formation known as the Pinnacles. Here fragile sand gullies capped with red clay form an unusual eroded gully off Long Beach.

Fishing, diving and surfing are popular pastimes along this coast and there are some great walks in the northern section of the park, including a 1 km nature trail to the Pinnacles. The nearby woodchip mill has an excellent tour each Thursday.

Access to both sections of the park is possible in conventional vehicles.

There are no camping facilities in the northern section. In the south, basic facilities (pit toilets and fireplaces) are provided at Saltwater Creek and Bittangabee Bay. Booking for camp sites in holiday periods is essential.

For more information, contact the National Parks and Wildlife Service, Merimbula, on (02) 6495 5001.

Beautiful beaches with clear waters are hallmarks of Ben Boyd National Park, which edges the Sapphire Coast. The area is excellent for both beach and estuary fishing.

Border Ranges National Park

SIZE: 31 683 ha
MAP: NSW 4 M1

This unique area of rainforest and mountain wilderness straddles the Queensland–New South Wales border and shares a common boundary with the better-known Lamington National Park to the north.

This area is home to large numbers of grey kangaroos and red-necked wallabies which can often be seen feeding. The Tweed Range scenic drive winds up through the lush rainforest for about 60 km and can be comfortably driven in about 2 hours.

There are a number of walking trails and picnic areas in the park.

Access is either via Kyogle or Murwillumbah.

Camping in the park is free and permits are not required. There are camping grounds at Sheep Station Creek and at Forest Tops. Bush camping is possible west of the Bar Mountain rest area.

Phone the National Parks and Wildlife Service, Kyogle, (02) 6632 1473 for more information.

The restless flycatcher (Myiagra inquieta) is a small bird similar to the willie wagtail. In Border Ranges National Park it lives in the eucalypt forests in the southern part of the park.

Morton National Park

SIZE: 170 635 ha
MAP: NSW 7 M2

Bushwalking and sightseeing are the most popular activities in Morton National Park. Around the spectacular 82 metre high Fitzroy Falls are easy walking trails, some accessible by wheelchair. There are also several great walks around the escarpment behind Bundanoon. The best walks though are around Pigeon House and the Castle.

The easiest and most popular access into the park is via Moss Vale, or from near Nowra or Ulladulla. If you intend to explore further you will need a 4WD vehicle, or be a keen bushwalker.

Car-based camping is available (for a fee) at Gambells Rest at Bundanoon—bookings essential, (02) 4887 7270—with hot showers, toilets and barbecues.

In the southern section there are small camping sites at Blue Gum Flat near Pigeon House, where the road crosses the Yadboro River, and on Long Gully Road. No camp fees apply here.

For more details, contact the National Parks and Wildlife Service, Nowra, (02) 4423 2170, or the Fitzroy Falls Visitor Centre, (02) 4887 7270.

Mount Kaputar National Park

SIZE: 36 817 ha
MAP: NSW 4 E7

This park is dominated by the tall peaks of Mount Kaputar (1520 metres) and Mount Coryah (1400 metres).

Great walking trails (that vary greatly in length and difficulty), lookouts and unusual rock formations are the features that attract visitors.

All visitors must approach the park from Narrabri. It is 30 km of good gravel road to the entrance and another 20 km of steep, winding road (too narrow for caravans) to the main camping grounds.

A small fee, payable on an honour system, applies to the camp sites at Dawsons Spring. There are also two huts that can be hired. At Bark Hut, you must leave your vehicle in the car park and walk into the camp ground with all your gear.

For more information, contact the National Parks and Wildlife Service, Narrabri, (02) 6799 1740.

Mungo National Park

SIZE: 27 847 ha
MAP: NSW 5 F4

The arid Mungo National Park is unique. Set in outback New South Wales, it is part of the Willandra Lakes World Heritage Region. Evidence of Australian Aboriginal occupation dates back more than 60 000 years and the bones of some of the oldest known humans in Australia have been found here.

The major point of interest in the park is the landform known as the Walls of China, while the nearby dry lake bed

Sawn Rocks, in the northern section of Mount Kaputar National Park, are towering basalt 'organ pipe' formations created by volcanic eruptions eons ago.

is an archaeological goldmine of bones, middens and artefacts.

While road access is unsealed, it is open to conventional vehicles, as are the tracks inside the park.

There are camp sites at the park entrance and at Belah Camp. Bring your own firewood and water. Bunk-style accommodation is available at the shearers' quarters in the park, and just outside the park at Mungo Lodge, phone (03) 5029 7297.

Contact the National Parks and Wild-life Service, Mungo, (02) 5029 7292, or Buronga, (03) 5021 8900, for additional information.

An example of the Australian Aboriginal rock art found in Mutawintji National Park. As well as its visual impact, this art has symbolic meaning.

Mutawintji National Park

SIZE: 68 912 ha
MAP: NSW 1 D6

There are several outstanding Australian Aboriginal art sites at what is known as the Mutawintji Historic Site, and the surrounding area has been declared a national park.

Mutawintji has a great deal to offer the visitor. There is the colour and grandeur of the real outback, ancient art sites and ceremonial grounds, the incredible Aboriginal Mutawintji Historic Site (486 hectares), and hidden rock pools amid deep red gorges.

The main features of the park are best seen on foot and there is a good network of walking trails, including wheelchair accessible tracks.

The 2 hour drive from Broken Hill is mostly along dry gravel roads that become impassable to all vehicles after rain. There is good camping with basic facilities at Homestead Creek. Contact the National Parks and Wildlife Service, Broken Hill, (08) 8088 5933, for more details.

The Walls of China, an outstanding 30 km long area containing unusually shaped sand dunes, is a highlight of a visit to Mungo National Park.

don't miss

At the Mutawintji Cultural Centre, near the entrance of the park, you can sit on the floor in the dark while a Dream-time story is told. You can also learn more about Mutawintji, which became the first national park in the state to be returned to its traditional owners in 1998.

Myall Lakes National Park

SIZE: 44 172 ha
MAP: NSW 6 L4

Myall Lakes National Park is a great place to enjoy water sports. Sailing, windsurfing and canoeing are very popular. Fishing, and netting fresh prawns late at night are also favourite pastimes.

Bushwalking is well catered for and everyone should experience the unique rainforest trail at Mungo Brush. Houseboats are another great way to experience the peace of the lakes.

Drivers of 4WD vehicles have beach access at designated points along the Mungo Brush Road. Permits for travel along the beach north from Hawks Nest are available from the Great Lakes Tourist Information Centre, Forster, phone (02) 6554 8799, or Tea Gardens, phone (02) 4997 0111.

Broughton Island, off the coast, is also within the national park and the fishing and diving are excellent.

One of New South Wales' most popular parks, Myall Lakes is 230 km north of Sydney and about 1 hour's drive from Newcastle.

Boating is one of the best ways to appreciate the vast and tranquil waterways of Myall Lakes. Anglers can fish for mullet, bream, flathead and luderick.

The National Parks and Wildlife Service, Hunter area, (02) 4987 3108, has provided good camping facilities at a number of places.

Oxley Wild Rivers National Park

SIZE: 92 926 ha
MAP: NSW 4 K8

The Oxley Wild Rivers National Park preserves an area that includes up to 10 separate river gorges. These gorges are separated by farming and forestry land on the higher plateaus.

The waterfalls tumbling off the escarpment into the wild gorges of the many river beds are spectacular and the lookouts over Wollomombi, Apsley, Dangars and Tia Falls are all easily accessed by vehicle. The adventurous bushwalker will also find the park extremely rewarding. Canoeing is possible on the rivers, especially at Georges Junction where access is easiest.

Travellers can access the park from many different points, including along the Oxley Highway.

Remote camping is permitted anywhere in the park except at designated

picnic areas and there are many beautiful spots to choose from.

Contact the National Parks and Wildlife Service, Armidale, (02) 6776 4260 or (02) 6776 0000, for more details.

Royal National Park

SIZE: 15 000 ha
MAP: NSW 6 J9

Royal National Park, gazetted in 1879, was Australia's first national park. It was severely affected by the Christmas 2001 bushfires.

Bushwalkers will find a huge number of trails to explore in the park and while the coast track is the most spectacular, its total length of 30 km would require an overnight camp.

There are many beaches where swimming is very popular, as are beach and rock fishing.

The park can be accessed by car, train and ferry. Road access is from the Princes Highway. There are walking trails into the park from the railway stations at Engadine, Loftus, Heathcote and Waterfall. A ferry service runs from Cronulla to Bundeena.

There is limited camping in the park at Bonnie Vale. Bookings are essential. There is bush camping or undeveloped sites at various spots including Werrong Beach, Curracurrang, Winifred Falls, Uloola Falls, Deer Pool and Karloo Pool.

For more information contact the National Parks and Wildlife Service, Visitor Centre, on (02) 9542 0648.

Washpool National Park

SIZE: 58 320 ha
MAP: NSW 4 K4

This park is a wilderness area that protects the largest area of old-growth, warm-temperate rainforest in New South Wales. Declared a national park in 1983, it has since been included on the World Heritage List.

Visitors wishing to see a wide variety of wildlife will not be disappointed as the region is one of the richest fauna areas in New South Wales.

A number of interesting walks within the park range from a pleasant one hour stroll along the banks of Coombadjha Creek to difficult 3 day hikes in more remote areas.

Washpool is on the Gwydir Highway between Grafton and Glen Innes in northern New South Wales. The park is accessible to conventional vehicles.

The main camping ground at Bellbird Camping Area has fireplaces, firewood, picnic tables and toilets. There are walk-in camp sites at the Coombadjha Camping Area.

For more details, contact the ranger at Glen Innes on (02) 6732 5133.

Above: *Although much of Washpool National Park is trackless wilderness, there are some easily accessible areas along Coombadjha Creek.*

The wonga pigeon (Leucosarcia melanoleuca) is one of the 260 species of birds found in Washpool National Park. It roosts in trees at night, but spends most of the day on the ground.

Left: *Coast banksias (Banksia integrifolia) can be seen in abundance on the Royal's magnificent Coast Track which follows the park's cliffs, escarpments and beaches.*

Willandra National Park

SIZE: 19 386 ha
MAP: NSW 5 L3

Willandra, 64 km northwest of Hillston, was once famous for merino wool. Now the flat country is home to numerous red kangaroos, while the sheep station homestead and other outbuildings have been retained to preserve this part of the state's outback history.

There are a number of walks in the park, with details available from the National Parks and Wildlife Service.

The Merton Motor Trail provides an unsealed road tour of the park. The western section of the park has no vehicle access and is restricted to bushwalkers only.

Access is via unsealed roads that are impassable in wet weather. It is possible to stay in the 'Men's Quarters' where bunks and cooking utensils are provided, but bookings must be made in advance, on (02) 6967 8159. Camping is also available near the homestead. Remote camping within the remainder of the park is possible for backpackers. The area becomes extremely hot in summertime.

The recently discovered Wollemi pine (Wollemia nobilis) was hidden in a sheltered rainforest gorge in Wollemi National Park. Only three small stands of the trees are known to exist.

For further information, contact the National Parks and Wildlife Service, Willandra, (02) 6967 8159, or Griffith, (02) 6966 8100.

Wollemi National Park

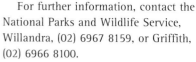

SIZE: 492 220 ha
MAP: NSW 6 H5

Wollemi is the second largest park in New South Wales and while it is primarily a wilderness park, it is within 2 hours of the busiest city in the country. In 1994, the Wollemi pine was found deep in the park. This is significant because this previously unknown species of tree can trace its descent directly from plants from the Jurassic period.

The park's major feature is its wilderness value and the intrepid bushwalker will find a fascinating range of places to enjoy amid stunning scenery.

For those interested in history the Newnes shale mine site has plenty to offer, while birdwatching, canoeing, liloing and swimming are popular activities in a number of places in the park.

Vehicle access is restricted to the park's perimeter; after that the park is really only for the fit, experienced and self-sufficient bushwalker.

On the eastern side there is camping at Wheeney Creek, while on the western boundary there is a pleasant large camping area at Newnes. Dunns Swamp is another good camping spot.

For more details contact the National Parks and Wildlife Service, Muswellbrook, (02) 6543 3533; Blackheath, (02) 4787 8877; or Mudgee, (02) 6372 7199.

Quietly floating or canoeing down the Colo River in Wollemi National Park provides an opportunity to observe wildlife that might not otherwise be seen.

Popular Parks at a Glance

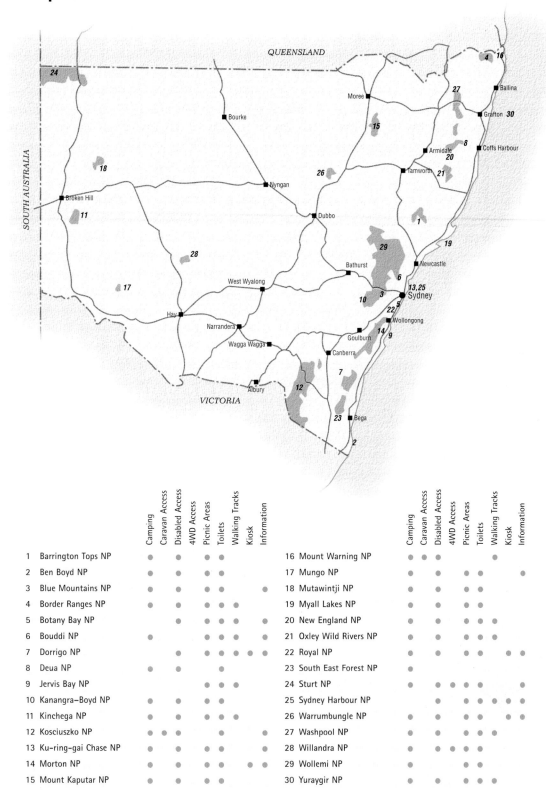

	Camping	Caravan Access	Disabled Access	4WD Access	Picnic Areas	Toilets	Walking Tracks	Kiosk	Information
1 Barrington Tops NP	●		●		●	●			
2 Ben Boyd NP	●		●		●	●			
3 Blue Mountains NP	●		●		●	●			●
4 Border Ranges NP	●		●		●	●	●		
5 Botany Bay NP			●		●	●	●		●
6 Bouddi NP	●				●	●	●		●
7 Dorrigo NP			●		●	●	●	●	●
8 Deua NP	●			●	●	●			
9 Jervis Bay NP					●	●	●		
10 Kanangra–Boyd NP	●			●	●				●
11 Kinchega NP	●	●		●	●	●			
12 Kosciuszko NP	●	●	●		●				●
13 Ku-ring-gai Chase NP	●				●	●			●
14 Morton NP	●				●	●		●	●
15 Mount Kaputar NP	●			●	●	●			
16 Mount Warning NP			●		●		●		
17 Mungo NP		●		●	●	●			●
18 Mutawintji NP	●			●	●	●			
19 Myall Lakes NP	●				●	●			
20 New England NP	●				●	●	●		
21 Oxley Wild Rivers NP	●				●	●	●		
22 Royal NP	●				●	●	●	●	●
23 South East Forest NP	●				●	●			
24 Sturt NP		●		●	●	●	●		●
25 Sydney Harbour NP			●		●	●	●	●	●
26 Warrumbungle NP	●				●	●	●		●
27 Washpool NP	●				●	●	●		
28 Willandra NP					●	●			●
29 Wollemi NP	●				●	●	●		
30 Yuraygir NP	●				●	●	●		

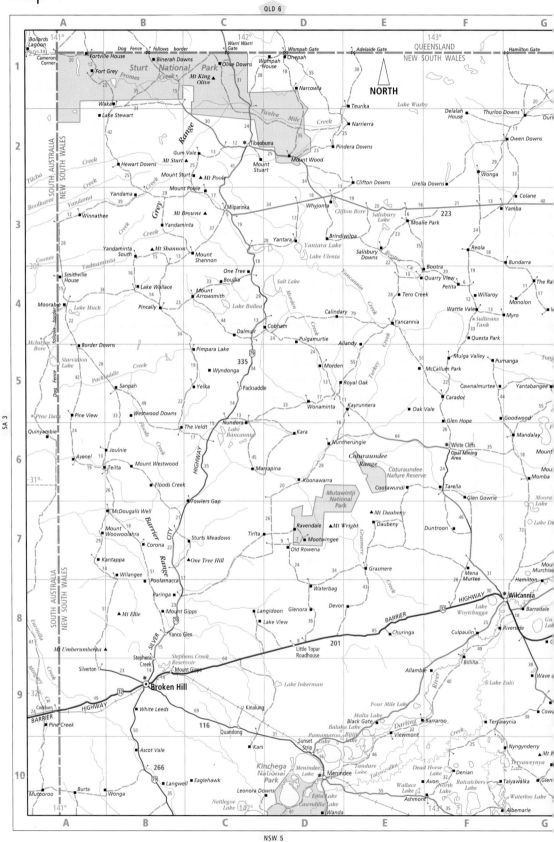

0 10 20 30 40 50
kilometres

H   J   K   L   M   N   P

Currawinya National Park
144°
145°
146°
QUEENSLAND
NEW SOUTH WALES
29°

ry Gate
ly Gate
Hungerford
Lake Womban
Cuttaburra Basin
Barringun
Rostella
Eureka Plains
Morton Plains
Jobs Gate
13
10

averley Downs
24
51
31
Brindingabba
Cuttaburra
Wirrawarra
Waratah
22
14

Nungunyah
Glenhope
22
Thoura
Comeroo
16
29
Enngonia
19
Gerara
47

33
23
20
Mooleyarran
Yantabulla
44
30
Beulah
Dalwood
62

33
Nardoo
7
Mooreland Downs
102
Back Springs
Strathern
Ella Vale
63

37
Dungarvon
24
Warrego River
River

21
Wampra
19
Minetta
Fords Bridge
Garlands
135
Corella
19
Collerina

Wanaaring
10
25
Wangareena
Rainbar
Lake Nichebulka
Lauradale
The Lagoon
Culgoa

31
Nocoleche
Nocoleche Nature Reserve
15
6
20
42
Romani
Pine View
Belvedere
42
Yambacoona
Mt Druid
28

den Vale
Janina
Barrakee
191
Goonery
Yandaroo
15
12
38
28
North Bourke
Moculta
Kamilaroi
98
Bogan

Emaroo
Salt Lake
Glenora
32
Lake Mere
25
Nulty
44
26
Bourke
Hastings
41
51

onnamah
Avondale
Utah Lake
Uteara
Toorale
64
Mulga
47
Woodstock
Mt Oxley
Tarcoon
34

rimpa
Mount Mulyah
View Point Outstation
22
28
Mt Burragurry
Hamilton Park
49
Murramburra Dam
Dwyers
Wave Hill
Wyuna Downs
Compton Downs
42

New Chum
21
Myrtle Vale
Toorale East
23
43
Belah
Ben Lomond
15
Wyuna Downs
18

Louth
31
Mt Gunderbooka
Byrock
31
52

Napunyah
37
Keelambra
Carney
Campamooka Mtn
Winbar
26
Mt Gunderbooka National Park
Curraween Hill
Wilga Downs
Coronga Peak
Little Peak
207
Glenariff

Green Lake
Myall
Polocara
Tara
92
Mt Deerina
Mulya
32
19
Bald Hills
Coronga Peak
168

olka
Tallalara
Kallara
Darling River
33
Wilgaroon
Yanda
40
Windera
El Trune
Dowling Bore
31
Coolabah

oo
Marra
41
Nangara
Mt Booroondarra
Booroondarra Downs
54
32

40
Dunoak
Innesowen
Gidgee
Mt Buckwaroon
Glen Hope
36

62
Tilpilly
Tiltagoona
55
Mount Gap
Mount Grenfell
Buckwaroon
59
Moquilambo
CSA Copper Mine
35
26
Sussex
Wilgalong

lga
Tilpilly Lake
Manara
Windara
Tambua
15
30
Cobar
16
Florida
22
Hermidale
21

a
258
Lilyvale
Meadow Glen
30
Boppy Mount
Canbelego
133
18

44
Cultowa
Emmdale Roadhouse
Bulla
Barnato
Lerida
33
Hill View
Mt Nurri
Mangalore
8

Wongalara
Coomeratta
Noona
44
Double Gates
17
The Rookery
62
Kopyje
Mount Lewis
34
Quanda Nat Res

56
Kaleno
43
The Bluff
32
Kidman
31
Babinda
31

16
Belarabon
13
Bindi
Bloomfield
13
Yarrama
14
Nymagee
40

Paddington
32
Garranvale
48
Glenwood
48

Baden Park
Kiama
Keewong
30
49
Taringo Downs
WAY
Gilgunnia

54
Berangabah
19
Yallock
41
Karwarn
Yathong Nature Reserve
38
Bedooba
14
57
Nangerybone
Bobadah
Walkers Hill

Mount Manara
Marfield
Tasman
31
21
48
144°
145°
34
254
146°
30
Eremaran
Burthong

0 10 20 30 40 50
kilometres

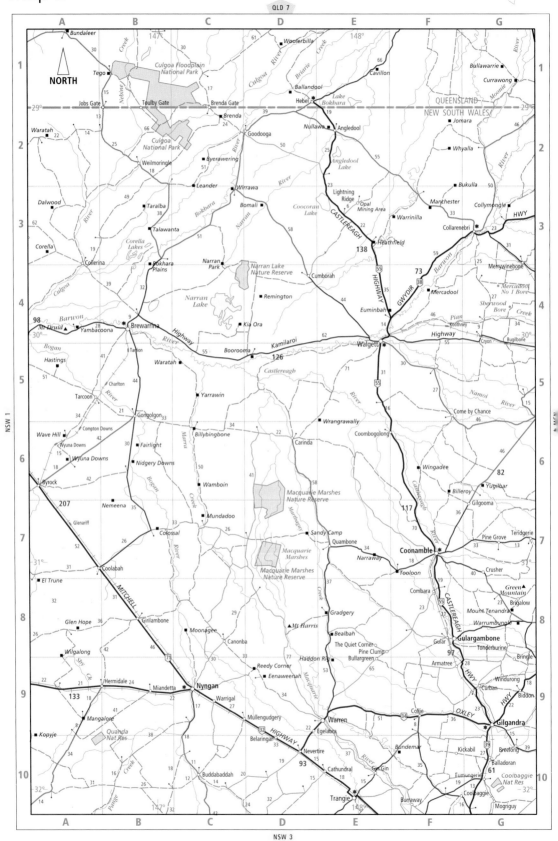

NSW 1

0 10 20 30 40 50
kilometres

NORTH

Bundemar · Kickabil · Breelong
Nevertire · Cathundral · Gin Gin · Eumungerie · Balladoran
Buddabaddah · Trangie · Burraway · Coolbaggie · Coolbaggie Nat Res · Mogriguy
Five Ways · Tabratong · Dandaloo · Narromine · Minore · Dubbo · Eulomogo · Brocklehurst · Barbigal · Beni
Lansdale · Tottenham · Albert · Farrendale · Cumboogle · Wongarbon · Glengarra · Geurie · Ponto
Bombah · Mogal Plain · Keriwah · Terowie · Mungery · Tanners Spring · Walmer · Arthurville
Nangerybone · Bobadah · Walkers Hill · Yellow Mtn · Ballatta · Yethera · Warge Rock · Bulgandramine · Tomingley · Obley · Yeoval · Curra Creek
Eremaran · Vermont Hill · Kerein Hills · Boona Mountains · Tullamore · Eribung · Dunmore · Peak Hill · Trewilga · Goobang National Park · Yullundry · Eurimbula · Cumnock
Mt Tallebung · Tallebung · Melrose · Kadungle · Fifield · Boor Hill · Mckibrin · Alectown · Baldry · Larras Lee
Flamingo · Woggoon Nature Reserve · Ghost Hill · Trundle · Goobang · Gumble · Molong
Gunebang · Kiacatoo · Mt Tilga · Byong Hills · Blow Clear · Nanardine · Bindogundra · Cudal · Boree
Euabalong West · Condobolin · Derriwong · Bogan Gate · Gunningbland · Parkes · Bumberry · Manildra
Euabalong · Ootha · Yarrabandai · Broigan · Warregal · Tichborne · Cookamidgera · Mandagery · Bowan Park
Murrin Bridge · Wallaroi Hill · Fairholme · Corridgery · Back Yamma · Daroobalgie · Nangar Nat Pk · Toogong · Longs Corner
Lake Cargelligo · Wargambegal · Burgooney · Tullibigeal · Banar Lake · Warroo · Bedgerebong · Forbes · Cumbijowa · Eugowra · Mogong · Cargo · Lockwood
Weja · Winnungra · Ungarie · Bena · Burcher · Corinella · Bundaburrah · Garema · Mulyandry · Nanami · Canowindra
Hannan · Gubbata · Kikoira · Thulloo · Girral · Blow Clear · Wambayne · Lake Cowal · Pinnacle Reefs · Wirrinya · Warraderry · Goologong · Billimari · Walli
Narriah Mtn · Calleen · Clear Ridge · Marsden · Pullabooka · Driftway · Piney Range · Yambira Mtn · Conimbla Nat Pk · Holmwood · Woodstock
Erigolia · Taleeban · Weethalle · Yalgogrin · Caragabel · Grenfell · Wireqa · Greenethorpe · Cowra · Noonbinna · Darbys · Morongla Creek
Tallimba · Wyalong · West Wyalong · Bland · Quandialla · Weddin Mts NP · Wattamondara · Koorawatha · Crowther · Breakfast Creek
Buddigower Nat Res · Alleena · Yiddah · Bimbi · Liramenga · Thuddungra · Wirrimah · Bendick Murrell · Godfreys Creek
Bellarwi · Barmedman · Bribbaree · Morangarell · Memagong Hill · Monteagle · Dandabilla Nat Res · Frogmore
Barellan · Moombooldool · Kamarah · Mirrool · Big Brush Nat Res · Gidginbung · Trungley Hall · Narrabutra · Tubbul · Burrangong · Murringo · Mt Geegullalong
Ardlethan · Ariah Park · Pullawan · Grogan · Milvale · Young · Wombat · Boorowa
Colinrooble · Uley · Walleroobie · Temora · Combaning · Springdale · Kingvale · Murrumburrah · Cunningar · Binalong
Leeton · Yanco · Cowabbie West · Mimosa · Stockinbingal · Yeo Yeo · Wallendbeen · Jindalee · Harden · Galong · Kangiara
Narrandera · Grong Grong · Matong · Ganmain · Methul · Sebastapol · Dirnasser · Bethungra Mtn · Cootamundra · Brawlin · Beggan Beggan · McMahons Reef · Goondah · Bowning
Corobimilla · Marrar · Old Junee · Junee Reefs · Ulandra Nature Res · Muttama · Jugiong · Bookham
Sandigo · Kywong · Galore · Coolamon · Downside · Harefield · Eurongilly · Coolac · Pettit · Gobarralong · Burrinjuck · Cavan
Birrego · Greenvale · Currawarna · Millwood · Malebo · Wantabadgery · Nangus · Goondial · Burrinjuck Waters SP · Wee Jasper
Boree Creek · Bullenbong · Wagga Wagga · Alfred Town · Mundarlo · Gundagai · Adjungbilly · Wee Jasper
Yulama · Lockhart · Uranquinty · Forest Hill · Mount Adrah · Tumblong · Brungle · Tumorrama Nat Res
Gregadoo · Borambola · Mount Horeb · Gocup

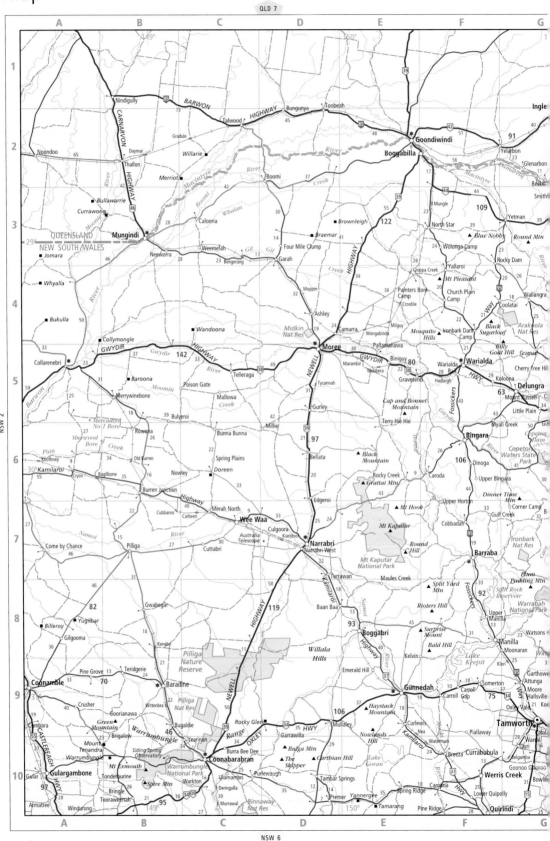

kilometres
0 10 20 30 40 50

H J K L M N P

1 Laravale · Numinbah Valley · Springbrook NP · Burleigh Heads · Coolangatta
Main Range National Park · Rockbrae · Mt Barney Nat Park · Tamrookum · Numinbah Nat Res · Tweed Heads · Fingal Head
Warwick · Emu Vale · Koreelah Nat Pk · Rathdowney · Limpinwood Nat Res · Lamington Nat Park · Bilambil · Banora Point · Chinderah · Kingscliff

2 Karara · Lake Leslie · Killarney · Mt Barney · Dalman · Woodenbong · Cougal · Lindesay View · Border Ranges NP · Mount Lion · Mt Warning Nat Pk · Numinbah · Chillingham · Uki · Murwillumbah · Tumbulgum · Condong · Bogangar · Pottsville Beach
Stanthorpe · The Summit · Rivertree Peak · Liston · Tooloom · Urbenville · Grevillia · Old Grevillia · Roseberry · Wiangaree · Horseshoe Creek · Cawongla · Nimbin · Rosebank · Modanville · Goonengerry · Wooyung · Ocean Shores · Brunswick Heads · Mullumbimby

3 Pikedale · Glen Aplin · Amosfield · Paddys Flat · Boonoo Boonoo Nat Pk · Old Bonalbo · Dyraaba · Ettrick · Kyogle · Cedar Point · The Channon · Dunoon · Rock Valley · Goolmangar · Byron Bay · Bangalow · Suffolk Park
Ballandean · Wallangarra · Sandy Hill · Bonalbo · Theresa Creek · Doubtful Creek · Fairy Hill · Bentley · Lismore · Bexhill · Wollongbar · Lennox Head · Ballina · Empire Vale

4 Tank Mtn · Sundown National Park · Glen Innes · Tenterfield · Drake · Mallanganee Nat Res · Coombell · Rappville · Tabbimble · Pacific Hwy · Woodburn · Evans Head · Snapper Point · Bundjalung National Park · Broadwater NP · Tabbimoble Swamp NP
Mt Gunyan · Silver Spur · Glenlyon · Lake Glenlyon · Black Mtn · Bluff Rock · Billyrimba · Mt Pikapene Nat Res · Mt Neville Nat Res · Camira Creek · Whiporie · Banyabba Nat Res · Chatsworth · Harwood · Mororo · Iluka · Mulloway Point

5 Mole River · Riverton · Mingoola · Tarban · Torrington · Deepwater · Emmaville · Strathbogie · Washpool National Park · Gibraltar Range NP · Glen Elgin · Cangai · Tortis Ck Nat Res · Copmanhurst · Koolkhan · Ulmarra · Grafton · South Grafton · Tyndale · Maclean · Yamba · Angourie · The Bald Knob · Yuraygir National Park · Brooms Head

6 Tent Hill · Dundee Rail · Dundee · Bald Nob · Barool Nat Pk · Newton Boyd · Dalmorton · Louis Point · Buccarumbi · OBX Creek · Coutts Crossing · Braunstone · Halfway Creek · Red Rock · Corindi Beach · Arrawarra · Wooli · Bare Point · Minnie Water · Pillar Valley · Yuraygir National Park

7 Guyra · Black Mountain · Aberfoyle · Wongwibinda · Ebor · Dundurrabin · Tyringham · Dorrigo · Bostobrick · North Dorrigo · Cascade · Megan · Ulong · Brooklana · Coramba · Korora · Coffs Harbour · Woolgoolga · Sandy Beach · Emerald Beach · Moonee Beach · Moonee Beach Nat Pk

8 Armidale · Uralla · Waterfall · Hillgrove · Jeogla · Wollomombi · New England National Park · Bellingen · Urunga · Valla Beach · Nambucca Heads · Macksville · Warrell Creek · Scotts Head · Grassy Head · Stuarts Point · PACIFIC · TASMAN · SEA

9 Walcha Road · Walcha · Moona Plains · Daisy Plains · Carrai Nat Res · Toorooka · Bellbrook · Willawarrin · Eungai · Turners Flat · Clybucca · Smithtown · Kinchela · South West Rocks · Arakoon · Smoky Cape · Kempsey · South Kempsey · Hat Head NP · OCEAN

10 Walcha · Kangaroo Flat · Werrikimbe Nat Pk · Oxley Wild Rivers NP · Mt Banda Banda · Kumbatine Nat Pk · Upper Rollands Plains · Rollands Plains · Maria River Nat Res · Frederickton · Gladstone · Koragoro Point · Crescent Head · Kundabung · Bellangry · Pappinbarra · Pembrooke · Telegraph Point · Blackmans Point · Wauchope · Port Macquarie · Point Plomer · Saltwater Lake
Mount Seaview · Raffles Peak · Kindee · Yarras · Ellenborough · Beechwood · Bagnoo

NORTH

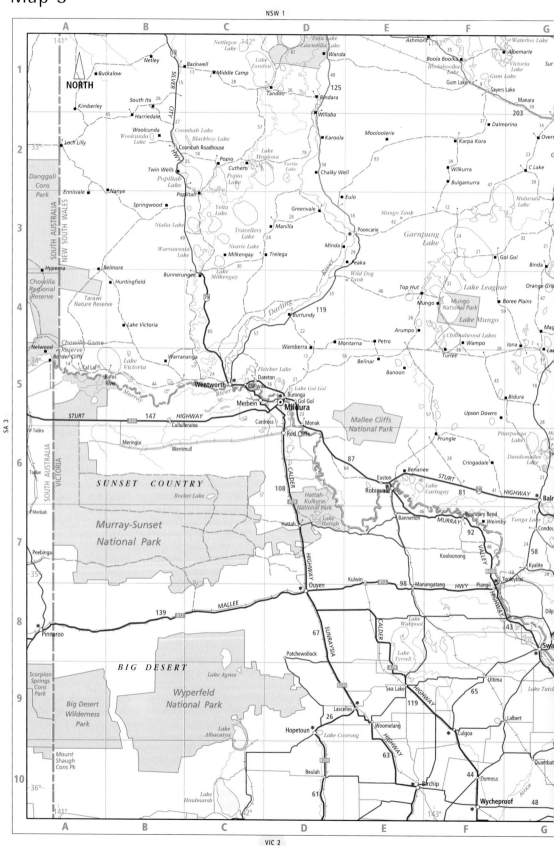

©Global Book Publishing Pty Ltd & Universal Press Pty Ltd

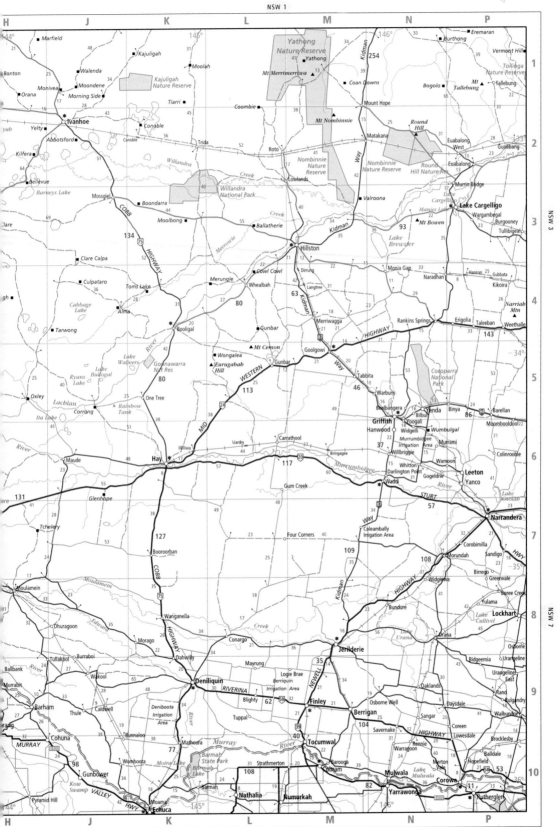

Map 6

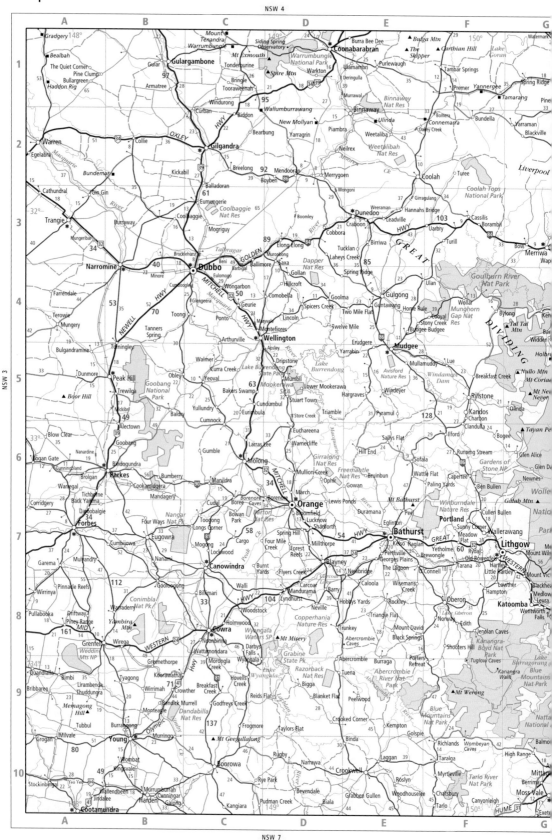

kilometres

0 10 20 30 40 50

NSW

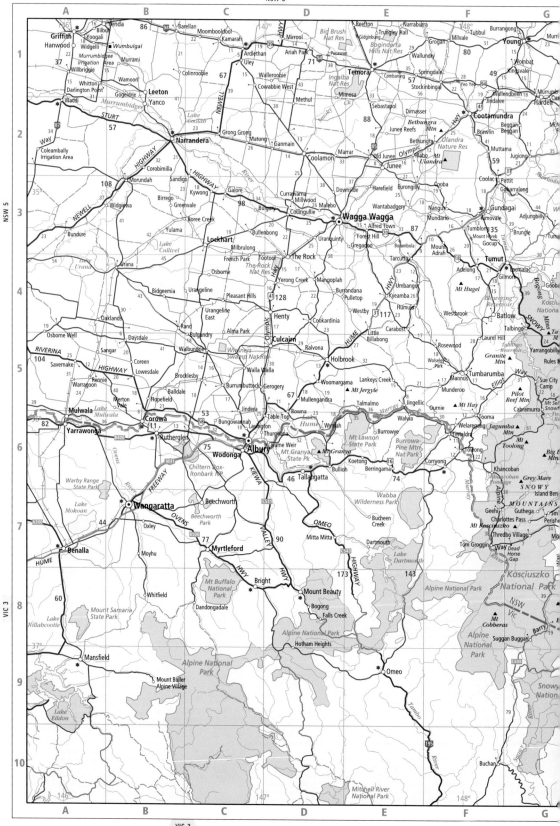

kilometres
0 10 20 30 40 50

NORTH

NSW

SOUTH

TASMAN

SEA

PACIFIC

OCEAN

Victoria

The small state of Victoria is truly a wonderland for outdoor enthusiasts, with over a tenth of its area devoted to national or state parks, reserves and protected historical sites. Its natural beauty extends from the mountainous High Country and large tracts of rugged forests to coastlines offering white sandy beaches, remote stretches of seashore and the magical Great Ocean Road. It encompasses the wonderful Gippsland lakes and the Little Desert, the magnificent Grampians and the open plains and low scrub of the mallee. Victoria is indeed fortunate to have such a large number of diverse multi-use parks, where walkers play alongside campers, climbers, horseriders and four-wheel drivers—all joined by their common love of the outdoors and their interest in its conservation.

Alpine National Park

Covering a vast area of 646 000 hectares, the Alpine National Park is Victoria's biggest, and one of Australia's finest parks, offering rugged mountains, powerful rivers, remote snowfields, open plains and deep gorges which open out to reveal green valleys. Reaching far across the Dividing Range, this park forms an important natural corridor for its unique flora and fauna and is best treated in six different sections: Mount Hotham–Feathertop; Wombargo–The Cobberas; Tingaringy; Bogong High Plains; Wonnangatta–Moroka; and Mount Buller–Stirling.

fact file

WHERE: Extends across the Great Dividing Range from Mansfield, through to the border with New South Wales, with access 230–500 km from Melbourne
Map: Vic 4 D4

WHEN: All year

WHY: Mountain scenery, skiing in winter, swimming, walking, 4WD tours, cycling, horse-riding, canoeing, nature study, photography, historical interest

SIZE: 646 000 ha

RANGER: Parks Victoria in Bright (03) 5755 1577, Dargo (03) 5140 1243, Omeo (03) 5159 1660, or Mount Beauty (03) 5754 4693

Right: The crimson rosella (Platycercus elegans) is found in and around the tall trees in the eucalypt forests and woodlands of the park.

In the Past

Australian Aboriginals resided in this mountain region for thousands of years, but it was in 1824 that Hume and Hovell explored and named the Australian Alps.

Many different types of people were to venture across and inhabit the peaks, including miners during the mining booms, loggers, graziers and workers on hydro-electric schemes.

The push to protect the region as a national park first came from the newly formed Victorian National Parks Association during the 1960s, but it wasn't until December 1989 that the Alpine National Park was proclaimed.

A Diversity of Life

The alpine region is ever-changing; snow covers the upper reaches for most of winter, while summer brings heat to both the lower reaches and the mountain tops. The weather can change from extreme heat to freezing temperatures very quickly, and snow is not uncommon during the warmer months.

Perhaps the most enduring image of the High Country is that of tall timbers. The park is dominated by eucalypts such as the mountain gum and stringybark,

then further up on the peaks the alpine ash, and above the snow line, the colourful, gnarled, stunted snow gum.

During spring, as the winter snow melts, a carpet of alpine daisies, alpine marsh marigold and the alpine hovea greet walkers who utilise the ski tracks for their forays on foot.

The changing weather and the different types of vegetation lead to diversity in the wildlife. An abundance of bird life will be found on a visit to the park. Species include the noisy gang-gang cockatoo, colourful crimson rosellas and the distinctive long-beaked wattlebird.

Patient visitors will be rewarded by chance meetings with kangaroos, bats and echidnas. Wombats can be found foraging at night.

Many species of animals are endemic to this region, including the brush-tailed

rock wallaby and the mountain pygmy possum. At one time the latter was thought to be extinct.

Mount Hotham–Feathertop

Mount Feathertop and Mount Hotham are among Victoria's highest peaks and provide a perfect playground for skiers and snowboarders in winter, and walkers and cyclists during the summer months.

The Hotham Heights village caters for the downhill skier, while the surrounding area boasts a remote mountain range for the ski tourer. Many cross-country skiers base themselves at nearby Dinner Plain, and the adventurous head cross-country along the Razorback trail to Mount Feathertop.

Walking tracks abound after the snow melts, and the Alpine Walking Track cuts through this region towards Falls Creek.

For up-to-date information, contact the Alpine Resorts Commission.

Above: *By far the highest mountain range on this relatively flat continent, the Australian Alps form a distinctive ecological zone, with several plant and animal species only found here.*

Left: *Snow gums (Eucalyptus niphophila) dominate the woodlands above the snow line. Its bark sheds in ribbons, leaving a smooth whitish-grey surface.*

VIC

Hiking at Falls Creek. When the snow melts, there are many accessible walking tracks. The 650 km Alpine Walking Track passes through the park and can be joined at Falls Creek.

Wombargo–The Cobberas

With only one access road suitable for conventional vehicles, this section in the north of the state abuts the New South Wales Kosciuszko National Park. Visitors with conventional vehicles should use Black Mountain Road to access the popular camping areas of Native Dog Flat, Willis on the Snowy River and the Cobberas Wilderness Area. Four-wheel drivers have a much greater choice of tracks and routes through this region.

The peaks of Mount Cobberas One and Two are popular bases for walks, as is Cowombat Flat with its wreckage of a DC-3 aircraft that crashed in 1954.

Tingaringy

As the highest peak east of the Snowy River, Mount Tingaringy offers commanding views of the New South Wales Kosciuszko Range and the peaks down south towards the Snowy River. Most of this region is classified as a wilderness area and at the border of New South Wales adjoins the Kosciuszko National Park and Byadbo Wilderness Area. Because mechanical means of transport are not permitted, it is mainly bushwalkers who use this remote and inhospitable region. Water can be scarce here in summer, so bushwalkers need to be well prepared and self-sufficient.

Bogong High Plains

The early graziers brought their cattle to the lush, grassy Bogong High Plains during summer and these plains were one of the first places you could ski in Victoria in the early 1900s.

Today the area is popular with visitors in both summer and winter as it still offers snow skiing, and also provides bushwalking, bike and horseriding, and trout fishing in the Rocky Valley Dam and Pretty Valley Pondage.

Wallace's Hut, built by the Wallace Brothers in 1889, is the oldest of the cattlemen's huts still standing in the park and it is classified by the National Trust. This building is not far from the Bogong High Plains Road, near Falls Creek.

Opposite page: Visitors to the Alpine National Park can gain access to beautiful Bindaree Falls from Mount Stirling Circuit Road which winds through sub-alpine and alpine forest.

[Map of the Alpine National Park region showing Victoria (VIC) and New South Wales (NSW), with locations including Myrtleford, Mitta Mitta, Mt Benambra, Dartmouth Reservoir, Mt Kosciuszko, Thredbo, Tom Groggin, Mt Bogong 1986 m, Alpine Walking Track, Mt Cobberas 1 & 2, Cobberas Wilderness Area, Mt Tingaringy, Lake Buffalo, Mt Beauty, Bogong, Hotham Heights, Mt Hotham 1868 m, Falls Creek, Mt Selwyn, Anglers Rest, Benambra, Native Dog Flat, MacKillops Bridge, Lake William Hovell, Lake Cobbler, Mt Stirling, Mt Howitt, Mt Buller, Mt Sarah, JB Plain, Dinner Plain, Omeo, Grant Historical Area, Alpine National Park, Swifts Creek, Lake Tali Karng, Dargo, The Sentinels, Avon Wilderness Area, Licola, Bruthen, Buchan, To Orbost 37 km, To Jindabyne 56 km, To Mansfield 10 km, Delatite River, Ovens River, Kiewa River, Buffalo River, Snowy River, Tambo River, Timbarra River, Mitchell River, Wonnangatta River, Macalister River, Caledonia River, Howqua River, Jamieson River, Barkly River, Avon River. Scale 0–20 kilometres.]

1 Cope Hut
2 Ropers Hut
3 Dibbens Hut
4 Nankervis Hut
5 Craigs Hut
6 Wallace Hut
7 Bluff Hut
8 Davies Hut

Wonnangatta–Moroka

This section of the park is one of the more popular, offering a wide range of walking and 4WD tracks, ski trails in winter for cross-country skiers, and excellent camping areas, many of which have access for conventional vehicles. For many, the main attraction is the Wonnangatta Valley with its majestic green valley floor where many pioneers settled last century.

Hidden deep in the mountains at the head of the Wellington River is the jewel of the High Country, Lake Tali Karng, which is accessible on foot and can only be viewed from the Sentinel and Echo Point on Rigalls Spur. Many walkers enjoy the 28 km hike, spending more than one night camped by the beautiful sapphire blue lake.

did you know?

Victoria's high country is the stuff of legends. The film *The Man from Snowy River*, based on A. B. 'Banjo' Paterson's poem of the same name, was made at Craig's Hut and other locations in the Alpine National Park. The Snowy River runs through the north-east of the park and into New South Wales.

Mount Buller–Stirling and Lake Cobbler

Only 2 hours drive from Melbourne, Mount Buller and Mount Stirling are two of the state capital's favourite playgrounds, with Stirling offering excellent cross-country skiing and popular walking trails, while Buller caters for Melbourne's downhill ski enthusiasts. With many trails surrounding the two

mountains and leading up to Lake Cobbler, 4WD touring and cycling are popular pastimes.

High Country Huts

Scattered throughout the park are a number of huts, most of which once belonged to the pioneers that grazed their cattle on the high plains during summer and which are part of the rich cultural heritage of the alpine region.

The most popular huts to visit include Wallace's Hut on the Bogong High Plains, and Bluff Hut and Craig's Hut in the region near Mansfield. Off the Howitt Road you will find Guy's Hut and the ruins of the Old Wonnangatta Station, while Davies Plain Hut is in the northern part of the park.

Activities

4WD touring is a very popular way to enjoy the park, especially where access is impossible by conventional vehicles.

While there are many walks within the park, by far the most impressive is the Alpine Walking Track which extends 650 km from the old goldmining town of Walhalla, across the rugged mountain range, into New South Wales, finishing in the Australian Capital Territory.

The Alps of Victoria also offer premium fishing, mountain-bike riding, horseriding and canoeing country. In fact, here in this vast park, there is something for everybody.

Access and Camping

Many bitumen and good quality roads lead to the major regions within the park.

The Mount Buller–Stirling area can be reached via Mansfield, north of Melbourne, along good quality gravel roads, while the Wonnangatta–Moroka area is accessed via Licola, on a well-maintained gravel road, or from Dargo on 4WD tracks.

Mount Hotham is serviced by a good bitumen road from Harrietville to the north and Dargo from the south. The Snowy River Road provides access for the Tingaringy unit, while Benambra and the Black Mountain Road lead to the Cobberas region in the north-east of the park.

Remote camping is the best way to experience the magnificent Alpine Park in areas where there are no facilities provided. There are, however, some popular camping sites (with toilets and fireplaces) accessible to conventional vehicles. These include MacKillops Bridge on the Snowy River, Sheepyard Flat and Lake Cobbler near Mount Buller, along the Wellington River north of Licola and at Anglers Rest, north of Omeo.

For details of camping locations, contact the regional Parks Victoria office or Parks Victoria, phone 131 963.

Camping in the high country. Many bitumen and good quality roads give access to camping sites with facilities, but hikers have the best opportunity to access more remote wilderness areas.

One of the favourite areas to visit, Wonnangatta Valley, is in the centre of the park, north of Licola. There is camping aplenty in the valley and attractions include the site of a burnt-out station on the banks of Conglomerate Creek and a cemetery perched on the hillside under towering pine trees.

Other interesting tours in the alpine park include Dargo and the Crooked River–Talbotville area, Jacksons Crossing on the Snowy River and the Deddick Trail. The more adventurous and experienced might like to tackle Butcher Country Track or the mountain country around Davies Plain.

This park is very popular with walkers. Popular short walks include the return trek from the Bogong High Plains to Wallace's Hut and another fairly easy walk from Howitt Road to Bryces Gorge.

Left: The Victorian Alps are famous for their skiing. Enthusiasts can enjoy cross-country skiing at Mount Stirling and Mount Feathertop, with downhill skiing being popular at Mount Buller and Mount Hotham.

VIC

tourist info

Alpine Resorts Commission, Mount Hotham (03) 5759 3550

Grampians National Park

A series of jagged blue peaks forms a striking outline on the horizon, perched on the western plains of Victoria. A closer inspection reveals the ruggedness and grandeur of massive sandstone sculptures interspersed with a mosaic of colourful wildflowers. The Grampians make up this series of ranges which extend more than 80 km in length and 50 km at their widest point; they signal the end of the Great Dividing Range that starts near Cooktown in far north Queensland.

These rugged mountains offer outdoor enthusiasts the base for most activities, including walking, rock climbing, cycling and abseiling.

The sculptured structures started to emerge more than 400 million years ago when the land rose to form large areas of mountain. These rock formations have since been weathered by wind and rain and are now the main attraction of the Grampians National Park.

One of the more noticeable features of the range is that the western slopes are modest, while the eastern slopes are very steep. Excellent examples of this can be found on the Wonderland Range, near Halls Gap in the park's centre. This region has not always been protected under national park status, but has long been recognised for its rugged beauty.

In the Past

Early evidence of Australian Aboriginal settlement can be seen in the park's many art sites; it is also believed that these early inhabitants utilised the rock formations and caves for their cere-monies. Many of the line drawings at the art sites such as Wab Manja and Billimina shelters depict animal tracks, human figures and handprints.

Thomas Mitchell was the first European to explore this region in 1836 and it was not long after that graziers

occupied the foothills of the mountains. Other settlers included gold miners and loggers, the latter harvesting timber dur-ing the area's time as a state forest until the national park was formed in 1984.

Since then, visitor numbers have noticeably increased, and now strict controls are in place to protect the region from the effect of the extra visi-tors as well as from feral animals, weeds and soil erosion.

Sandstone Formations

The 167 000 hectare national park con-sists of four main systems of ranges: Victoria and Mount William in the park's lower sections, Mount Difficult in the north, and Serra, which cuts through the centre of the park from Dunkeld to Halls Gap. A smaller range to the south-west of Halls Gap is the Wonderland

VIC

Left and below: *Halls Gap is perhaps the most popular area of the Grampians National Park, which is not really surprising as it is the main tourist centre for the region. From Halls Gap you can look at unusual rock formations and towering cliffs, start walking trails, stop in at the Visitor Centre, and go bush camping.*

Range. This range is popular with visitors, and its unusual rock formations and towering cliffs can be appreciated in a variety of walks that begin around Halls Gap.

The rugged sandstone peaks and valleys are home to an extremely diverse plant life, with many rare species of wildflowers. Spring heralds the wildflower season. From August to November the colourful blooms carpet the rocky slopes and valleys, and include species such as the brilliant red flame heath which is widespread on the hillsides and the rare spectral duck orchid.

High up, the plateaus are covered in thick heathlands, while the hillsides and most of the park are covered in woodland forests and eucalypts such as messmate and brown stringybarks. In contrast, the moist valley floors and folds within the rocks provide the nutrients needed for the swamp gums, succulent ferns and silver banksias to flourish.

The diversity of plant life provides a habitat for a large number of birds, with more than 200 different species recorded in the Grampians. Flowering gums attract lorikeets, while yellow-tailed black cockatoos soar above the stringybarks. Walkers will see crimson rosellas and honeyeaters in the heathlands, and campers will often be rewarded with the antics of kookaburras.

Left: *The rainbow bee-eater (Merops ornatus), which can be seen in much of mainland Australia, can eat hundreds of bees each day. Over 200 bird species have been recorded in the Grampians.*

The most common marsupial spotted within the park is the swamp wallaby, but other species such as the grey kangaroo and a number of possums inhabit the park. Zumstein picnic area in the centre of the park is popular for viewing kangaroos, but visitors are asked not to feed these friendly natives. Platypus also reside in many of the creeks, but it takes a keen eye and a great deal of patience to spot one of these reclusive mono-tremes.

A Bushwalker's Paradise

With more than 200 km of maintained walking tracks throughout the park, it is no wonder that walkers head to this region to sample the many trails and the spectacular scenery. These trails range from short strolls through to overnight treks over rough terrain that are only suitable for the ambitious and fit.

One of the most popular walks for tourists is the Wonderland Long Walk. This walk starts at the Halls Gap camp ground and climbs along the Pinnacle Track

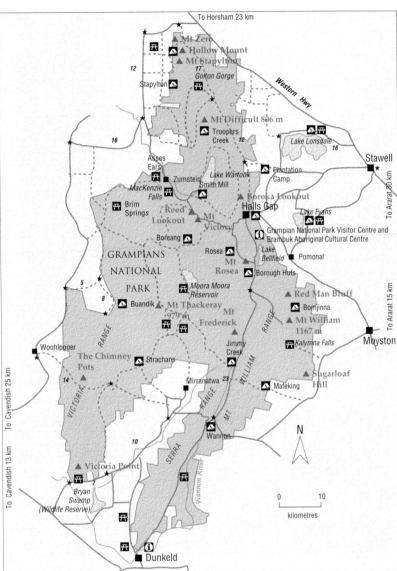

through eucalypt forests to the Pinnacle Lookout, which rewards the energetic walker with spectacular views. Continuing along the Wonderland Track on the return walk to Halls Gap takes in the Grand Canyon, Silent Street and the famous Elephant's Hide. This 10 km walk is of moderate difficulty and should take a day to complete.

Another walk is Briggs Bluff, which is best undertaken by those without a fear of heights, as it follows the cliff edge. This 10 km walk begins at the car park near Rose Gap and follows the Beehive Falls track and then climbs steeply

up onto the plateau for spectacular views of the Wimmera Plains.

The Balconies, which offers scenic views of the Victoria Valley, can be reached via a track from the Reed Lookout car park. This easy walk is less than 2 km long.

Information on all the walks are available from the Grampians National Park Visitor Centre at Halls Gap.

Rock Climbing and Abseiling

Featuring a multitude of large, majestic sandstone formations, the Grampians have a number of popular rock climbs.

don't miss

The Grampians offers some of the most spectacular climbing sites in the whole of Australia. There are many tour operators that can take you climbing, with the climbs ranging from easy to the more difficult, for the experienced climber.

the vehicular tracks that were used during the logging era have now been closed, so there is little to attract keen four-wheel drivers. Cycling is the next best form of transport and there are a number of pleasant rides in the region.

A popular one-day ride is the Wonderland Trail that leaves from Zumstein picnic area and heads to Wonderland car park before returning to Zumstein. The length of this trek is 53 km and will take a day to complete. The trail takes in MacKenzie Falls and the Pinnacle Lookout.

For the more adventurous, there is a 100 km 3-day ride, leaving also from Zumstein, which heads to the Victoria Range in the south of the park, taking in the Glenelg River, Wallaby Rocks and various Australian Aboriginal sites.

The two lakes in the park—Wartook and Bellfield—offer the visitor canoeing, swimming and fishing. Brown trout, redfin, blackfish and the occasional rainbow trout can be taken; nearby Rocklands Reservoir, Lake Fyans and Lake Toolondo are also popular. Yabbying is also a favourite pastime of the locals in many of the dams and waterholes in and around the park area. Victorian fishing licences must be obtained from Parks Victoria for all waters.

Wartook offers restricted powerboat use, while Rocklands and Lake Fyans are the main bodies of water for powered watercraft and water-skiers.

The park offers a cultural experience through a number of ancient Australian Aboriginal rock art sites, some of which are accessible to visitors.

MacKenzie Falls is the most popular of the several waterfalls in the Grampians. After rain, torrents of water rush over 40 metre cliffs into a deep pool.

Hollow Mountain, in the north of the park, is very popular, while Mount Rosea, near Halls Gap, offers one of the best collections of sandstone climbs. For something different, nearby Bundaleer has a range of climbs.

For details on climbing in the Grampians, or nearby Mount Arapiles, contact Parks Victoria 131 963, and the Victorian Climbing Centre. Guided climbing tours can be organised through Base Camp and Beyond at Halls Gap.

Other Activities

There are a number of scenic drives through the ranges. However, most of

Brambuk Aboriginal Cultural Centre near Halls Gap gives its visitors an insight into the indigenous culture through displays, bush tucker and performances given by the local Australian Aboriginal people.

The Grampians National Park Visitor Centre and its extensive displays should be your first stop at the beginning of your exploration of the park. Rangers are on hand to answer any questions.

Access

The park is 260 km from Melbourne, and Halls Gap can be reached via Ararat or Stawell. Access to the park's southern section is via Dunkeld, and through Wartook to the west.

Camping

There are bush camping areas throughout the park and a number of excellent camps where fees apply. Most are operated on a self-serve system, where campers fill out forms and deposit them at the camp site.

Camp grounds in the central part of the park include Borough Huts, Mount Rosea and Boreang. To the south-east, covering the Serra and Mount William Ranges, you will find Bomjinna, Jimmy Creek, Mafeking and Wannon Crossing. Victoria Range to the south-west offers camping at Buandik and Strachan Hut. Camping in the northern sector can be found at Troopers Creek, Smith Mill, Hollow Mountain and Mount Stapylton. The most popular camping areas are those at Halls Gap.

tourist info

Brambuk Aboriginal Cultural Centre, Halls Gap (03) 5356 4452

Base Camp and Beyond, Halls Gap (03) 5356 4300

Grampian National Park Visitor Centre (03) 5356 4381. Open daily 9.00 a.m. to 5.00 p.m.

Stawell Tourist Information Centre (03) 5358 2314

Victorian Climbing Centre, Seaford (03) 9782 4222

VIC

Right: *Casting for brown trout, redfin or blackfish in the Rocklands Reservoir, a popular fishing spot in the Grampians. Fishing licences must be obtained before you begin.*

Below: *Superb stretches of water in the Grampians include Lake Bellfield, which is the closest to Halls Gap. Water sports, including swimming, canoeing and fishing, are popular.*

Croajingolong National Park

The Croajingolong National Park is a remote wilderness area where cool freshwater streams trickle down from the mountains and from within pockets of temperate rainforest, through the tablelands of the park, before filtering through the sand dunes to finally emerge on the rugged windswept coastline of eastern Victoria.

Above: *The rugged south-eastern coast of Victoria, near Point Hicks. The Thurra River winds through the national park to meet the sea here. A small boat or a canoe will give access to the estuary.*

Right: *A seagull or silver gull (Larus novaehollandiae) on the Croajingolong coast. Over 300 species of birds can be found in the park, including pelicans, lyrebirds, parrots and cockatoos.*

Australian Aboriginals are thought to have lived in the Croajingolong area for over 40 000 years and it's not hard to understand why. With prolific plant life and an abundance of birds, fish and marsupials, this area provided a perfect food source for the local tribal groups.

Croajingolong was established in 1979 from a number of smaller parks. The natural, unspoilt beauty of this park attracts hundreds of visitors each year, especially to the freshwater estuaries of the Thurra, Mueller and Wingan Rivers.

The park features woodlands that lead down into gullies where temperate rainforest plants such as tree ferns, mosses, orchids and vines can be found. As you venture closer towards the coastline, the large trees give way to smaller plants, which offer a riot of colour in spring and, finally, stunted banksias and tea-trees on the windswept cliffs.

Nature study and birdwatching are popular pastimes among park visitors, and over 300 species of birds can be found, including many waterbirds.

Walking, Canoeing and Fishing

The area is a popular bushwalking destination with the long beaches, relatively good access and availability of fresh water being attractions to those who revel in remote lonely beaches.

Popular shorter walks within the park include the 2 hour Dunes Walk which takes you over the high sand dunes and offers a superb view over Point Hicks. In the same area is the Lighthouse Trek, which is easier and takes 3 hours to explore Point Hicks. From Wingan River camp site you can take the 5–6 hours return Petrel Point Track which explores the eastern coastline, while for a full day's walk, take the Easby Track from Wingan Point.

To get a different and enjoyable view of the area a small boat or a canoe will give you access to many sections of delightful river and estuary country, its wildlife and fishing.

Keen anglers will be rewarded with a large variety of species, taken from river, beach and headland, with nearby

Below: *Genoa Falls, located in the northern part of the park, form a multi-deck cascade. Water dragons can sometimes be seen sunning themselves on the rocks by the falls.*

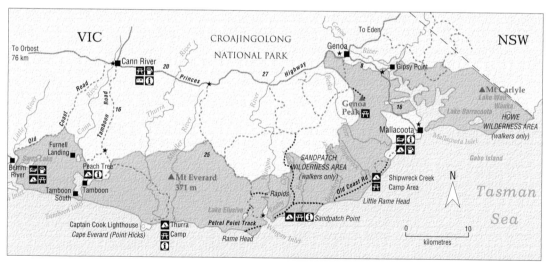

Mallacoota being a popular spot to catch flathead, bream and sand whiting.

Access and Camping

The road to Mallacoota is sealed but the generally good unsealed roads into the park from the Princes Highway may close after rain. Check with the ranger.

Camping is allowed at Peach Tree Camping Area on Tamboon Inlet, Ship-wreck Creek, Wingan River, Mueller River and Thurra River. Camping is also allowed outside the park at Cape Conran, Bemm River, Marlo and Mallacoota. Most of the camp sites have basic facilities (pit toilets, fireplaces and tables).

During the peak holiday periods, a ballot system is used for allocation of camping sites. Contact the ranger for camping information.

Dandenong Ranges National Park

Reaching upward from Ferntree Gully on the outskirts of Melbourne, over Mount Dandenong, lies the verdant sanctuary of the Dandenong Ranges National Park. Four large areas of natural bush plus smaller sections in the immediate vicinity have been combined to form the park. Over 130 species of birds and 31 mammal species have been recorded, while there are more than 350 plant species, 16 of which are either rare or restricted in distribution.

Activities

Apart from lazing underneath the forest canopy on a hot summer's day, the most popular recreation in the park is bush-walking, and a number of excellent trails are on offer.

The Ferntree Gully block offers a variety of interesting walks including the 1000 Steps to the top of the range. There are three picnic areas, including the wheelchair accessible Ferntree Gully and One Tree Hill picnic areas.

The Sherbrooke section boasts natural bushland and the tumbling Sherbrooke Falls. This block also features the Hardy Gully Nature Trail near the Grants Picnic Ground. This walk is about 700 metres and should take visitors only half an hour to complete. Nearby is the Margaret Lester Forest Walk, of similar length, which has a hard surface that is suitable for wheelchairs.

Mount Dandenong itself is in the section known as Doongalla, which means 'place of peace'. It is aptly named, with spectacular views and rugged bush trails leading down the western side of the mountain. Near-

Lush tree ferns contrasting with trickling water-falls and tall eucalypts provide part of the appeal of the Dandenong Ranges National Park.

by is a kiosk and the Mount Dandenong Observatory. The Doongalla Homestead site is accessible by car, along Doongalla Road, and its lawns and exotic plants make an idyllic picnic area.

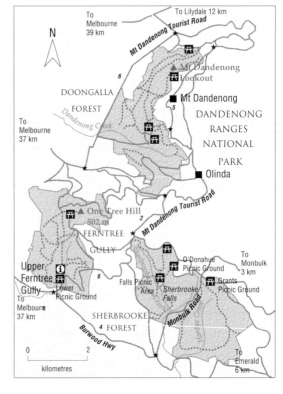

To the east is the Olinda Forest block that joins with the Silvan Reservoir Water Reserve and the R. J. Hamer Forest Arboretum. While the water reserve is closed to the public there are a large number of trails and a couple of picnic areas through the rest of the area.

There are some long walks in the park, including the 15 km Western Trail and the 18 km Olinda Forest Trail from Mount Dandenong to Kallista.

In the surrounding area there are other parks and reserves including the William Ricketts Sanctuary and the National Rhododendron Gardens.

The Doongalla block can be reached off the Mount Dandenong Tourist Road, or from the Mountain Highway. The Falls Road off the Mount Dandenong Tourist Road gives access to the Olinda Forest section of the national park.

Camping is not permitted within this metropolitan parkland, but there is plenty of accommodation, including charming bed-and-breakfast places, in the hills of the Dandenong Ranges.

Left: *The eastern yellow robin* (Eopsaltria australis) *is one of the many birds that inhabit the park. Visitors will also hear bellbirds, kookaburras and the amazing song of the lyrebird.*

Access

From the city, the Burwood Highway is the best access to the park. The major Melbourne street directories detail access, picnic areas and walking trails in the park.

The first and most accessible section of the park is the Ferntree Gully block, which is just off the Burwood Highway in Upper Ferntree Gully.

Further along the Mount Dandenong Tourist Road, and flanking the Monbulk Road, is the Sherbrooke Forest section.

This park is less than an hour's drive from Melbourne. Access to the park is easy along the Mount Dandenong Tourist Road, but once there, walking is the best way to enjoy the natural bushland.

VIC

Wilsons Promontory National Park

One of the most attractive and popular national parks in Victoria, 'The Prom', as it is affectionately known, is one of the country's oldest parks, being established in 1898. The park encompasses 130 km of coastline and has an immense diversity of landscapes, with huge granite headlands protecting secluded white beaches while marshland and sand dunes give sanctuary to a multitude of bird and animal life.

fact file

WHERE: South Gippsland on the Victorian coast, 200 km south-east of Melbourne
Map: Vic 6 J8

WHEN: All year

WHY: Camping, walking, photography, scuba diving, snorkelling, swimming, overnight bushwalking (permit required)

SIZE: 53 000 ha

RANGER: Tidal River (03) 5680 9555

did you know?

The native plants and animals of The Prom have not always been conserved. Sealers Cove was named by George Bass, who sent his men to shoot seals for supplies there in 1798, and in the early 1840s Refuge Cove housed a whaling station. Later, in the 1850s, a timber mill was set up at Sealers Cove.

Further inland, the land reaches up to form rugged forested mountain ranges that play host to fern-filled gullies and temperate pockets of rainforest. The east and west coasts of The Prom have been protected in a Marine Park (some fishing allowed) while a 300 metre wide Marine Reserve (totally protected, no fishing allowed) protects the southern coast and nearby offshore islands.

Water Activities and Walks

Apart from photography, which is a popular pastime in the park, bushwalking is the favoured activity, and the only form of transport, as bicycles are not permitted past vehicle boundaries. There are walks of every degree of difficulty, from short 10 minute strolls to rugged overnight hikes that require overnight permits.

Popular walks include Squeaky Beach to Picnic Bay, while a more difficult 38 km return walk leads to the Lighthouse on the southernmost tip of the Australian mainland.

On the east coast, an energetic and popular 37 km 2–3 day walk, starting at the car park at Mount Oberon, takes in Sealers Cove, Refuge Cove and Waterloo Bay.

Many water activities can be enjoyed in the surrounding ocean and the freshwater streams, including swimming, snorkelling and scuba diving. Fishing is also popular but restrictions apply in the marine parks and reserves. Check with the ranger at Tidal River for details.

Boats can be launched off the beach at Tidal River. A key is available from the ranger.

Access and Camping

The park can be accessed from the South Gippsland Highway via Foster or Meeniyan and Fish Creek.

Tidal River offers the only vehicle access to the park and has camping and caravan sites, along with cabins, flats and group lodges. Demand for the sites and accommodation is extremely heavy, especially during peak holiday times when a ballot is drawn. Facilities for campers include unpowered sites, fireplaces, a kiosk, toilets, showers and picnic tables.

Accommodation is also available in the Lighthouse Cottages, but access is only by walking.

More remote camping areas in the park, which are accessed by walking tracks and have toilets, include Oberon Bay which is close to the Tidal River site, Roaring Meg in the south of the park, and Waterloo Bay. As well there's Refuge Cove and Sealers Cove on the east coast, while in the north of the park is Tin Mine Cove.

There are also some other sites which have no toilet facilities. They include Johnny Souey Cove, Five Mile Beach, Lower Barry Creek and Barry Creek.

Many of the northern camp sites are often closed in summer due to lack of fresh water.

For camp and accommodation bookings or further enquires, contact the Visitor Information Centre at Tidal River on (03) 5680 9555.

Left: *Wilsons Promontory National Park now includes 130 km of unspoilt coastline. The park has been expanded considerably since its establishment in 1898.*

VIC

The dramatic granite bluffs and slabs of The Prom are popular with climbers. Whale Rock overlooks the magnificent coastline of the park.

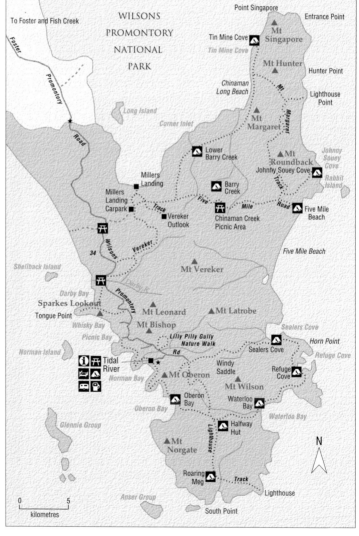

Wyperfeld National Park and Lake Albacutya Regional Park

Wyperfeld National Park was established in the early twentieth century and has now become the third-largest park in Victoria. Lake Albacutya Regional Park adjoins the national park on its southern boundary and boasts a size of 8300 hectares. With much of the north-west of Victoria cleared for grazing and wheat farming, these parks protect one of the last large expanses of mallee country left in the state.

Above: *The raucous sulphur-crested cockatoo* (Cacatua galerita) *can be seen among the red gums and heathlands in the park.*

fact file

WHERE: 450 km north-west of Melbourne, 47 km from Hopetoun
Map: Vic 2 D3

WHEN: March to May; September to November, particularly for wildflowers

WHY: Walking, cycling, scenic drives, 4WD, birdwatching, wildflower study

SIZE: 357 017 ha

RANGER: (03) 5395 7221

The basis of these parks is the large number of occasionally flooded lakes which are connected by Outlet Creek that runs north through the park from the northern end of Lake Albacutya.

The parks are host to a wide variety of bird and animal life. Emus and kangaroos are common, while the mallee fowl makes its nest amongst the remote mallee-covered dunes.

Activities

There are two self-guided walks within the Wyperfeld Park, both of which are of an easy standard. One trail is located at Lake Brambruk, the other at Black Flat Lake and the return trip takes from 2 to 3 hours.

The Desert Walk is a relatively easy 6 km circuit walk along a sandy track near Nine Mile Square and offers excellent views of the Big Desert and Outlet Creek during the 3 hours it takes.

For more remote walks, use the Casuarina camp ground as your base and seek local information from the park ranger.

Bicycles can be used on the firmer tracks such as the Outlet Creek Track, Lowan Track and Dattuck Track, but other tracks will probably be too sandy.

Drivers of 4WD vehicles will enjoy the drive north from the main Wonga

Right: Camping facilities are provided at the Wonga Hut site in Wyperfeld. This is near Wonga Lake, which now holds water only rarely, after extremely heavy flooding further north.

Camping Ground via the Eastern Lookout Road and the Dattuck, North–South and Eagle tracks to Pine Plain and beyond. There's some good remote camping in this northern area.

At Lake Albacutya a 4WD track circles the lake. Duck shooting is also permitted during the season. Dogs are allowed on a leash in the camping areas around the lake only.

West of Lake Albacutya two 4WD tracks cut through this remote region—the Chinaman Well Track and the Milmed Rock Track— and both lead to the main Murrayville–Nhill Road.

Access and Camping

The best access is from the Henty Highway, then west from Hopetoun.

The northern section of the park can be easily accessed via Hopetoun and Patchewollock. The western boundary of the park is along the Murrayville–Nhill Road, a graded dirt road that can be closed after rain.

The main camping area is at Wonga Hut, which has a picnic shelter, limited water, washing block, pit toilets and fireplaces. It is suitable for caravans, although there is no power.

Broken Bucket, on the Murrayville–Nhill Road, has toilets and water. In the north of the park, Casuarina has pit toilets, limited water and fireplaces and is accessible by 4WD vehicles. Remote bush camping for walkers is allowed.

There are also three camping grounds on the shores of Lake Albacutya and these have toilets and picnic tables only.

Water supplies are limited and you may need to bring your own.

Left: Red kangaroos (Macropus rufus) graze on the grassy plains of the park. Emus and grey kangaroos are also often seen, and there are small desert animals in the mallee areas.

VIC

don't miss

There are many ways to explore the beauties and wonders of this park. You can try birdwatching, canoeing, 4WD touring, camping and even duck shooting when in season. Bushwalking is popular in the park and there are two self-guided trails.

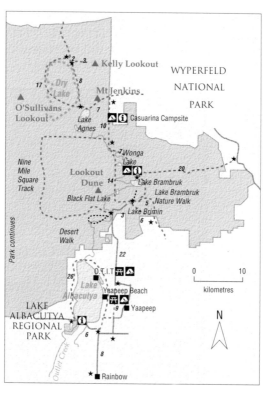

Mornington Peninsula National Park

The Mornington Peninsula National Park covers some 2686 hectares, mainly along the coast from Point Nepean to Cape Schanck in the east, and features craggy headlands, spectacular sandy beaches and an abundance of marine life and history.

This park includes the old Port Nepean Quarantine Station, which incorporates an historic fort, cemetery and quarantine station that was set up in 1852. The fort was erected in 1882, but only two shots were ever fired in the fort's 63 year history of active duty—at the start of each World War.

Activities

Exploring Point Nepean is possible by boarding the transporter service, or you can cycle any day of the year taking in all the sights. This section of the park is popular and visitor numbers are limited so it is advisable to book ahead.

The back beaches of Sorrento, Portsea and Gunnamatta are well known among surfers, beach lovers and fishermen.

The Cape Schanck area was originally protected by the Cape Schanck Coastal Reserve, but is now part of the Mornington National Park.

Popular walks include the Farnsworth Track that covers the area between Portsea and London Bridge and offers superb coastal views, while the inland section of the park can be enjoyed along a walking track from Cape Schanck.

Access and Facilities

There's good and easy access to places along the coast including Portsea, the Sorrento Back Beach and Cape Schanck.

The park is for day-use only; toilets and picnic facilities can be found throughout the park.

Cheviot Beach is on the southern side of Point Nepean. It was named after a ship wrecked there in 1887. The surf here can be dangerous, and only experienced scuba divers should explore the wreck.

Murray–Sunset National Park

Located in the far north-west of Victoria, the Murray–Sunset National Park is the second-largest park in the state. It offers salt flats and sand dunes to the north, and thick mallee scrub to the south. Proclaimed in 1991, the park takes in four important wilderness zones.

Located only 6 hours from Melbourne, this vast park offers visitors an insight into the arid desert regions of Australia. It is renowned for the magnificent Pink Lakes, and this easily accessible spot is the ideal base for a series of day trips by 4WD, bicycle or on foot.

It is, however, the remoteness of the region that has a lasting impact on visitors, and four-wheel drivers are best equipped to take advantage of this.

Experienced walkers can also take advantage of the wilderness areas, while easier, shorter walks are available near the designated camping areas.

The word 'mallee' is the term used to describe the unusual growth form of the eucalypts in the area. About 20 species of mallee eucalypts grow in this region.

The Pink Lakes derive their hue from carotene, a pigment secreted by algae (Dunaliella salina). The colour is brightest in spring and summer.

VIC

Access and Camping

The Mallee Highway borders the south of the park, while the Calder Highway borders the eastern side.

Camping is very pleasant at Pink Lakes where you will find reasonable facilities. If you have a 4WD vehicle you can reach the camping areas of Mopoke, Pheneeys Track, Mount Crozier and Rocket Lake. These remote camping areas offer basic facilities. Water is not available through most of the park.

Heavy rain can make the tracks inaccessible for conventional vehicles.

Along the northern edge of the park, the Murray and Lindsay Rivers regularly flood the neighbouring plains, creating sizable billabongs.

Snowy River National Park

The powerful Snowy River forces its way through deep, rocky gorges and the rugged Victorian High Country before it finally settles into a large, wide, tranquil waterway and trickles quietly out to the ocean. Covering 98 700 hectares, this remote area is considered to be extremely significant and its remoteness has allowed two wilderness areas to be incorporated within the park.

Canoeing is the best way to enjoy the Snowy River, and to observe the park's river scenery, impressive deep gorges and diverse vegetation.

fact file

WHERE: Far East Gippsland, 390 km from Melbourne via the Princes Highway
Map: Vic 4 G6

WHEN: All year, though the Snowy River is best in the warmer months

WHY: Snowy River, MacKillops Bridge, canoeing, camping, bushwalking, scenic drives, mountain bike riding, 4WD, fishing, rafting

SIZE: 98 700 ha

RANGER: Bendoc (03) 6458 1456

Near MacKillops Bridge. The walks in this northern part of the park show the harsh grey rock faces and dense vegetation around the Snowy River valley.

tourist info

Victorian Canoe Association, (03) 9459 4251

Activities

Although the Snowy Mountains Hydro-Electricity Scheme takes much of the water from the river, there are still rugged gorges and rapids to thrill the most experienced canoeist. The section from MacKillops Bridge to Buchan, which flows through three gorges, is a 3- to 4-day trip.

For walkers there are a number of trails to enjoy. There's the hard 18 km Silver Mine Walking Track and the easier Snowy River Nature Walk from MacKillops Bridge.

Experienced four-wheel drivers will enjoy the Deddick Trail.

Access and Camping

Park access is either from the Buchan–Gelantipy road to the turn-off past Seldom Seen and onto the road to MacKillops Bridge, or via the 4WD Deddick Trail, which is seasonally closed and runs from the south of the park to MacKillops Bridge. There is also access from the north-east via Bonang and the Bonang–Gelantipy road. The road in, however, has very steep drop-offs.

The camping grounds at MacKillops Bridge, Waratah Flat and Balley Hooley have basic facilities; Raymond Falls and Hick's camp sites have none. Camping permits are required.

More National Parks of Importance

Baw Baw National Park

SIZE: 13 300 ha
MAP: Vic 6 J3

Apart from the Alpine National Park, the Baw Baw National Park is the only other Victorian park with large areas of subalpine vegetation and a habitat suitable for the rare Leadbeater's possum.

During winter, skiers enjoy the downhill slopes or the many cross-country trails that lead as far afield as Mount St Gwinear. In the milder months, bushwalkers enjoy the trails scattered over the mountain tops or traversing part of the long-distance Alpine Walking Track. The Silvertop Picnic Ground has excellent views of the Thomson Dam.

The main access to the park is from Drouin through Nerrim South and Tanjil Bren where a narrow, winding bitumen road leads to the village. The Mount Erica car park or Mount St Gwinear are accessible off the Thomson Valley Road.

Dispersed bush camping is allowed on the Baw Baw Plateau, while there are also motels and lodges at the Mount Baw Baw Alpine Village.

For more information contact the ranger at Erica on (03) 5165 3204.

Errinundra National Park

SIZE: 25 600 ha
MAP: Vic 4 J7

In eastern Victoria, high on the Errinundra Plateau, you will find the largest stand of cool temperate rainforest in the state. Scenic drives and boardwalks help visitors appreciate this priceless beauty. The self-guided nature walk gives a good insight into the park.

Access is restricted in wet conditions, when closures may apply. The main entry is via the Errinundra Road from

Club Terrace to the south, or the Bonang Highway from the east, taking the Errinundra Road. The main roads into the park are unsealed and winding, and should be driven with caution. They are unsuitable for caravans.

Camping sites can be found at the Gap Scenic Reserve in the north, on the Bonang River near the intersection of the Bonang Highway and the Gap Road. Goongerah Camping Area is to the west.

Be prepared for wet weather, even in the warmer months.

For further information, contact the ranger at Orbost, on (03) 5161 1222, or at Bendoc, on (03) 6458 1456.

The snow gum (Eucalyptus pauciflora) is a cold-climate tree. Baw Baw and Alpine are the only Victorian parks where it can be seen.

Most of the Errinundra National Park is above 1000 m and is inaccessible during winter due to snow and rain. Springtime also brings heavy rain to the area.

Hattah–Kulkyne National Park

SIZE: 48 000 ha
MAP: Vic 1 F6

The Hattah–Kulkyne National Park takes in a typical mallee environment of native cypress pine woodland and vast mallee scrubland. The park is bordered by the Murray River and the Murray–Kulkyne Regional Park to the east.

In all but the driest years a series of small riverlets feed water from the Murray River along the Chalka Creek, which in turn provides an oasis for the wildlife in the park: birds, kangaroos and other animals can be found in abundance.

The lakes are best explored by canoe, but walking and cycling are also both excellent ways to explore the park.

Access to the park is via the Sunraysia Highway or Robinvale Road east of Hattah. Good gravel roads stretch through the park. Delightful camping areas can be found on the shores of Lake Hattah and Lake Mournpall and along the Murray River.

For more information contact Parks Victoria, on 131 963.

Right: The sacred king-fisher (Todiramphus sanctus) is one of 200 species of birds living in Hattah–Kulkyne National Park. The park has both dry and lake environments, unlike others in this part of the state.

The trees in the northern part of Kinglake National Park are mainly stringy-barks, peppermint gums and other eucalypts.

Right: Mallee vegetation on the shores of Lake Hattah, one in the series of lakes connected by small waterways that are the main feature of the Hattah–Kulkyne National Park.

Kinglake National Park

SIZE: 21 600 ha
MAP: Vic 6 E2

The Kinglake National Park provides Melburnians with a cool respite from the summer heat and offers magnificent views of the city, densely forested mountain tops and fern-filled gullies.

For walkers, the Wombelano Falls on Hirts Creek can be accessed via an easy short walk through the cool, fern-filled gullies; ferns and messmate forests can be seen on the short walk to Mason Falls. The more spectacular journey by foot is the 20 km moderate to hard Everard Circuit Walk. If you want a great view, without the energetic walk, the Frank Thomson Lookout is just out of town.

The park is divided into three sections surrounding Kinglake township and can be accessed via the Melba Highway, or from any of the roads leading to Kinglake.

The region caters more for day-visitors, but there is a camp area at the Gums. The area is small, and sites need to be booked ahead through the ranger. Contact Parks Victoria, on 131 963.

Lake Eildon National Park

SIZE: 27 750 ha
MAP: Vic 3 J9

Lake Eildon National Park is a natural playground for campers, walkers and wildlife enthusiasts. It offers steep, rugged mountains and freshwater rivers leading into the vast reservoir of Lake Eildon with its many arms and bays.

Fishing is popular in the lake and the streams that flow into it, while four-wheel drivers can tour the remote parts of the park. Bushwalkers, water-skiers and canoeists will also enjoy the lake, rivers and surrounding forest country.

The park can be accessed via the Eildon–Jamieson road or from Goughs Bay via Mansfield.

Camp sites are located at Fraser Camping area and Jerusalem Creek and should be pre-booked during peak times. Boat-based camp sites are at Taylors Creek, Mountaineer Inlet and Coopers Point. Camping permits are required. Contact the ranger at Fraser Camping Ground, on (03) 5772 1293.

There are a number of bushwalks in the southern section of Lake Eildon National Park, varying from energetic five-hour treks, to relaxed one-hour trails.

Little Desert National Park

SIZE: 132 000 ha
MAP: Vic 2 C8

The Little Desert National Park conserves an important region of the mallee in far western Victoria. The sandy soils support typical mallee vegetation and heathland areas, and the park has a diverse range of animal and bird life, and vegetation. In spring there is a spectacular display of wildflowers.

As most of the tracks in the sandy region are unsuitable for conventional vehicles, this remote area is perfect for 4WDs. Tracks are often closed due to wet weather and the park ranger at Wail, phone (03) 5389 1204, should be contacted for information on track conditions and closures.

Many walks in the area accommodate the day or overnight hiker, while short walks can be taken from the camping areas.

Access to the park is along well-formed gravel roads from Dimboola, Horsham or Edenhope.

Remote bush camping is allowed in the central and western blocks, while at the Horseshoe Bend camping ground on the Wimmera River, you will find sites for caravans and tents. Ackle Bend also has basic camping facilities.

don't miss

Try to time your visit to Little Desert National Park to coincide with the spring blooming of wild-flowers. Apart from the typical mallee vegetation, you can see smaller plants and shrubs, such as holly grevillea, flame heath and the colourful broom bush.

VIC

Lower Glenelg National Park

SIZE: 27 300 ha
MAP: Vic 5 C6

Before it meets the Southern Ocean in western Victoria, the Glenelg River carves a magnificent gorge lined with tall limestone cliffs that form the most popular feature of this park. With plenty of overnight camps and easy paddling, the Glenelg River offers newcomers the perfect canoeing adventure.

The Glenelg River Gorge and the river itself are popular for canoeing, fishing and boating. The Princess Margaret Rose Caves, which are open for guided tours, are another attraction— phone (03) 8738 4171. Limited camping and accommodation are also available at the caves.

Many walking tracks crisscross the park, and bushwalkers can see large number of plants and animals as well as wildflowers in spring.

Dartmoor and Nelson give easy access to all the sections of the park. Camp grounds are scattered along the Glenelg River and also at Dartmoor. Camping is by permit only, from the Nelson Visitor Information Centre, (03) 8738 4051.

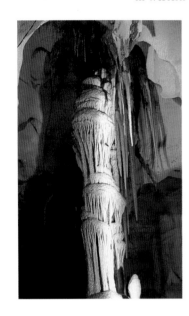

A limestone column in Princess Margaret Rose Caves in the Lower Glenelg National Park. The caves were discovered in 1936.

Right: An Australian king parrot (Alisterus scapularis) in Mitchell River National Park. They join about 150 other bird species in the park, which includes excellent forest country.

Mitchell River National Park

SIZE: 11 900 ha
MAP: Vic 4 C8

The Mitchell River National Park offers a remote mountain wilderness just north of the Princes Highway in East Gippsland, 300 km from Melbourne.

Many visitors come to raft or canoe down the Mitchell River. Such an adventure is best in spring. The park also has 4WD tracks.

Apart from the river, the best known feature of this park is the Den of Nargun, where a steep walking track, about 1 km long, leads from the car park at the south of the park to a limestone cave featuring stalactites. This car park is the most accessible and most favoured entry into the park. Other points of interest are the Bluff Lookout and Billy Goat Bend.

Access is from the Princes Highway before Bairnsdale, taking the Dargo Road.

Numerous bush camping sites can be found throughout the park, particularly along the Mitchell River.

For more information contact the ranger at Bairnsdale, on (03) 5152 0400.

Mount Buffalo National Park

SIZE: 31 600 ha
MAP: Vic 3 M7

Encircled by the Ovens, Buffalo and Buckland Rivers, this year-round park offers snow-covered mountain tops for skiing in winter, and clear, warm days for walking in summer.

It is the rugged nature of this park that beckons a wide variety of outdoor enthusiasts. There's excellent bushwalking with more than 90 km of marked trails in the park, and for the more adventurous there are some fantastic long rock climbs.

During the winter months cross-country skiers are well catered for, while downhill skiers have many trails to choose from. Anglers will find brown trout in Lake Catani, and mountain-bike riders have use of the vehicle access roads through the park.

Access to the park from Melbourne is via the Hume Highway on a sealed road through Porepunkah. Camping is restricted to the camp ground at Lake Catani. Motel or lodge-style accommodation is available at the Chalet, phone (03) 5755 1500, or the Tatra Inn, phone (03) 5755 1988.

For more information contact the ranger at Bright on (03) 5755 1577.

Otway National Park

SIZE: 12 876 ha
MAP: Vic 5 L9

The Otway National Park stretches from just west of Apollo Bay along the coastline to Princetown where it merges with the Port Campbell National Park. This park has impressive mountain ash trees, waterfalls and lush, fern-filled ravines as well as its rugged coastline.

Fishing and surfing are popular along the coast and in the rivers, and there are numerous walks to enjoy. Swimming should be restricted to the lakes and rivers, as there are strong sea currents. Horseriding with a permit is allowed, as is mountain-bike riding.

The park can be accessed from the Princes Highway, then south through Apollo Bay or Lavers Hill, or via the Great Ocean Road.

Campers are catered for at the beachside Blanket Bay camping area at Point Lewis. Further west is the Johanna camping area, while Aire River also has camp sites.

Camp sites can be very popular, especially during summer, and should be booked in advance with the ranger. Contact Parks Victoria on 131 963.

Above: *The huge granite plateau of Mount Buffalo towers over the surrounding river valleys. It was named by the explorers Hume and Hovell.*

Fog along the Great Ocean Road in the Otway National Park. In summer and autumn the park's forests are a cool haven from the heat.

Above: *The Twelve Apostles in Port Campbell National Park. This landmark was once part of a limestone cave system. Gradually the outer limestone wore away, creating these stacks.*

Right: *The Lakes National Park and Gippsland Lakes Coastal Park are ideal family holiday locations, offering seaside fun as well as lakes and forest areas.*

Port Campbell National Park

SIZE: 1750 ha
MAP: Vic 5 J8

The weather-beaten coastline of the Port Campbell National Park stands as a headstone for the numerous shipwrecks that lie on the nearby ocean floor. But it is the significant landmark of the Twelve Apostles that most people remember from their visit to this spectacular coast. These sea stacks—small, sheer-sided islands just off-shore—dominate this coast and the drive along it.

The historic ship-wreck-trail drive from Port Fairy all the way to Lavers Hill follows the Great Ocean Road. There are many interesting walks in the area, and the famous Glenample Homestead is now open to visitors.

The park is accessed via the Great Ocean Road, between Princetown and Peterborough. Camping is available at all the towns. Bookings are essential over the main holiday periods. For more information contact Parks Victoria on 131 963, or call into the Visitor Centre at the Twelve Apostles.

The Lakes National Park and Gippsland Lakes Coastal Park

SIZE: 2390 ha/17 584 ha
MAP: Vic 6 N4

Encompassing the coastal region from Seaspray to Lakes Entrance, the Gippsland Lakes Coastal Park boasts such natural features as Ninety Mile Beach and the vast inland coastal lakes system. The smaller Lakes National Park adjoins it, while other reserves are dotted throughout the immediate area.

Visitors can take one of the many walks along the beach or stroll through banksia woodlands. Birdwatchers can use the bird hides in the park, while a trip to Murphy's Hill will reward the energetic with fantastic views of Bass Strait. Wildflowers flourish and visitors in October can enjoy the fine displays. There's also plenty of water to swim in.

There is boat access from Paynesville, and the eastern end of the park is reached from Bairnsdale. Rotomah Island is accessed by boat.

There are many camping areas within the coastal park, but camping in the national park is only allowed at Emu Bight.

Contact Parks Victoria on 131 963 for more details.

Popular Parks at a Glance

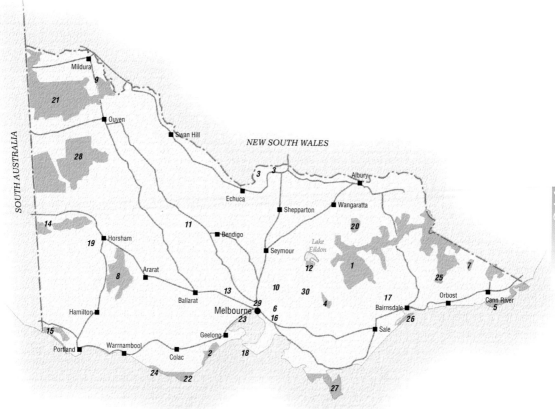

#	Park	Camping	Caravan Access	Disabled Access	4WD Access	Picnic Areas	Toilets	Walking Tracks	Kiosk	Information
1	Alpine NP	●			●	●	●	●		
2	Angahook–Lorne SP	●		●	●	●	●			●
3	Barmah SP	●		●	●	●	●			●
4	Baw Baw NP	●						●		
5	Croajingolong NP	●			●	●		●		
6	Dandenong Ranges NP				●	●		●	●	●
7	Errinundra NP	●			●	●		●		●
8	Grampians NP	●		●	●	●	●	●		●
9	Hattah–Kulkyne NP	●	●		●	●	●			●
10	Kinglake NP	●		●	●	●	●	●		●
11	Kooyoora SP	●		●	●	●	●			
12	Lake Eildon NP	●			●	●	●	●	●	
13	Lerderderg SP	●			●	●		●		●
14	Little Desert NP	●	●		●	●	●	●		
15	Lower Glenelg NP	●						●		
16	Lysterfied Lake Park				●	●	●	●		●
17	Mitchell River NP	●	●			●	●	●		
18	Mornington Peninsula NP			●		●	●	●		
19	Mount Arapiles–Tooan SP	●				●	●	●		
20	Mount Buffalo NP	●	●							●
21	Murray–Sunset NP	●			●	●	●	●		●
22	Otway NP	●				●		●		●
23	Point Cook CP			●		●	●			●
24	Port Campbell NP							●		●
25	Snowy River NP	●			●	●	●	●		●
26	The Lakes NP	●			●	●	●	●		●
27	Wilsons Promontory NP	●				●	●	●		●
28	Wyperfeld NP	●	●		●	●				●
29	Yarra Ranges NP					●	●	●		
30	Yarra Valley Parklands				●	●	●	●		●

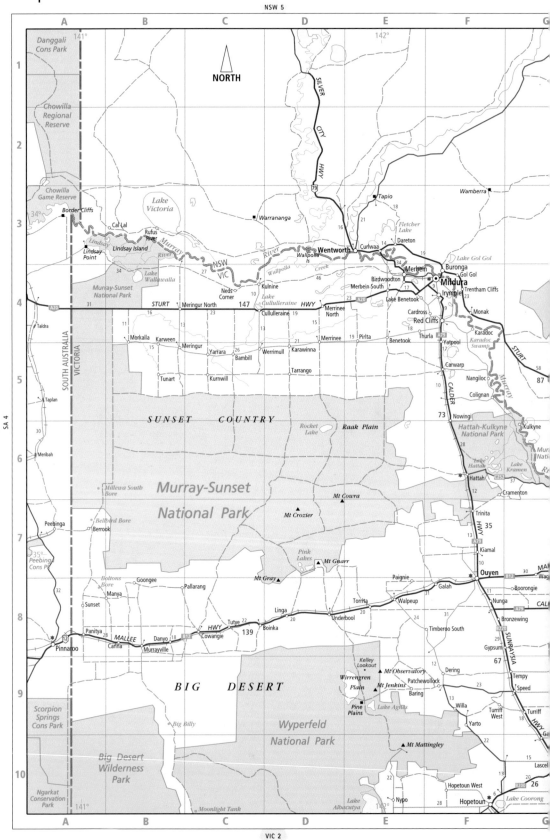

NORTH

| | A | B | C | D | E | F | G |

Danggali
Cons Park

Chowilla
Regional
Reserve

Chowilla
Game Reserve

Border Cliffs

Cal Lal

Rufus River

Lindsay Island

Lindsay Point

Lake Wallawalla

Murray-Sunset
National Park

Taldra

Morkalla Karween
Meringur

Yarrara Bambill

Tunart Kurnwill

Taplan

Meribah

Millewa South Bore

Peebinga
Berrook

Peebinga
Cons P

Boltons Bore Goongee
Manya Pallarang

Sunset

Panitya MALLEE
Pinnaroo Canna Danyo
Cowangie Murrayville

Scorpion
Springs
Cons Park

Big Billy

Ngarkat
Conservation
Park

SOUTH AUSTRALIA

VICTORIA

Lake
Victoria

Warrananga

NSW
VIC

Wallpolla Is

Neds Corner

Meringur North STURT 147

Cullulleraine

Bambill

Werrimull Karawinna

Tarrango

SUNSET COUNTRY

Rocket Lake Raak Plain

Murray-Sunset
National Park

Mt Cowra

Mt Crozier

Pink Lakes Mt Gnarr

Mt Gray

Linga

Tutye Boinka
HWY 139

BIG DESERT

Moonlight Tank

Tapio

Wamberra

Fletcher Lake

Curlwaa Dareton

Wentworth

Wallpolla

Creek

Lake Cullulleraine HWY

Merrinee North

Merrinee Pirlta

Birdwoodton
Merbein South

Benetook

Merbein Buronga
Gol Gol

Mildura
Irymple Trentham Cliffs

Lake Benetook

Cardross
Red Cliffs

Thurla Yatpool

Karadoc
Karadoc Swamp

Carwarp

Nangiloc

Colignan

Nowingi

Hattah-Kulkyne
National Park

Lake Hattah Lake Kramen

Hattah Cramenton

Trinita 35

Kiamal

Ouyen Boorongie

Nunga

Bronzewing

Timberoo South Gypsum

Underbool

Torrita Walpeup

Paignie Galah

Kelley Lookout
Wirrengren Plain Mt Observatory
Mt Jenkins Patchewollock
Baring

Pine Plains Lake Agnas

Wyperfeld
National Park

Mt Mattingley

Nypo

Lake Albacutya

Dering

Willa

Yarto

Tempy
Speed

Turriff West Turriff

Lascel

Hopetoun West

Hopetoun Lake Coorong

Murray

STURT 87

Mildura

CALDER 73

HWY 35

SUNRAYSIA 67

| | A | B | C | D | E | F | G |

0 10 20 30 40
kilometres

143°
144°

1

2

Chibnalwood Lakes

■ Turlee

−34°
3

■ Prungle

Pitarpunga Lake
Lake Macommon

Ganaway Lake

Lachlan   *River*
Ita Lake

Penarie
Dundomallee Lake

Maude

4

Lake Benanee
34

Waldaria Lake

Lake Tala

Murrumbidgee

River

18

River
55

5

Robinvale
81   20   41

Lake Caringay

✱ Balranald

HIGHWAY   131

3
Bannerton   Kyndalyn
MURRAY   29   Boundary Bend
Mangooya

92   VALLEY   25   Narrung

41   STURT
35

69

6

19   Koorkab   Piambie

Condoulpe

Yanga Lake

Annuello
Kooloonong   Kenley
13   Haysdale   58
Condoulpe Lake

7
Koimbo
23   Bolton   Natya

HWY   Kyalite

Perekerten

−35°

lwyne   Prooinga
✱ Mahangatang   HWY   43   812   Piangil North   Tooleybuc
Piangil

Moolpa

Wakool   71

Moulamein

River
110

8

Cocamba   17   Tudor
25
trap   Chinkapook
13   Chillingollah   26
Towan   16   Wood Wood
Koraleigh
39
Nyah   Koraleigh
Nyah West   Vinifera   Speewa
43   Pira   Beverford   16
Woorinen   Tyntynder   Central
North   11   Murray Downs

Stony Crossing

River
Edward

River

69   66

9

Lake Tyrrell
Lake Wahpool
Tyrrell   Waitchie   23   *Channel*   22
Downs   12
19   Long   *Tims*   Gowanford   9
Plains
19   43   Ultima   18
Sea Lake

✱ Swan Hill   6
10   *Lake Boga*   Fish Point
13   1400   *Lake Tutchewop*
Lake Boga   17   Winlaton
Goschen   Tresco   24
25   Lalbert   Kunat   Mystic Park
Meatian   Road   Beauchamp   *Kangaroo Lake*

Murray   *River*

Ballbank

Benjeroop

Murrabit

103

27   Wakool

10

Boigbeat   34
18
179   12   ✱
Culgoa
23   8
142°

Lake Timboram

Lake Lalbert   Lalbert
29   18   17

57   *Lake Charm*   15
Lake Charm   Capels   24   Culfearne
Lake Cullen   Crossing   21
Bael Bael   *The Marsh*   Westby   27
17   *Middle Lake*   11
Sandhill Lake   *Lake Bael Bael*   9   ✱ Kerang
Koroop

Myall   10   Barham
Koondrook
Teal Point   NSW
VIC   14
71
Gannawarra

V I C

NSW 5

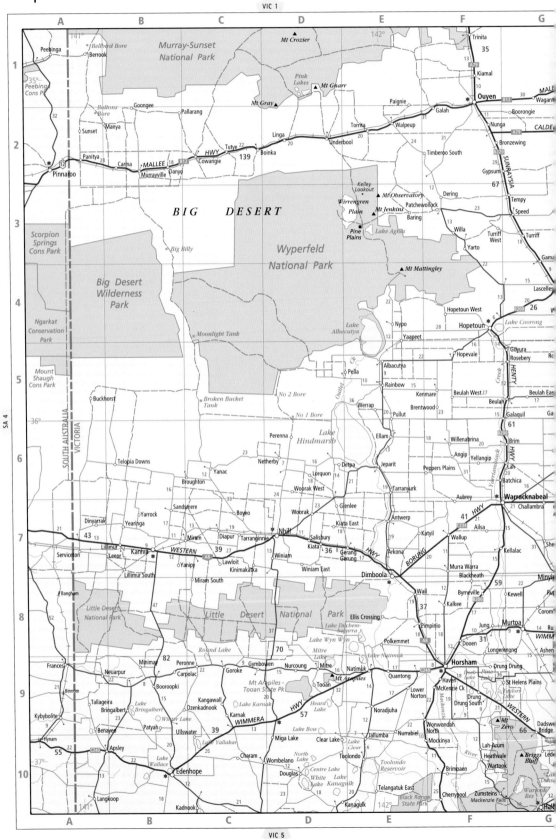

0 10 20 30 40
kilometres

NORTH

—35°

143°

Koimbo
nuello
Bolton
Kooloonong
Haysdale
Kenley
lwyne
Mahangatang
Prooinga
Piangil North
HWY 43
Piangil
Kyalite
Moolpa
Perekerten
Cocamba
Natya
Tooleybuc
Wood Wood
ytrap
Chinkapook
Tudor
Towan
Koraleigh
Nyah
Stony Crossing
Wakool
Moulamein
Moulamein
Creek
Chillingollah
Nyah West
Pira
Vinifera
Speewa
Beverford
Tyntynder
Central
Edward
River
110
Lake
Tyrrell
Waitchie
Nowie
North
Woorinen
Murray Downs
103
Tyrrell
Downs
Gowanford
Ultima
Channel
Tims
SWAN HILL
Lake
Boga
Fish Point
Murray
River
Ballbank
Wakool
Long
Plains
Goschen
Lake Boga
Tresco
Winlaton
Benjeroop
Murrabit
Sea Lake
Boigbeat
Lalbert
Road
Kunat
Mystic Park
Kangaroo
Lake
Lake Charm
Lake Cullen
Myall
Culfearne
Barham
Koondrook
Berriwillock
Meatian
Beauchamp
The Marsh
Lake Charm
Capels
Crossing
Westby
Tea Point
Lake
Lalbert
Lalbert
Bael Bael
Middle
Lake
KERANG
Koroop
Gannawarra
Culgoa
Warne
Cokum
Tittybong
Budgerum
Sandhill
Lake
Lake
Bael Bael
Kerang East
Mead
COHUNA
Sutton
Kalpienung
Normanville
Dingwall
98
Wee Wee Rup
Jil Jil
Nullawil
Towaninny
Quambatook
Langville
Tragowell
Leitchville
Gunbower
Kinnabulla
Whirily
Dumosa
Lake Meran
Leaghur
State Pk
Macorna
Mt
Hope
Kow
Swamp
Patho
Karyrie
Narraport
Towaninny South
Oakvale
Meran
West
Appin
South
Loddon Vale
Mincha
Bald Rock
Torrumbarry
Birchip
Thalia
Ninyeunook
Gredgwin
Leaghur
Barraport
Canary Island
Gladfield
Pyramid Hill
Terrick Terrick
Morton
Plains
Bunguluke
Catumnal
Minmindie
Yando
Terrick Terrick
National Park
Watchem
Massey
WYCHEPROOF
Glenloth
Narrewillock
Lake Marmal
Boort
Boort East
Dutham Ox
Yarrawalla
Mologa
Mt Terrick
Mitiamo
Corack East
Chirrup
Teddywaddy
West
Teddywaddy
Buckrabanyule
Wychitella
Mysia
Fernihurst
Yarrawalla
South
Banyenong
Wooroonook
CHARLTON
Barrakee
Borung
Jarklin
Calivil
Prairie
Piavella
Tennyson
Litchfield
Mt Jeffcott
Yeungroon
East
Woosang
Korong Vale
Bears Lagoon
Millloo
Laen North
Donald
Dooboobetie
Yeungroon
Richmond
Plains
Wedderburn
Junction
Serpentine
East
Loddon
Dingee
Tandarra
Diggora
West
Laen East
Wedderburn
Powlett
Plains
134
Kamarooka
Laen
Cope Cope
Gooroc
Coonooer Bridge
Berrimal
Kurraca West
Glenalbyn
Kurting
Woolshed
Corner
Kamarooka
National Park
Kamarooka East
Rich Avon
Swanwater
Sutherland
Slaty Creek
Gowar East
Kooyoora
State Park
Inglewood
Raywood
Summerfield
Bagshot North
Goornong
Banyena
Swanwater
West
Traynors Lagoon
Gre Gre North
ST ARNAUD
Koore
Fentons Creek
Wehla
Bridgewater
Derby
Yarraberb
Woodvale
Campbells Forest
North
Huntly
Bagshot
Fosterville
Marnoo
Gre Gre
Logan
Rheola
Kingower
Arnold
Leichardt
Myers Flat
Epsom
Huntly
Marnoo
East
Beazleys Bridge
Carapooee
Emu
Burkes Flat
Cochranes Creek
Llanelly
Newbridge
Marong
Maiden
Gully
EAGLEHAWK
Junortoun
Axedale
Wallaloo
65
Rostron
Moliagul
Tarnagulla
Woodstock
BENDIGO
Longlea
Wallaloo
East
Kanya
Tottington
Winjallok
Stuart Mill
Bealiba
Goldsborough
Dunolly
Laanecoorie
Shelbourne
Lockwood
KANGAROO FLAT
Big Hill
Strathfieldsaye
Eppalock
Axe Creek
Callawadda
Paradise
Archdale
Laanecoorie
Res
Eastville
Sedgwick
Emu
Creek
Morri Morri
Navarre
Kara Kara
State Park
Archdale
Junction
Redbank
Bet Bet
Betley
Eddington
Nuggetty
Ravenswood
39
Lake
Eppalock
Campbells
Bridge
Greens
Creek
Tulkara
Wattle Creek
Landsborough
Natte Yallock
Rathscar
Wareek
Havelock
Timor
Baringhup
Maldon
Ravenswood South
Sutton Grange
Harcourt
Stawell
Concongella
Joel
Landsborough
West
Joel South
Barkly
Warrenmang
Homebush
MARYBOROUGH
Alma
Simson
Carisbrook
49
Cairn
Curran
Res
Barkers Creek
Welshmans Reef
CASTLEMAINE
Chewton
Barfold
Metcalfe
Mt Avoca
AVOCA
Bung Bong
Adelaide
Lead
Moolort
Joyces
Creek
Campbells
Creek
67
Elphinstone
Crowlands
Glenlofty
Glenpatrick
Lamplough
Amherst
Daisy Hill
Majorca
Strathlea
Newstead
Fryerstown
Taradale

143°
144°

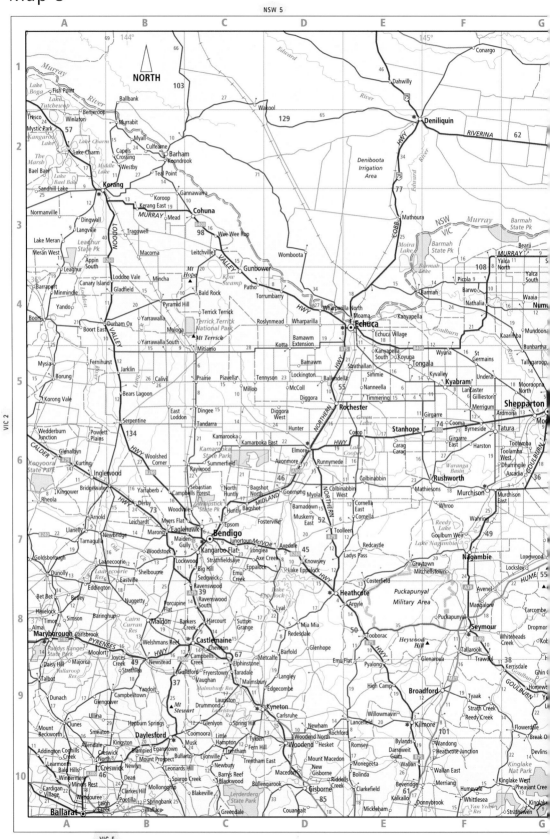

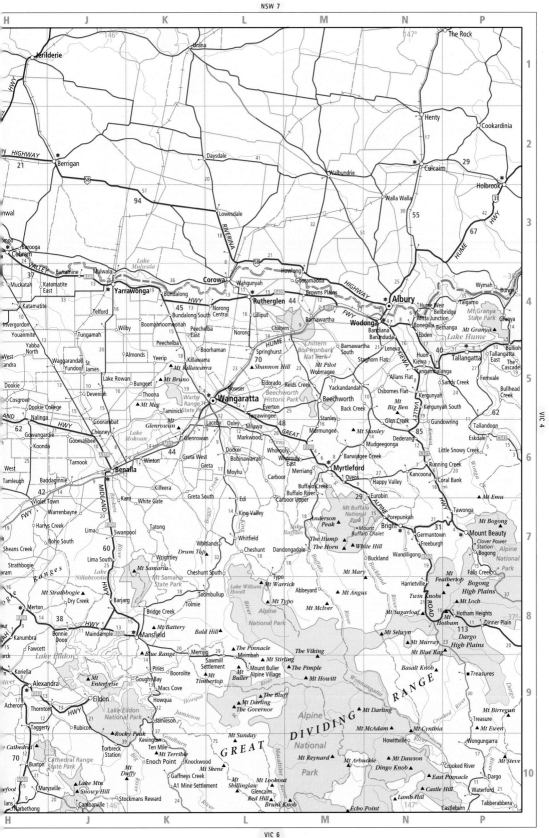

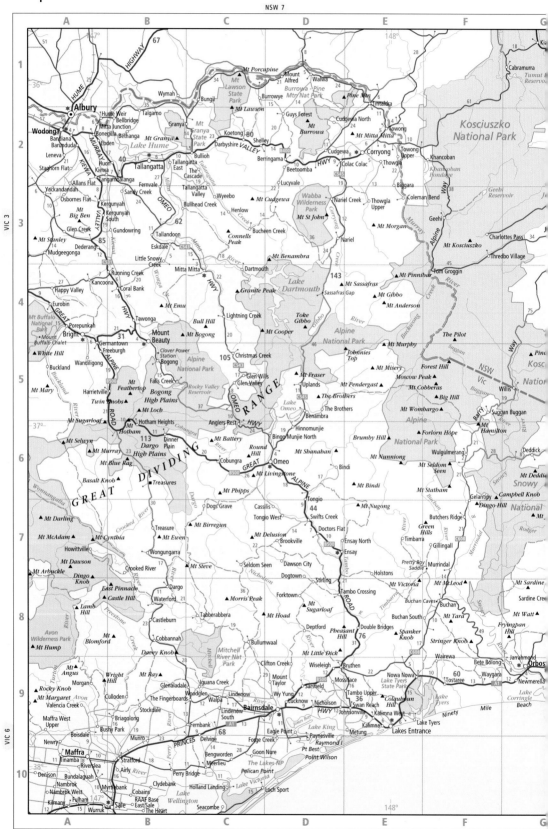

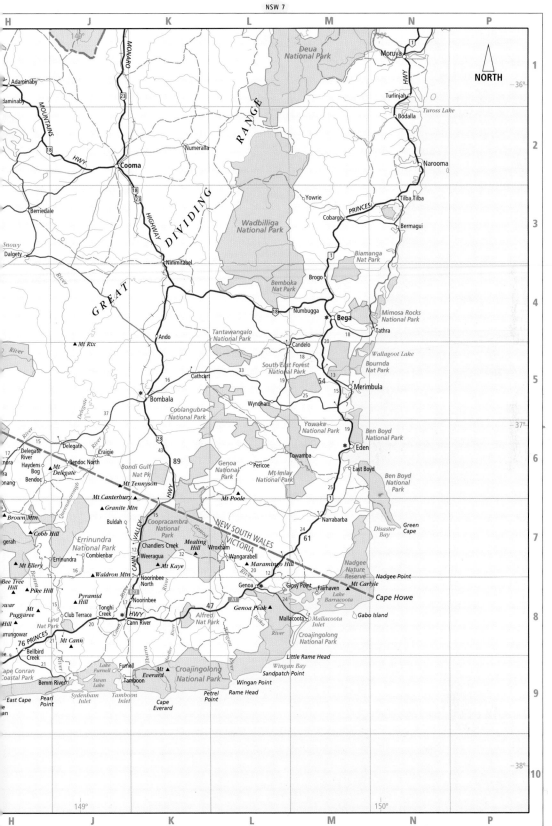

0 10 20 30 40
kilometres

NORTH

V/C

—36°

—37°

—38°

H   **J**   **K**   **L**   **M**   **N**   **P**

1   2   3   4   5   6   7   8   9   10

149°   150°

Adaminaby
daminaby
MONARO
SNOWY
MOUNTAINS
HWY
18
23
Cooma
Numeralla
Berriedale
18
23
Highway
Snowy
Dalgety
River
Nimmitabel
GREAT
DIVIDING
RANGE
Mt Rix
Ando
Cathcart
16
33
Bombala
37
Coolangubra
National Park
Delegate
River
15
17
Delegate
Craigie
Bendoc North
Haydens
Bog
Mt
Delegate
Bendoc
89
23
43
Mt Tennyson
HWY
Mt Canterbury
Granite Mtn
Brown Mtn
Buldah
Cobb Hill
Errinundra
National Park
gerah
Errinundra
Combienbar
Mt Ellery
Waldron Mtn
16
15
12
CANN VALLEY
Cooracombra
National Park
Chandlers Creek
Weeragua
Mt Kaye
Bee Tree
Hill
Pike Hill
15
Pyramid
Hill
Mt
Puggaree
owar
15
Tonghi
Creek
Club Terrace
Noorinbee
North
Noorinbee
20
HWY
Cann River
47
rrungowar
Hill
76
PRINCES
21
Mt Cann
Bellbird
Creek
21
Cann
River
Lind
Nat Park
Lake
Furnell
Furnell
Mt
Everard
Tamboon
Sydenham
Inlet
Tamboon
Inlet
Susan
Lake
Bemm River
ape Conran
Coastal Park
East Cape
Pearl
Point
Cape
Everard
Croajingolong
National Park
Bemm River
Thurra River
Cann River
Genoa River
Mealing
Hill
Wroxham
Wangarabell
Maramingo Hill
20
12
Genoa
A1
Noorinbee
47
Genoa Peak
Alfred
Nat Park
24
Gipsy Point
Fairhaven
Lake
Barracoota
Mallacoota
Inlet
Mallacoota
Betka
River
Genoa
River
Petrel
Point
Rame Head
Wingan Point
Wingan Bay
Sandpatch Point
Little Rame Head
Croajingolong
National Park
Mt Carlyle
Gabo Island
Cape Howe
Nadgee Point
Nadgee
Nature
Reserve
61
24
25
1
Narrabarba
NEW SOUTH WALES
VICTORIA
Genoa
Valley
Ben Boyd
National
Park
Disaster
Bay
Green
Cape
East Boyd
Eden
19
Towamba
Pericoe
Mt Imlay
National Park
Genoa
National
Park
Mt Poole
Yowaka
National Park
7
5
25
15
54
Merimbula
18
7
13
Wyndham
South East Forest
National Park
19
Candelo
20
Bega
18
Tathra
Numbugga
18
Bemboka
Nat Park
Tantawangalo
National Park
Brogo
1
Biamanga
Nat Park
Cobargo
PRINCES
Yowrie
Wadbilliga
National Park
Bermagui
Tilba Tilba
Narooma
Bodalla
Turlinjah
HWY
1
Moruya
Deua
National Park
Bondi Gulf
Nat Pk
Queensborough River
Mimosa Rocks
National Park
Wallagoot Lake
Bournda
Nat Park
Tuross Lake

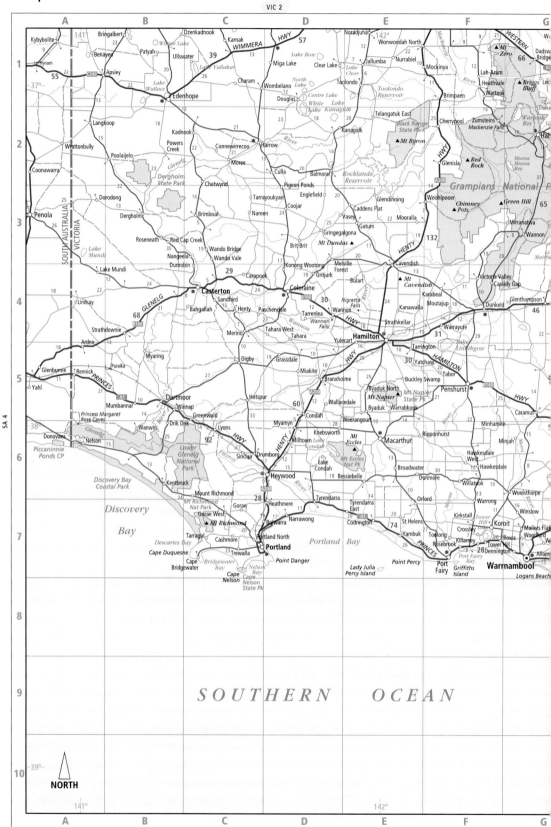

VIC 2

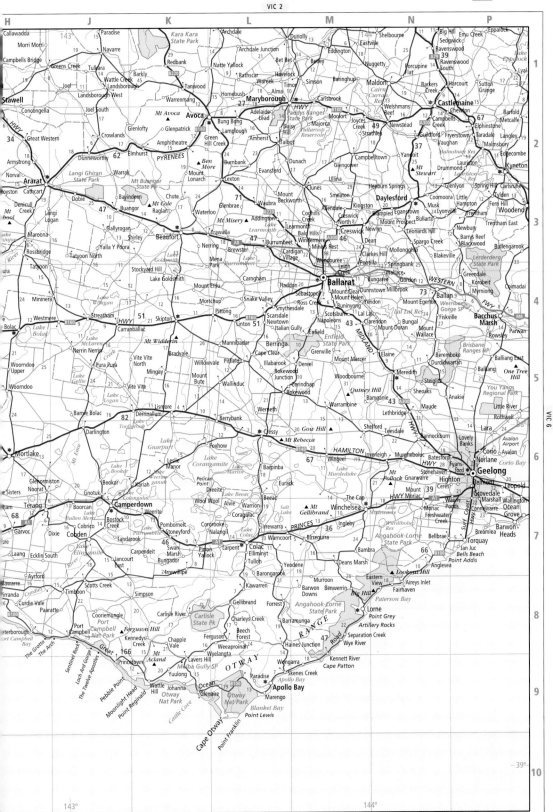

0   10   20   30   40
kilometres

143°

144°

143°

144°

39°

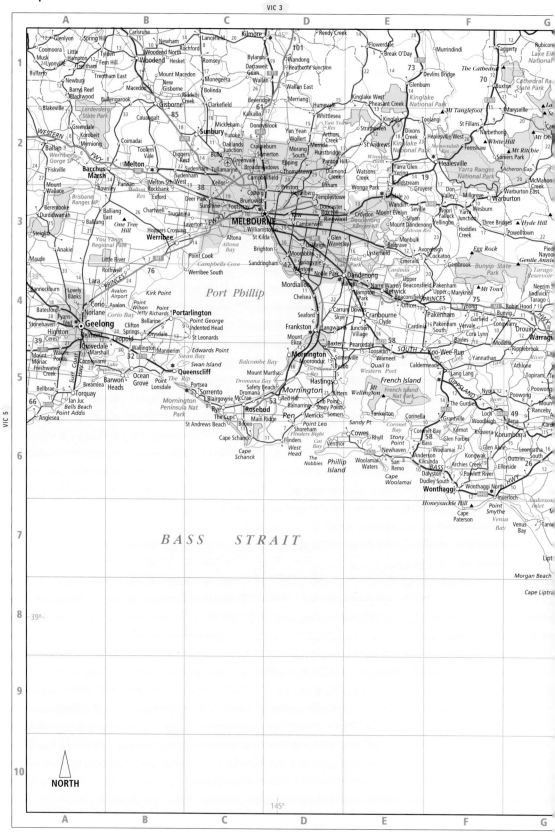

VIC 3

VIC 5

A B C D E F G

Port Phillip

BASS STRAIT

NORTH

145°

39°

38°

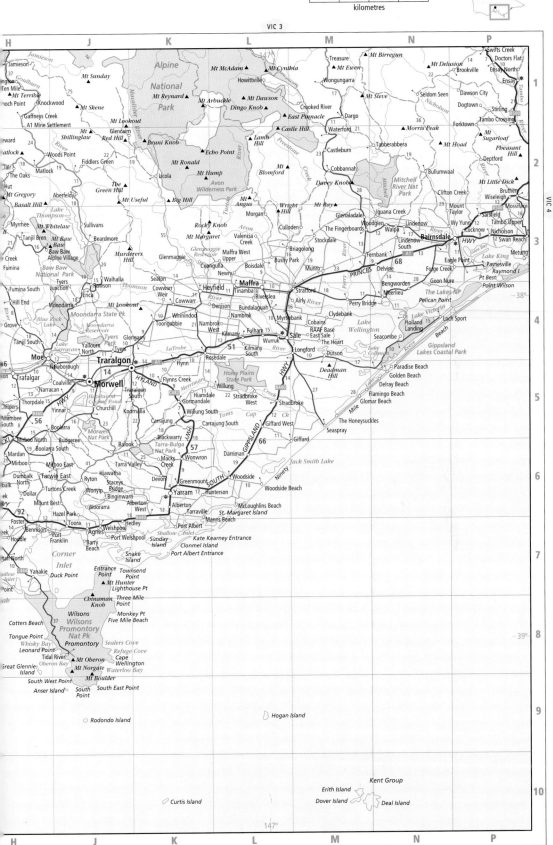

Tasmania

With over one-quarter of the state set aside as national parks, state reserves, historic sites and similar, Tasmania offers a wonderfully rich diversity of protected wilderness, startling natural beauty and amazing history. A National Parks Holiday Pass, valid for two months, gives you entry into all 33 national parks and is available for a small fee. The parks offer a variety of activities, from gentle strolls to week-long bushwalks, from river and lake cruises to scenic flights. You can ski; fish; canoe; sail; dive; abseil; ride a horse, a jet boat or camel; four-wheel drive along vast ocean beaches and giant sand dunes; or raft down wild rivers. Tasmania's parks are blessed with a wealth of attractions and facilities; lacking only deserts and coral reefs, there really is something here for everyone.

Cradle Mountain–Lake St Clair National Park

Cradle Mountain–Lake St Clair National Park is one of the most famous and spectacular national parks in Australia. Part of the Tasmanian Wilderness World Heritage Area, it is listed by the World Heritage Commission as one of the most precious places on earth. This stunningly beautiful area contains rugged mountain peaks, steep forested gorges, moorlands, rainforest, glacial lakes and tarns.

fact file

WHERE: Cradle Valley is 85 km (about 1 hour's drive) from Devonport via Sheffield or Wilmot, or from Burnie airport; Lake St Clair is 175 km from Hobart, via the Lyell Highway and Derwent Bridge. Roads may be closed in winter
Map: Tas 1 J9

WHEN: November to April

WHY: Bushwalking, rock climbing, fishing, canoeing, windsurfing, trail rides, boat cruising, wildlife, 4WD

SIZE: 161 204 ha

RANGER: Cradle Mountain (03) 6492 1133; Lake St Clair (03) 6289 1172

Erosion by glaciers and water, which took place more than 500 000 years ago, carved out the valleys and lakes. Plants in the area reflect their ancient heritage, bearing a closer relationship to species found in New Zealand and South America than to those seen on the mainland of Australia. With snow gums and giant grass trees, or moss- and lichen-clad pencil pine forests, the varied terrain contains a wide range of flora including buttongrass sedges, daisies and herbs.

The Twisted Lakes were created over 500 000 years ago, during a glacial period. Their calm surface mirrors the beauty of their surrounds.

Left: *Plants in Cradle Mountain–Lake St Clair National Park add to its incredible beauty. The deciduous beech (Nothofagus gunnii) creates a splash of golden colour during autumn.*

Below: *Pencil pines (Athrotaxis cupressoides) are found throughout Cradle Mountain–Lake St Clair National Park. This hardy species survives in an extremely harsh environment.*

TAS

With rain falling on an average of 275 days per year and snowfalls occurring on around 54 days a year, you can expect clear and sunny weather only on about 32 days! But even in winter the park has a unique splendour and beauty; under a mantle of snow it takes on a fantasy land appearance.

Cradle Mountain

Father of Cradle Mountain

Gustav Weindorfer, an Austrian naturalist, is considered the 'father' of this 161 204-hectare national park. He built his forest home, Waldheim Chalet, in the wilderness at Cradle Valley in 1911 when everything, including the bathtub, had to be carried in on foot.

After Weindorfer's death in 1932, Waldheim was purchased by his friends and continued to be run as a guesthouse until 1975 when it was closed because of its dilapidated state. Faithfully restored by the Parks and Wildlife Service, with woodwork fashioned from native King Billy pine trees, it is now a monument to this far-sighted pioneer.

Wildlife

The national park is a veritable magnet for all lovers of nature. Prolific wildlife found in the region incorporates many migratory species of birds, such as wrens, honeyeaters and robins, which depart the high country in winter and head towards coastal areas, leaving the park to the resident birdlife, which includes eagles, currawongs and parrots.

A largely nocturnal marsupial population includes wombats, possums, spotted-tailed quolls (tiger cats), and Tasmanian devils. During the day the many Bennett's wallabies and pademelons will approach people, looking for handouts.

don't miss

While you're in Cradle Mountain–Lake St Clair National Park, take the opportunity to test your angling skills against the famous Tasmanian rainbow and brown trout that are found in the lakes and streams.

A lone bushwalker enjoys the view from the top of Barn Bluff overlooking Cradle Mountain–Lake St Clair National Park. There are many walking tracks crisscrossing the park.

Walking

There are numerous signposted walks within Cradle Valley, starting with a reasonably gentle half-hour return stroll along the Enchanted Walk. The King Billy Track (one hour return) takes you through beautiful moss-clad forests of myrtle beech, sassafras, celery-top pine and ancient—1500 to 1700 years old—King Billy pines.

There's also the very easy, 500-metre Rainforest Walk starting from behind the visitor centre, which takes you right around roaring Pencil Pines Falls, while a very popular 3-hour return walk goes to the Ballroom Forest. This superb walk follows the western shore of Lake Dove, which reflects the craggy peaks of Cradle Mountain, to a primeval wonderland full of myrtle, sassafras and deciduous beech.

The Pencil Pine Falls near Cradle Mountain Lodge flow downstream through Cradle Valley from Lake Dove, one of the many glacial lakes scattered throughout the park.

Mountain guides from the Cradle Mountain Lodge lead regular daily walks, but if you are trekking independently, it's important to register at the Ranger's Office in the visitor centre for any walk over an hour. Weather in these regions is notoriously fickle and you'll need to be well prepared for sudden changes. Japara coats, waterproof pants and even gumboots can be hired from the store if necessary.

The Overland Track

For the dedicated trekker, the 60-km Overland Track from Cradle Valley to Lake St Clair offers one of the world's great walks. Evocative names, such as Cathedral Mountain, the Acropolis and Mount Olympus, indicate the reverence which trekkers, from the earliest times, have accorded this stunning area.

The track winds around Lake Dove and Cradle Mountain to Barn Bluff, past many glacial lakes, around Mounts Pelion (both East and West) and Mount Ossa—Tasmania's highest peak at 1617 metres—and down to Lake St Clair, headwater of the Derwent River.

The Overland Track requires a minimum of 5 days and is not for the unfit

or ill-prepared. Although there are some public huts found along the trail, tents should always be carried.

Guided treks are available from Craclair Tours. Those seeking a little luxury can indulge themselves in a fabulous 'walk on the wild side' with Cradle Huts, a Launceston-based company which has four well-appointed lodges along the Overland Track—it is the only private accommodation allowed in this wilderness area.

Cradle Huts run 6-day walks, averaging a daily walking time of 5 hours, including a full day at Pelion (midway) to rest—or, if you are feeling

energetic, you can climb Mount Ossa. A 17-km boat trip down Lake St Clair completes the trek which begins and ends in Launceston. You can contact Cradle Huts in Launceston on (03) 6331 2006.

Other Activities

Tasmania's lakes and streams are renowned as some of the best in the world for chasing the elusive trout. All the major waterways are open to the public for fishing from July until April (an annual Inland Fisheries licence is necessary).

Other activities within Cradle Valley include canoeing, whitewater rafting,

Left: *Fly-fishing is one of the big drawcards of the Cradle Mountain–Lake St Clair National Park. The deep, crystal-clear lakes are brimming with trout.*

Below left: *A 6-km track winds around the shores of Lake Dove and past the imposing spires of Cradle Mountain. Many believe it to be one of Tasmania's premier walking trails.*

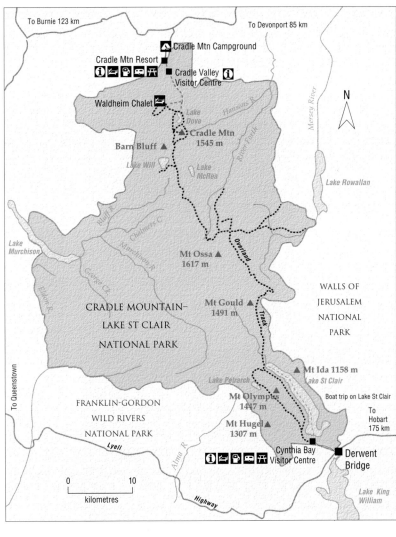

panning for gold, 4WD tours, trail rides on mountain ponies, and even abseiling for the more adventurous.

The Cradle Mountain Visitor Centre, at Cradle Valley (open from 8 a.m. to 5 p.m. daily), has a wealth of information on this World Heritage Area, while the store in Cradle Valley has a wide range of souvenirs plus enough provisions so you can handle your own catering. Petrol (unleaded only) is also available. Scenic flights are on offer from a small runway nearby.

Within the national park itself there are no roads, apart from the road to Lake Dove. There are numerous 4WD tracks around Cradle Valley, to places such as Lake Lea and over the Middlesex Plains, but most tracks are on private property and permission must be granted before use. Cradle Mountain Lodge runs regular 4WD tours of the area.

Weather-beaten and covered in moss, some of the King Billy pines (Athrotaxis selaginoides) found in the park are up to 1500 years old.

Wilderness Retreat

Cradle Mountain Lodge is also a wonderfully relaxing wilderness retreat, offering a wide range of accommodation options from camping—in one of the prettiest and best-equipped camp grounds in the country—through to dormitories and the self-contained Waldheim Cabins to the upmarket Cradle Mountain huts.

The highlight of an evening at Cradle Mountain Lodge is the 9.30 p.m. animal feeding on the 'Critter Stand' outside the Tavern Bar. Fresh fruit and vegetables are offered to the rufous wallabies, quolls, brush-tail possums, tiger cats, Tasmanian devils and wombats. The very fat possums are so tame they climb onto the verandah railing to be hand fed and are not even fazed by blinding camera flashes! You can contact Cradle Mountain Lodge on (03) 6492 1303.

Cradle Mountain Lodge offers the weary traveller a warm haven against the fickle and often inclement weather of the Tasmanian highlands.

Lake St Clair

This beautiful lake in the south of the national park is an easy half-day drive from Hobart. Surrounded by magical mountains, Lake St Clair is Australia's deepest lake (up to 200 metres in places) and is very cold. Its beauty and serenity, where its shallow fringes lap large boulders and sandy beaches, backed by gnarled cypress pines and eucalypts, create a very contemplative mood. Lake St Clair is one of the prettiest spots in Tasmania and one of the most popular with day visitors, particularly people passing through to the west coast, but it is not hard to escape the tourist hordes to find peace and quiet.

Facilities

Cynthia Bay on the south-west corner of the lake is a popular picnic area, with barbecues, toilets, picnic shelter, kiosk, and frequently, hordes of tourist buses and mobs of wallabies.

The visitor centre has interpretation displays of the geology of the region, a video on glaciers and a giant hologram of a family of thylacines (the Tasmanian tiger). The centre also houses the offices of the Parks and Wildlife Service, a shop and a restaurant. It is a fantastic place for children to learn about animals and places in Tasmania. Information on trout fishing is also available here.

TAS

Walking

A beautiful, 3- to 4-hour (return) walk following the roaring Hugel River leads to the lovely Shadow and Forgotten Lakes. Two short, new walks at Cynthia Bay are the Platypus Bay Loop (1 hour return) and the Woodland Nature Walk (1 hour return).

Another easy track, suitable for families, (45 minutes return) is the Watersmeet Nature Trail which leads to the start (or the end) of the Overland Track, passing through eucalypts, rainforest and across buttongrass plains to the Hugel and Cuvier Rivers. Abundant native wildlife, particularly birds and wallabies, can be seen along all these tracks.

Other Activities

A ferry runs regular cruises to the mouth of the Narcissus River at the northern end of the lake and is frequently utilised by walkers finishing the Overland Track. Lake St Clair is a great spot for canoeing, windsurfing, trout fishing and swimming (if you're feeling brave!).

Camping

Phone the ranger's office or the National Parks and Wildlife Service Information Centre on (03) 6492 1133 for details of camp sites. On the Overland Track it is preferable to camp near the huts to prevent degradation of the country. There is no camping in the Cradle Mountain day-walk areas.

Shadow Lake has camp sites where you can enjoy superb lake and mountain views, and Lake St Clair Wilderness Holidays, 5 km north of the Derwent Bridge, has camp sites, backpackers' accommodation and luxury cabins for four to eight people. Contact them for more information on (03) 6289 1137.

Spikes of vibrant scarlet flowers from the Tasmanian native kerosene bush (Richea scoparia) cover the lower slopes of Cradle Mountain–Lake St Clair National Park during summer.

Franklin–Gordon Wild Rivers National Park

Born out of the greatest environmental battle fought in this country, the Franklin–Gordon Wild Rivers National Park now protects the Franklin River and much of the lower reaches of the Gordon River. One of the greatest wilderness adventure trips in Australia is to raft down the often tranquil, sometimes rapid-churned Franklin River to its junction with the mighty Gordon River in south-west Tasmania.

Above: *Whitewater rafting is definitely not for the faint-hearted, especially on the wild rapids of the Franklin River. A safety helmet and a life jacket are essential items for those tackling the rapids.*

A Wild River

The Franklin River is the largest river in Tasmania to run free for its entire length, from its source in the Cheyne Range to its meeting with the Gordon River 45 km from the sea at Macquarie Harbour.

For many adventurers, a rafting trip on the Franklin begins on one of the Franklin's tributaries, the Collingwood. Once on the Franklin, the river begins its great arc around the sheer bluff of Frenchmans Cap before entering a series of gorges separated by rapids of varying intensity. These are known by such descriptive names as the Churn, Thunder Rush and the Cauldron. Once out of the Great Ravine the river is more placid, and below Big Fall the river slows and spreads out, waiting to join the Gordon.

A Mighty River

The Gordon is regarded by many as the monarch of all rivers. The lower reaches are magnificent, known for their fantastic reflections that, like the very best mirror, reflect the images of the dense forests crowding the pristine river bank.

Apart from the placid stretches of the lower Gordon (accessible from Strahan), much of the river is out of bounds as it is too dangerous to raft or paddle.

Access and Camping

Most people experience the wonders of the region on one of the many cruise boats which operate daily out of Strahan,

Right: *In the 1980s, the Franklin River was at the centre of a heated debate between conservationists and the state government, who wanted to dam the river. It was a debate that bitterly divided the state.*

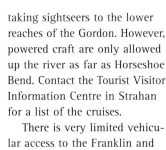

taking sightseers to the lower reaches of the Gordon. However, powered craft are only allowed up the river as far as Horseshoe Bend. Contact the Tourist Visitor Information Centre in Strahan for a list of the cruises.

There is very limited vehicular access to the Franklin and Gordon areas. Only the Mount McCall 4WD track gives access to the Franklin. This track goes through spectacular country and ends, 22 km later, near Mount McCall and well above the river! You need a permit and a key for the gate from the Queenstown office of the Parks and Wildlife Service.

A few walking trails delve into this wilderness, including short ones off the Lyell Highway and others that are only suitable for well-equipped, experienced bushwalkers. A number of companies with float planes, such as Wilderness Air, operate out of Strahan taking tourists over the rivers and peaks. This is a great way to see this rugged area.

Camping is limited in the park but there are a few bush camps scattered through the area suitable for bushwalkers. The bridge over the Collingwood is one such spot, Irenabyss Camp on the Franklin is another, along with Warners Landing on the Gordon. Otherwise you pitch a tent where you find room in amongst the dense forest or on a flattish slope on the edge of a cliff!

The town of Strahan has all facilities and is really quite a delightful place to spend a few days.

tourist info

Tasmanian Wild River Adventures
0409 977 506

Visitor Information Centre, Strahan
(03) 6471 7622

Wilderness Air
(03) 6471 7280

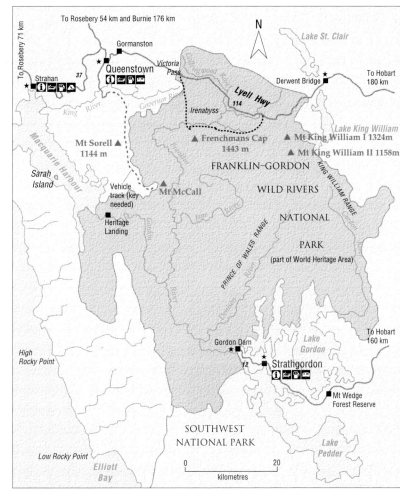

Freycinet National Park

Spectacular coastal scenery is everywhere you look on the Freycinet Peninsula, where dramatic red granite peaks are reflected in clear blue waters lapping sands of dazzling white. The three peaks of the Hazards dominate the skyline, and long before you reach the peninsula they beckon across the expanse of Great Oyster Bay. Such breathtaking panoramas, abundant wildlife and a wealth of outdoor activities make this national park a great holiday area.

fact file

WHERE: 39 km south of Bicheno, via the Tasman Highway; limited vehicular access
Map: Tas 3 P1

WHEN: November to May

WHY: Walking, wildlife, fishing, water sports, sightseeing cruises, 4WD

SIZE: 16 803 ha

RANGER: (03) 6257 0107

The lookout at Cape Tourville affords visitors a magnificent view of the rugged granite coastline along the eastern side of Freycinet National Park.

Freycinet National Park consists mainly of coastal heathland, which becomes a veritable artist's palette of vibrant colours in spring, dominated by awe-inspiring peaks and cliffs. Magnificent pure white, sandy beaches, such as Wineglass Bay (mostly accessible only by boat or on foot), alternate with towering cliffs above the rocky coastline.

The abundant wildlife is as rich as it is varied. Black cockatoos, green rosellas, yellow wattle-birds, butcherbirds and wedge-tail eagles are all seen, while gannets, fairy penguins and white-breasted sea-eagles are some of the many sea-birds. There are also wallabies, possums, echidnas and potoroos.

The Freycinet Peninsula was named in 1802 by the French explorer Nicholas Baudin to honour his cartographer Henri Freycinet, and became a national park in 1916. Together with Mount Field, it is Tasmania's oldest national park.

Activities

Freycinet National Park is largely a wilderness area with very little vehicular access. This is a bushwalker's paradise with a variety of walks ranging from 1 to 10 hours, and there are several camp sites for overnight hikers on the 27-km circuit track of the park.

Another popular walk with visitors— particularly at sunrise—is to the summit of Mount Amos for stunning views south across Wineglass Bay and the peninsula, or north across Coles Bay and beyond (2 hours return).

One of the few areas with vehicular access and one of the most spectacular is Cape Tourville, while Bluestone Bay is reached by a 4WD track.

The Hazards, about 485 metres high, present a real challenge to climbers. The fishing in the park is good, with fishing charters being available from the nearby Coles Bay township. Fuel, supplies, boat and sporting equipment hire are also found in the town. Water sports include swimming, water skiing, diving, sailing and canoeing.

To the north (about 10 km from the highway) are the delightfully named

With the cobalt blue waters of Wineglass Bay crowned by a sublime curve of white sand, it comes as no surprise that this beach is recognised as one of the most beautiful in the world.

don't miss

If you're feeling fit, climb the Hazards that form a formidable backdrop to the Freycinet Lodge. They are over 485 metres high and reward the adventurous climber with beautiful views over the entire national park.

TAS

Friendly Beaches, which are a great area for anglers and four wheel drivers. From here, Freycinet Experience runs 4-day walks in the national park starting with a boat ride to Schouten Island.

Access and Accommodation

The park is approximately a 3-hour drive from Hobart, and about the same from Devonport on the state's northern coast.

Accommodation ranges from the fantastic waterfront camp through youth hostels to B&Bs. The environmentally friendly Freycinet Lodge offers many nature-based and educational activities.

There is also a variety of accommodation available through the Freycinet Experience. They offer simple cabin accommodation for overnight walkers as well as more luxurious lodges—for longer stays—tucked away out of sight at the Friendly Beaches. Call (03) 6223 7565 for more information.

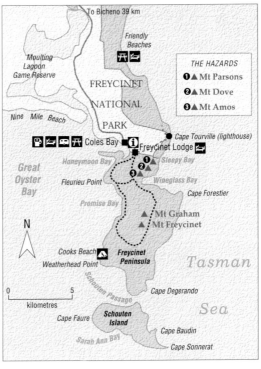

To Bicheno 39 km

Friendly Beaches

Moulting Lagoon Game Reserve

FREYCINET

NATIONAL

PARK

Nine Mile Beach

Coles Bay

Freycinet Lodge

Cape Tourville (lighthouse)

THE HAZARDS
1 ▲ Mt Parsons
2 ▲ Mt Dove
3 ▲ Mt Amos

Honeymoon Bay

Sleepy Bay

Great Oyster Bay

Fleurieu Point

Wineglass Bay

Cape Forestier

Promise Bay

N

Mt Graham
Mt Freycinet

Cooks Beach

Freycinet Peninsula

Weatherhead Point

Tasman

0   5
kilometres

Schouten Passage

Cape Degerando

Sea

Cape Faure

Schouten Island

Cape Baudin

Sarah Ann Bay

Cape Sonnerat

Mount Field National Park

This is Tasmania's oldest national park (along with Freycinet National Park) and is one of the state's prettiest, with a great variety of scenery from low-level rainforest to high-altitude moorlands, brooding mountain ranges, waterfalls and many beautiful lakes. Mount Field has something for everyone, from gentle walks to winter skiing. Lake Dobson, a beautiful mountain lake, is also accessible by car. There's abundant wildlife including Tasmanian devils, spotted-tail quolls and even platypus. Birdlife is also prolific.

The picturesque Russell Falls are the most recognisable and photographed feature of the Mount Field National Park.

fact file

WHERE: 75 km north-west of Hobart via New Norfolk Map: Tas 3 G4

WHEN: September to May; June to August

WHY: Wildlife, bush-walking, fishing, picnics, camping, scenic drives, cross-country skiing

SIZE: 16 977 ha

RANGER: (03) 6288 1149

Walking and Skiing

The whole of Mount Field National Park is a walkers' paradise with walks ranging from 10-minute strolls to overnight hikes. A large picnic area at the park entrance is the starting point for a 1-km Nature Walk which winds through giant tree ferns, swamp gums and a great variety of small ferns to the magnificent Russell Falls. Numerous other marked tracks lead to the many lakes and peaks in the national park. Some of these are overnight hikes but there are a number of hikers huts in the park.

Snow-covered in winter, the park offers good cross-country ski tours across the higher plateaus. There is no downhill skiing.

Access and Camping

The park is situated 75 km north-west of Hobart with the entrance 35 km from New Norfolk. There is 4WD access only in late autumn to early spring. Check road conditions before setting out.

At the entrance there is a visitor centre with information about the park. A pretty camping area nearby has full facilities.

The view of Mount Field National Park overlooking Lake Seal is breathtaking. In winter the park can become snow-covered, which adds a new dimension to the already harsh landscape.

More National Parks of Importance

Ben Lomond National Park

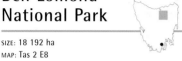

SIZE: 18 192 ha
MAP: Tas 2 E8

Ben Lomond National Park encompasses a 1300-metre high plateau, just 60 km from Launceston, and in winter it becomes the state's major ski resort offering cross-country and downhill skiing from beginners to advanced.

In spring Ben Lomond is a popular spot for day visitors and is a pleasant, unspoilt area for walkers, while the dramatic vertical dolerite columns here attract rock climbers. However, the road up to Ben Lomond is not for the faint-hearted: the final ascent is steep, winding and narrow.

Apart from private clubs, the only accommodation is at Creek Inn which has log-cabin style units. There are no formal camp sites but bush camping is allowed in the national park.

For more information contact the National Parks and Wildlife Service office in Launceston on (03) 6336 5312.

Maria Island National Park

SIZE: 11 550 ha
MAP: Tas 3 N4

This tranquil, beautiful and quite historic island, just 15 km off Tasmania's east coast, boasts magnificent coastal cliffs, dazzling white beaches, open forests and a mountain range that supports a delicate rainforest habitat.

Maria Island was named by explorer Abel Tasman in 1642. In 1825 a penal settlement was established on the island, but it was abandoned in 1832. It was declared a national park in 1972 and the restoration of many of the old buildings, a highlight of a visit here, began. For walkers there are a number of tracks to enjoy, and there is an abundance of tame wildlife to experience.

Ferries operate from Triabunna and Louisville Point, taking less than an hour to reach the island. Triabunna is 84 km from Hobart via the Tasman Highway.

Camp sites are available at the township of Darlington, plus basic dormitory accommodation. You can also camp at French's Farm and Encampment Cove. There is no transport or other facilities on Maria Island.

For more information or to book accommodation, phone (03) 6257 1420.

Ben Lomond National Park, only an hour's drive from Launceston, is Tasmania's only downhill skiing area. It is popular with both visitors and the local population.

TAS

The fossil cliffs on Maria Island are only one of the many natural features of this beautiful national park off the east coast. The island also has convict ruins dating back to the early nineteenth century.

Mount William National Park

SIZE: 18 439 ha
MAP: Tas 2 H4

Mount William National Park is an important area for the conservation of Tasmania's coastal flora, including the grass tree (Xanthorrhoea australis).

One of Tasmania's lesser known national parks, Mount William National Park combines natural beauty and abundant wildlife in a coastal setting. Originally set aside to protect the then-rare forester kangaroo, this park covers the north-east tip of Tasmania and encloses coastal heathland, dry sclerophyll forest and a bounty of beautiful beaches.

Swimming, surfing, fishing and diving are popular pastimes; long, white beaches and a network of fire trails allow for a variety of bushwalking. An easy 30-minute walk to the top of Mount William gives sweeping views of the park.

Camp sites are dotted among the sand dunes near Picnic Rocks and on a grassy area beside Deep Creek. In the north there are numerous camp sites around Stumpys Bay and north of Cape Naturaliste.

For more information, phone the ranger on (03) 6357 2108.

Walls of Jerusalem National Park

SIZE: 51 800 ha
MAP: Tas 1 L9

A subalpine wilderness, this national park forms part of the World Heritage Area, and is a gorgeous but fragile place. This park is also strictly for the very fit. Bushwalking, some rock climbing and cross-country skiing are the only activities.

From the car park a strenuous 3-hour walk entails a steep climb up to Trappers Hut and on to Solomons Jewels, a chain of beautiful little lakes. Another steep ridge brings you to Herods Gate and Lake Salome. The West Wall towers 300 metres above this lake, as does the Temple. Mount Jerusalem, the highest mountain in the park at 1458 metres, is to the north. At this altitude weather can be unpredictable at any time of year, so it is important to be well prepared.

There is no vehicular access into the park. There are no facilities in the park, but bush camping is allowed. Only fuel stoves are allowed. For more information, phone the National Parks and Wildlife Service at Moll Creek (03) 6363 5182 or Launceston (03) 6336 5312.

Visitors to the Walls of Jerusalem National Park who make the trip in winter need to be appropriately dressed to combat exposure and frostbite.

Popular Parks at a Glance

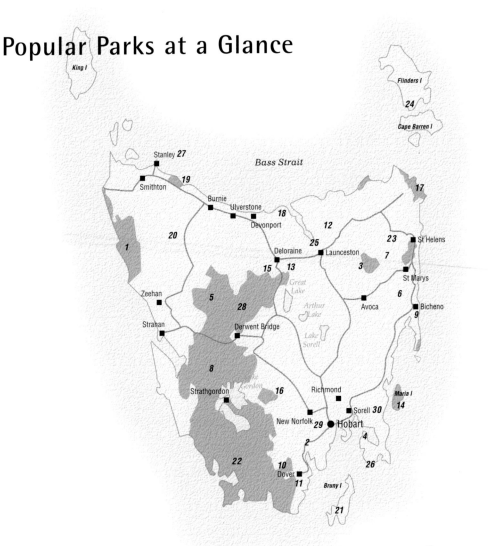

	Camping	Caravan Access	Disabled Access	4WD Access	Picnic Areas	Toilets	Walking Tracks	Kiosk	Information
1 Arthur Pieman PA	•	•	•	•		•	•		•
2 Arve River Road/Skywalk	•	•	•	•		•	•		
3 Ben Lomond NP	•				•	•	•	•	
4 Coal Mines HS and Lime Bay	•	•			•	•	•		
5 Cradle Mtn–Lake St Clair NP	•		•		•	•	•	•	
6 Douglas Apsley NP	•					•	•		
7 Evercreech FR				•	•	•	•		
8 Franklin–Gordon Wild Rivers NP	•		•		•	•	•	•	
9 Freycinet NP	•	•			•	•	•		•
10 Hartz Mountains NP	•				•	•	•		
11 Hastings Caves & Thermal Springs		•			•	•	•	•	•
12 Hollybank FR	•		•		•	•	•		
13 Liffey Falls					•	•	•	•	
14 Maria Island NP	•		•		•	•	•		•
15 Mole Creek Karst NP					•	•	•		•

	Camping	Caravan Access	Disabled Access	4WD Access	Picnic Areas	Toilets	Walking Tracks	Kiosk	Information
16 Mount Field NP	•	•	•		•	•	•	•	•
17 Mount William NP	•	•			•	•	•		
18 Narawntapu NP	•	•	•		•	•	•		•
19 Rocky Cape NP	•				•		•		
20 Savage River NP									
21 South Bruny NP	•	•			•	•	•		
22 Southwest NP	•						•		•
23 St Columba Falls						•	•		
24 Strzelecki NP	•	•			•	•	•		•
25 Tamar Island			•			•	•		
26 Tasman NP	•	•			•	•	•		
27 The Nut					•	•	•	•	
28 Walls of Jerusalem NP	•					•	•		
29 Wellington Park				•	•	•	•	•	
30 Wielangta Forest Drive				•	•	•	•		

Map 1

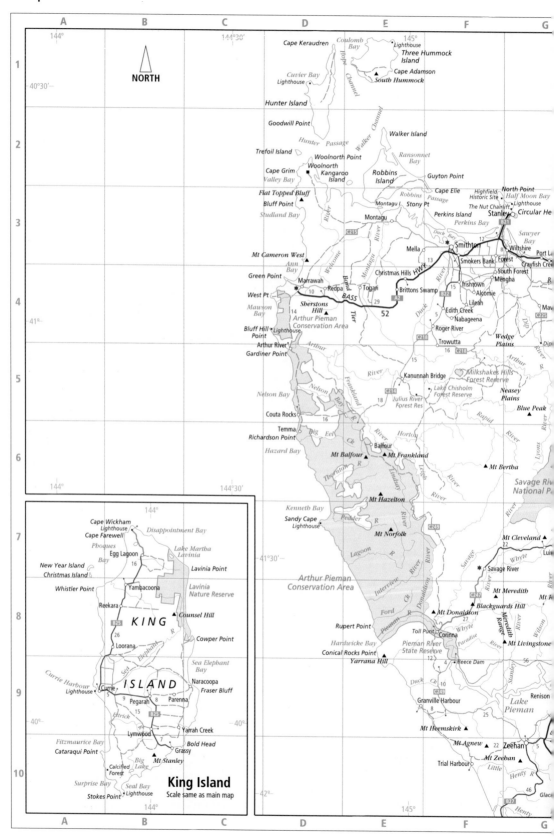

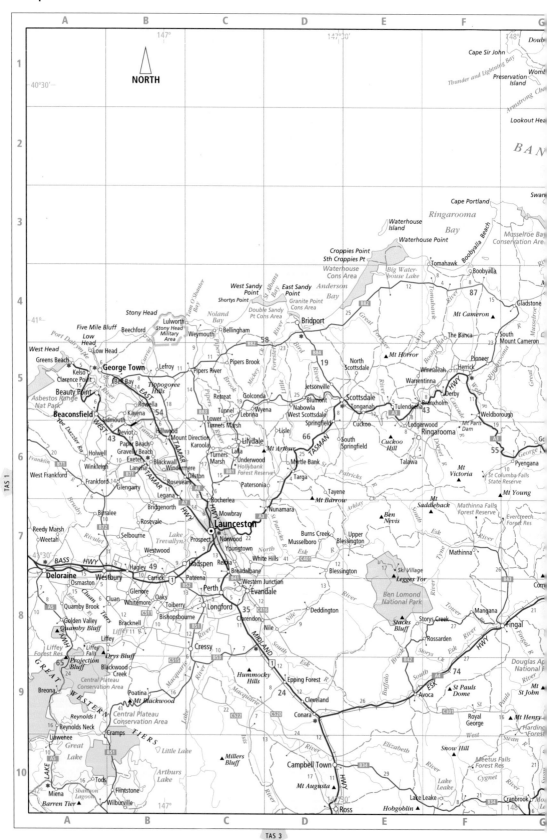

0   10   20   30
kilometres

Flinders Island
Scale same as main map

H   J   K   L   M   N   P

148°30'   148°30'

Mt Kerford ▲   Cape Barren

Inner Sister
Island

Outer Sister Island

Cone Pt
Passage
Island

Blyth Point   Palana

Lighthouse
Stanley Point

F
U
R
N
E
A
U
X

1

Killiecrankie
Bay   ▲ Mt Killiecrankie

○ Killiecrankie

AIT

Cape
Frankland   ▲ Mt Tanner   B85

Leeka ○

FLINDERS

30

ISLAND

Babel Island

Lighthouse
Cat Island

Sellars Point

2

Roydon
Island

Tanners
Bay

Marshall
Bay

40°-

Wybalenna
Historic Site

Prime Seal
Island

uraliste
s Bay

Emita

Furneaux
Lookout

Blue Rocks
19

Arthur
Bay

Memana

The
Patriachs ▲

C802

Pats R

Walkers
Lookout

▲ Mt Levensthorpe

Sellars Lagoon

Cameron
Inlet

-40°

G
R
O
U
P

3

od Bay

Purdon Bay

Eddystone Point Lighthouse
Eddystone Point

ons Bay

Sharon Point

ay of Fires
ons Area
Bay Of
Fires

e Gardens

-41°-

Chalky Island

Long
Point

Parrys
Bay

Whitemark

B85

Logan
Lagoon

Big Green
Island

East Kangaroo
Island

Fotheringate Bay

Trousers Point

Mt Chappell
Island

Goose Island

Lighthouse

Badger Island

Long Island

Ranga

Strzelecki ▲
Peaks

C803

24

Lady
Barron

Pot Boil Point

Little Green Island

Great Dog Island

Strzelecki NP

Franklin

Pigs Head Point

Sound

Little Dog I

Vansittart Island

Puncheon Pt

Anderson Island

Tin Kettle
Island

Apple Orchard Point

Deep Bay

Cape

4

5

oop Lagoon

Binalong
Bay   Humbug Point
       Cons Area
1   St Helens Pt
    St Helens Point
ns   Cons Area
○ Stieglitz
rnella
side ○ St Helens Island

Dianas Basin

eaumaris
der Forest Res

mander

nderson Lagoon
lmouth

Four Mile Creek
Ironhouse Point

nt Pass

Chain of Lagoons

Picaninny Point

emplestow Lagoon
rymour
Long Point

Maclean
Bay

life and Animal Park

Bicheno

Cape Lodi
Courland Bay

Freycinet
National Park

Friendly
Beaches
er

Cape Barren
Island

▲ Mt Munro

Barren Island

Harleys Point

Double Peak ▲

Cape Sir John

Thunder and Lightning Bay

Preservation
Island

Wombat Pt

Sloping Pt

Kent
Bay

Mt Kerford
▲

Cape Barren

Armstrong Channel

Lookout Head

Clarke
Island

Forsyth
Island

Black Point

Moriarty Bay

Moriarty Point

Cone Pt
Passage
Island

-40°30'

-40°30'

6

T A S

148°   148°30'

149°

149°30'

-41°30'

7

8

9

10

-42°

148°30'   149°   149°30'

H   J   K   L   M   N   P

Map 3

kilometres

0 10 20 30

—42°

—42°30'

—43°

—43°30'

TASMAN SEA

STORM BAY

Great Lake

Lake Sorell

Lake Crescent

Wilburville

Steppes

Interlaken

Ross

Tunbridge

Woodbury

Antill Ponds

Mt Franklin

Lake Leake

Hobgoblin

Cranbrook

Freycinet Nat Park

Friendly Beaches

Mt Peter

Mt Paul

Coles Bay

Lighthouse

Cape Tourville

Nine Mile Beach

Hepburn Point

Swansea

Great Oyster Bay

Spiky Bridge

Fleurieu Pt

Wineglass Bay

Cape Forestier

Mt Graham

Mt Freycinet

Freycinet Pen

Baldy Bluff

Cape Degerando

Schouten Passage

Schouten Island

Rooster Point

Cape Sonnerat

Freycinet National Park

Oatlands

York Plains

Vincent Hill

Callington Mill Historic Site

Pawtella

Lemont

Little Swanport

Faddens Tier

Tooms Lake

Mayfield Bay Cons Area

Mayfield Bay

Buxton Pt

Little Swanport

Seaford Point

Cape Faure

Table Mtn

Woods Quoin

Andover

Parattah

Northumbria Hill

Jericho

Pike Hill

Mount Seymour

Stonor

Whitefoord

Baden

Woodsdale

Little Swanport Hill

Buckland Military Training Area

Bluestone Tier

Boltons Beach Cons Area

Grindstone Point

Mt Murray

Bothwell

Green Hill Spring Hill

Melton Mowbray

Black Tier

Lake Tiberias

Rhyndaston

Tunnack

Eldon

Kempton

Colebrook

Levendale

Mt Hobbs

Triabunna

Cape Bougainville

Mt Reid

Hollow Tree

Mt Spode

Pelham

Elderslie

Dysart

Quoin Mtn

Craigbourne Dam

Louisville

Lighthouse

Orford

Spring Beach

Cape Boullanger

Maria Island National Park

Darlington

Brown Mtn

Buckland

Thumbs Picnic Area

Rheban

Return Pt

Johnsons Pt

Maria Island

Mt Maria

Mistaken Cape

Pelham

Bagdad

Mangalore

Lowdina

Campania

Runnymede

Mt Morrison

Prossers Sugarloaf

Pt Lesueur

Shoal Bay

Riedle Bay

Oyster Bay

Broadmarsh

Pontville

Brighton

Richmond

Orielton

Nugent

Sandspit River Forest Res

Cape Bernier

Cape Peron

Cape Maurouard

Gretna

Rosegarland

Mt Dromedary

Black Hills Dromedary

Granton

Old Beach

Grasstree Hill

Pawleena

Kellevie

Marion Bay

Glenora

Macquarie Plains

Hayes

Magra

Bridgewater

Sorell

Wattle Hill

Bream Creek

Copping

Cape Paul Lamanon

New Norfolk

Malbina

Molesworth

Otago

Risdon Vale

Cambridge

Midway Point

Forcett

Lewisham

Dodges Ferry

Dunalley

North Bay

Cape Frederick Hendrick

Glenfern

Glenlusk

Mt Rumney

Seven Mile Beach

Carlton

Primrose Sands

Dunalley Bay

Mt Forestier

High Yellow Bluff

Mount Lloyd

Lachlan

Collinsvale

Glenorchy

Rokeby

Frederick Henry Bay

Forestier Peninsula

Cape Surville

Collins Cap

Lookout

HOBART

Ridgeway

Lauderdale

Green Head

Sandford

Lime Bay Nat Res

Smooth I

Murdunna

Trestle Mtn

Blue Hill

Mt Wellington

Fern Tree

Neika

Taroona

Shot Tower

Sloping I

Cremorne

Chronicle Pt

Coal Mines Historic Site

Eaglehawk Neck

Tessellated Pavement

Pirates Bay

Mt Misery

Crabtree

Grove

Kingston

Blackmans Bay

Cape Deslacs

Clifton Beach

Norfolk Bay

Tasman Arch

Tasman Blowhole

Devils Kitchen

Waterfall Bay

Judbury

Lucaston

Ranelagh

Lower Longley

Sandfly

Howden

Opossum Bay

Saltwater River

South Arm

Tasmanian Devil Park

Taranna

Glen Huon

Huonville

Pelverata

Electrona

Margate

Kaoota

Tinderbox

Nth West Bay

Iron Pot Lighthouse

Betsey Island

Premaydena

Koonya

O'Hara Bluff

Tasman Trail

Fortescue Bay

Cape Huay

Franklin

Pelverata Falls

Woodstock

Snug

Snug Falls

Coningham

Killora

Dennes Point

Outer North Head

One Tree Point

Barnes Bay

Wedge Bay

Nubeena

Tasman Peninsula

Cradoc

Kettering

Oyster Cove

Woodbridge

The Yellow Bluff

White Beach

Highcroft

Palmers Lookout

Port Arthur Convict Ruins

Munro Bight

Tasman National Park

Geeveston

Glaziers Bay

Wattle Grove

Petcheys Bay

Lymington

Gardners Bay

Nicholls Rivulet

Birchs Bay

Trumpeter Bay

Curio Bay

Remarkable Cave

Cape Pillar

Cairns Bay

Waterloo

Surges Bay

Cygnet

Middleton

Variety Bay

Two Island Bay

Tasman I Lighthouse

North Bruny Island

Maingon Bay

South Franklin

Forbes Bay

Port Huon

Garden Island Creek

Gordon

Simpsons Bay

Isthmus Bay

Cape Queen Elizabeth

Glendevie

Police Point

Hideaway Bay

Surveyors Bay

Huon

Verona Sands

Simpsons Bay

Adventure Bay

Raminea

Dover

Strathblane

Maggot Pt

Esperance Pt

Alonnah

Fluted Cape

Ventenat Point

South Bruny

Lunawanna

Adventure Bay

Capt Cook's Landing Place

Bligh Museum

Cape Connella

Thermal Pool

Partridge Island

Hopwood Point

Bay of Islands

Lune River

Ida Bay

Southport

South Bruny Nat Park

Mangana Bluff

South Bruny National Park

Southport Lagoon

Historic Lighthouse

Mt Bruny

Boreel Head

Eliza Point

Recherche Bay

Cape Bruny

West Cloudy Head

Cloudy Bay

East Cloudy Head

Tasman Head

The Friars

Catamaran

Whale Sculpture

Cockle Creek

Whale Head

South Australia

When they think of South Australia, lovers of the outdoors will immediately call to mind such places as the Flinders Ranges, the Simpson Desert, or the cliffs lining the Great Australian Bight where the flat plains of the Nullarbor Plain plunge into the rolling swells of the Southern Ocean. There are many other natural wonders, and they have one thing in common—some form of park or reserve protects them all. With more than 17 per cent of South Australia protected in some form of conservation area, the state can boast one of the most dynamic and forward-thinking reserve systems in the country. From the parks in the remote north, to the Flinders Ranges, to the south-east and to the mighty Murray, there are many rare jewels hidden away in the vastness of South Australia.

Flinders Ranges National Park

This semi-arid mountain country is among the most spectacular regions of the Australian outback. The changing moods of these mountains enchant all who gaze upon them. The ranges stretch 300 km from near Gladstone in the relatively well-watered parts of the state, north to the low hill of Mount Hopeless on the edge of the Strzelecki Desert. But it is in the central Flinders, around the unique geological structure of Wilpena Pound, that the ranges take on their grandest and most distinctive character.

fact file

WHERE: 460 km north of Adelaide
Map: SA 3 K4

WHEN: April to October; September is best for wildflowers

WHY: Great camping, remote mountain scenery, wildflowers

SIZE: 92 746 ha

RANGER: Wilpena (08) 8648 0049; Oraparinna (08) 8648 0047

The little eagle (Hieraaetus morphnoides) feeds mostly on live prey such as reptiles, small animals and small birds.

While Wilpena Pound is the linchpin of the surrounding Flinders Ranges National Park, it really does vie with other natural wonders nearby to provide a seemingly never-ending extravaganza of scenery.

In the Past

The Adnyamathanha people, or 'Hill People', were the original inhabitants of this area and they have left a rich legacy of rock art sites in the region.

Although the mountains were named after Matthew Flinders, who was the first European to view the ranges on his circumnavigation of Australia in 1802, it was Edward John Eyre in 1839 and 1840 who settled the area. Other explorers and surveyors followed, and two doctors, the Browne brothers, opened up the area around Wilpena Pound and the Aroona Valley just to the north.

Since the early 1950s, the Pound has had a tourist resort located at the Wilpena Creek entrance. In 1970 a national park was founded to the north-east of Wilpena Pound, and two years later the new national park was amalgamated with the Pound. Since then the park has grown to its present size of 92 746 hectares.

Wilpena Pound

The centrepiece of the park is Wilpena Pound, which attracts most of the visitors and the acclaim. The name Wilpena is said to mean in the local Aboriginal dialect, 'a cupped hand', which is a perfect description of this huge natural amphitheatre, while a 'pound' was the early settlers' name for a stock enclosure. Nearly 5 km wide and 11 km long, the undulating grassland inside the Pound sweeps up on its edges to the lofty craggy peaks of the all-encircling Wilpena Pound Range, that on the edges plummet to the surrounding plains.

There are only two exits from the Pound. One, in the north-west, through Edeowie Gorge, is narrow, rocky and

Grassland sweeps up to the edges of the ranges which encircle Wilpena Pound in the Flinders Ranges. St Mary Peak, part of the range which forms the north-eastern wall of Wilpena Pound, is the highest point in South Australia.

Below: *Wilpena Pound, the centrepiece of this national park, covers over 83 sq km. This crater-like area with its more permanent waterholes, rich vegetation and bountiful wildlife provides a contrast to the stark, dry surrounding plains.*

cliff-strewn, while the other follows the gum-lined Wilpena Creek through a steep-sided valley on the eastern side of the Pound. The park's tourist resort and all the amenities are located close to this entrance.

Few people would come to this area and not take at least a short stroll through the gap carved by Wilpena Creek. Ancient, giant red gums tower over the track and crowd the rocky, often reed-shrouded creek bed, making the walk a shady delight, especially welcome after a long walk across rocky ridges or sun-scorched open plains.

The shorter walks take you to the old homestead and then up the ridge on a short but steep climb to Wangarra

The unusual bearded dragon (Pogona vitti-ceps). When threatened, this lizard intimidates predators by standing with its mouth open and puffing out the spiny pouch under its jaw.

Lookout. The return walk of 2 to 3 km takes 1 to 2 hours. From the entrance to the Pound there is also an hour-long walk along a nature trail and a more strenuous walk of about 2 hours to the lookout on top of Mount Ohlssen Bagge.

Longer walks of a day or more can take you south to Bridle Gap, on the edge of the park, or north to Edeowie Gorge, while a circuit route via the heart of the Pound and Cooinda Camp can take you north to Tanderra Saddle and the top of St Mary Peak. From there it turns south along the battlements of the range to bring you back to the starting point at Wilpena Creek.

Part of the long-distance Heysen Walking Trail cuts through the park, entering at the southern end of the Pound via Bridle Gap. It then heads north from Wilpena Creek along the ABC Range to the Aroona Valley and out of the park to Parachilna Gorge. You can enjoy this trail for a day, a week or even longer, but you need to be experienced and well equipped for extended forays.

Sacred Canyon

Sacred Canyon is one of the best Australian Aboriginal art sites in the Flinders Ranges and is only accessible via a good dirt road that heads off the main Blinman road, just north of the Wilpena Pound Resort turn-off.

A brief walk from the car park along a tree-lined creek brings you to the short narrow canyon. There are rock engravings, or petroglyphs, which can be seen on the sheer rock faces on both sides of the canyon. This ancient form of indigenous art includes animal tracks, circles and other symbols.

Aroona Valley

The scenic Aroona Valley tucks in beside the northern peaks of the ABC Range, but it is the Heysen Range immediately to the west that dominates the view. The partially restored mud brick and pine Aroona

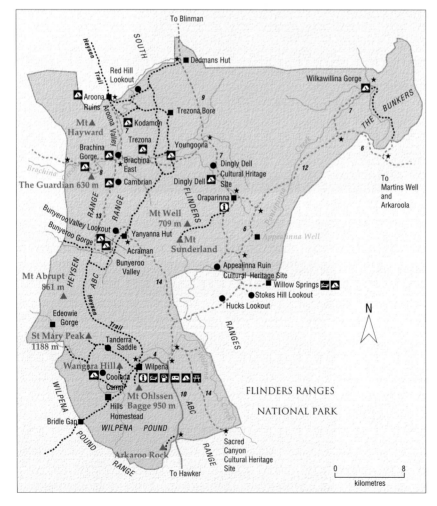

Opposite page: *White cypress pine (Callitris glauco-phylla) growing in the local rugged sandstone; its roots penetrate the rock crevices in their search for water.*

Grass trees (Xanthor-rhoea australis) grow on the rocky hillsides. In spring, their white flower spikes blend wih the pinks and reds of Sturt's desert pea, bottlebrush and Sturt's desert rose.

homestead is perfectly situated to make the most of the view and it also shows how hard life was here back in the boom days of the late 1800s.

You can enjoy a short or long stroll along the Heysen Walking Trail or along the nearby creek. Another walking trail leads out to Red Hill Lookout, a 9 km, 3 to 4 hour, return trip, while other walks will take you out to the Trezona Range or along the Yuluna loop and through the ABC Range.

Brachina Gorge

Where the Brachina Creek meanders through the Heysen Range it forms one of the most delightful features in the area. Gums line the creek, which often has a slow trickle of water running along it. In places, fairly large pools,

protected by a rugged bluff or group of shady trees, provide a permanent water source for the area's wildlife.

There are no designated walks, but a stroll along the creek is very pleasant and informative, as it is part of the Brachina Gorge Geological Trail which takes you right through the range. For those who feel energetic, a climb of one of the nearby peaks will give a grand view of the gorge and the surrounding mountains. This really is a special place.

Wilkawillina Gorge

Located in the very north-east of the park is Wilkawillina Gorge, where the Mount Billy Creek has cut its way through the Bunkers Range.

There is a camping ground close to the vehicle track end and a walk of about a kilometre will take you into the gorge proper. This part of the Flinders is much drier than the Wilpena side.

Spectacular Brachina Gorge was formed by Brachina Creek cutting through the ABC and Heysen Ranges. The tall white gums of the area were immortalised by artist Hans Heysen (1877–1968).

Recommended Drive

One of the best drives in the park is to take the Yanyanna Hut–Bunyeroo Valley road in the early morning. It is especially colourful after rain when the wildflowers bloom. Once you are off the main Blinman road, red kangaroos are very common, and as you get closer to the main range and the hills begin to crowd in, euros and western grey kangaroos may be seen.

The views are superb, with the pine-clad hills rolling away to the sheer bluffs of the Heysen Range. If you want to make a day of it, head up to the Prairie Hotel in Parachilna for lunch and then in the evening head back taking the Moralana Scenic Drive to Wilpena. Although this 36 km drive is actually out of the park, it gives wonderful views of the western walls of Wilpena—in the dying light of day, they are just fabulous.

Access

You can travel on bitumen all the way from Adelaide to the resort at the entrance to Wilpena Pound via Wilmington and Quorn (400 km), while the slightly shorter way (370 km) through Orroroo and Jamestown has a 40 km section of good dirt road south of Hawker.

Elsewhere, good dirt roads suitable for conventional vehicles lead through the park to all the points of interest.

Only after occasional heavy rains or floods are any of the roads closed, and then generally only for a short time.

Camping

At Wilpena Pound there is a well-established motel and caravan park, including a general store, fuel outlet, ranger base and visitor information centre.

There is some very good camping in the Aroona Valley, as well as along the headwaters of Brachina Creek, at Dingley Dell on the Blinman road 30 km north of Wilpena Pound, along the main road through Bunyeroo Gorge and at Wilkawillina Gorge in the far north-east of the park. A favourite camping area is along Brachina Gorge where you'll find a number of pleasant spots to stop a while.

No matter where you camp a fee is payable, and no firewood is allowed to be collected in the park. Gas fires are preferred.

Above: *Climbing the Great Wall, a sheer sandstone cliff face 50 m high. The Great Wall is one of the highlights of Moonarie, South Australia's most significant climbing site, on the outer wall of Wilpena Pound.*

Galahs (Cacatua roseicapilla) *range over grasslands and savannah throughout much of Australia, including the Flinders. These seed-eating parrots will travel as much as 15 km in a day to search for food.*

tourist info

Visitor Centre Wilpena
(08) 8648 0048

Coffin Bay National Park

This park takes up the whole of the Coffin Bay Peninsula, with its 30 380 hectares of sand and limestone country covered mainly with mallee, tea-tree and she-oak woodlands, and low swampy areas covered in samphire. In places, sterile white drifting sand dunes engulf all living things. On one side of the great T-shaped peninsula are the placid protected waters of Coffin Bay, an ideal place to swim, sail a boat or to fish for whiting.

fact file

WHERE: 625 km west of Adelaide, via Port Lincoln
Map: SA 4 B2

WHEN: October to April

WHY: Spectacular coastal scenery, good fishing, safe swimming, surfing, 4WD

SIZE: 30 380 ha

RANGER: National Parks and Wildlife Service (08) 8688 3111

On the opposite side of Coffin Bay Peninsula, along its south-western coast, the surf generated from the great Southern Ocean pounds the coast continuously.

Of course, such an untamed area has other attractions as well. The beaches, headlands, rich shallow coastal waters and scrub-covered sand ridges provide a rich and bountiful habitat for birds. Ospreys are common, rock parrots nest in the scrub above the cliff-lined beaches, and shearwaters skim the nearby waters; occasionally, the rare and elusive western whipbird can be seen.

In the Past

The Nauo people once inhabited the area around Coffin Bay, and shell middens along the coast are a reminder of their early way of life.

Matthew Flinders was the first European to see this coast in 1802 and the area was colonised in the 1840s. Early graziers shipped their hard-earned bales of wool from Morgans Landing, on the north-western coast of Coffin Bay.

Coffin Bay offers superb fishing, both from the protected bayside beaches and on the wilder sea coast. Fishing boat charters are also available.

Activities

There are a number of walking trails in the park, most of which follow old vehicle tracks. It is also very enjoyable to walk along the beaches.

At Yangie Bay there is a very short walk of just 300 metres to the Yangie Lookout, or a longer 1.5 km Kallara Nature Trail walk. Other walks from here include the 5 km walk to Yangie Island or to Long Beach.

In the Whidbey Wilderness area there are a number of short walks, while overnight walks include the 26 km walk south along the Whidbey Trail.

The fishing is superb everywhere. The protected bay beaches are a mecca for King George whiting, garfish, trevally,

The township is only 50 km from Port Lincoln.

The entrance to the park is just through the township. Buying an annual Eyre Park Pass will help you save a few dollars if you are visiting a few parks on Eyre Peninsula.

Conventional vehicles can get as far as Yangie Bay. From this point a series of soft, sandy 4WD tracks head west to the furthermost points of the peninsula. The Whidbey Wilderness area has no vehicle access.

There is a fair range of camping and accommodation in the nearby Coffin Bay township. The local general store can supply food and fuel, while Beachcomber Agencies, phone (08) 8685 4057, has tourist information.

In the national park you are only allowed to camp at Yangie Bay, Black Springs, Morgans Landing, The Pool, and near Sensation Beach.

Left: *Sand dunes at Coffin Bay National Park. The coastal landscape of barren drifting dunes contrasts sharply with protected bays backed by black tea trees.*

did you know?

There are wild ponies in this park! Managed by the Coffin Bay Pony Preservation Society and National Parks and Wildlife, SA, the ponies are believed to be descended from animals brought to the area by the early settlers in the 1840s.

Many conservationists believe that allowing the ponies to live in the park sends the wrong message about feral animals in national parks.

flathead and salmon, while along the wilder coast you can try your luck for salmon, snapper, whiting and a wide variety of reef fish.

Of course, swimming, surfing, diving and sailing are popular pastimes.

Access and Camping

Access to Coffin Bay is easy and on good roads from the main Flinders Highway.

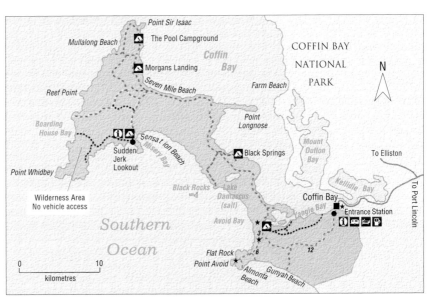

Flinders Chase National Park

The Flinders Chase National Park is renowned for its wildlife, as well as for the amazing view, through Admirals Arch, of a wild, turbulent Southern Ocean pounding a rocky inlet on the far western coast of Kangaroo Island. The park consists of 73 920 hectares of wild virgin scrub and bush country and takes up the whole of the western end of the island. Because of its undisturbed nature and its wide variety of habitats and fauna, it is one of South Australia's most important parks.

Amazing shapes of seemingly delicately balanced boulders sit on top of a remnant granite outcrop at the Remarkable Rocks area.

fact file

WHERE: On Kangaroo Island, 270 km south-west of Adelaide
Map: SA 4 E5

WHEN: November, December, March to May

WHY: Coastal scenery, wildlife, fishing

SIZE: 73 920 ha

RANGER: Rocky River
(08) 8559 7235 or
(08) 8559 7220

Wildlife

Kangaroos, koalas, ringtail possums and even platypus are commonly seen. Over a dozen species of mammals are native to the park including tammar wallabies, the southern brown bandicoot, the Australian sea lion and the Australian and New Zealand fur seals.

A number of reptiles also live in the park including Gould's sand goanna, a handsome monitor lizard that reaches 1.6 metres in length. Black tiger snakes and copperhead snakes can also be seen but these should be left alone.

There are nearly 200 species of birds found in the park with yellow-tailed black cockatoos and Cape Barren geese being the most common. The rare western whipbird and the glossy black cockatoo may also be sighted on occasion.

Activities

A number of pleasant, relatively easy walking trails can be found throughout the park including those at Cape du Couedic, Remarkable Rocks, Rocky River (where platypus waterholes may allow a viewing of this elusive monotreme) and Sandy Creek. The Ravine des Casoars trail to the wild and scenic west coast in the northern section of the park is a moderate-to-hard walk of 7 km. Well-equipped and experienced

The strikingly marked harlequin fish (Othos dentex). These are a reasonably common catch on the deeper reefs around Kangaroo Island.

walkers could attempt a much longer trek along the entire west coast.

Kangaroo Island is known for its great fishing. West Bay and Harveys Return are also popular and produce good catches of snapper, sweep, rock cod, whiting and salmon.

A number of wrecks have occurred along this coast including that of the *Loch Vennachar*, a 250-foot clipper which disappeared in 1905 and was finally discovered in 1976 a kilometre north of West Bay. A grave of an unknown sailor can be seen just up from the beach at West Bay.

Access

Access to Kangaroo Island is via the SeaLink ferry from Cape Jervis, 105 km south of Adelaide. The ferry takes you to the small island town of Penneshaw. Flinders Chase National Park is down the other end of the island from Penneshaw, 150 km away, either on bitumen or excellent dirt roads.

The park headquarters is located at Rocky River on the South Coast Road. Within the park most roads are good dirt, and the many points of interest are accessible in a conventional vehicle.

Camping and Accommodation

At Rocky River there is a good camping area with showers, toilets and limited supplies. West Bay, Snake Lagoon and Harveys Return all have small camping areas. Only gas fires are allowed in the Island parks. Accommodation is available at the old Rocky River homestead, in the lighthouse keeper's quarters at Cape Borda and Cape du Couedic, or at Flinders Chase Farmstay and Hostel, phone (08) 8559 7223.

Below: *The land bridge of Admiral's Arch at Cape du Couedic is one of the scenic highlights of Kangaroo Island. Many of the filaments hanging from the roof of the arch are actually fossilised tree roots.*

Entry fees and camping fees apply. If you are staying and touring the island an 'Island Pass' will work out more convenient and economical.

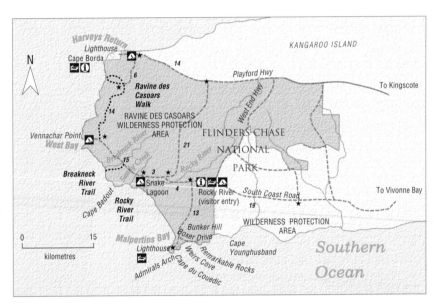

SA

Witjira National Park, Simpson Desert Regional Reserve & Park

Many people believe that there is no finer desert oasis in Australia than the warm waters of Dalhousie Springs located in the far north of South Australia, in the very west of Witjira National Park. Located on the western edge of the Simpson Desert, the group of 70 or so springs that make up the Dalhousie group of mound springs comprises the most significant natural outflowings of the vast artesian basin that underlies much of outback Australia.

In the Past

Several groups of Australian Aboriginals included different areas of the Simpson Desert in their tribal lands. Dalhousie Springs and the permanent water points on the western edge of the desert were of spiritual significance as well as an important water source to the Lower Southern Aranda people and the Wangkangurru people.

Charles Sturt was the first European to see the desert in 1845, but the Dalhousie Springs were not discovered until the early 1870s.

Interest in the desert was revived in the 1950s when oil exploration began and this continued through to the 1970s. All the tracks across the desert from Dalhousie east are the result of that exploration work.

In 1967 the Simpson Desert Conservation Park of 6927 sq km was proclaimed. In 1988 the Simpson Desert Regional Reserve of 29 642 sq km was declared linking all the parks, while the Witjira National Park of 7770 sq km, was also established at that time.

Places to Experience

It is the desert ambience, the peace and the solitude, that makes the great memories of a trip to the Simpson Desert parks. The springs around Dalhousie, once you can tear yourself away from the warm water, are worth exploring and the variety of birds is remarkable. Likewise, Purni Bore, deeper into the desert, is a gem and the wetlands created by this bore attract much wildlife.

The ruins of the old Dalhousie homestead should also be visited.

Access

No matter what direction you come from, only dirt roads lead to these parks. The area is really the realm of a 4WD, but in good conditions the main track from Oodnadatta is passable to a conventional vehicle, driven with care.

From Dalhousie the route across the desert strikes the first of the sand ridges

just over 50 km east. The French Line is the roughest but shortest track east (430 km to Birdsville), the WAA Line a good alternative, while the Rig Road is the longest. However, all are definitely 4WD routes and you need to be well prepared and equipped for a crossing of the desert to Birdsville.

All of these routes may be closed after rain. Check with the rangers before setting off.

Camping

In the very north of the park, 70 km from Dalhousie Springs, the old homestead of Mount Dare offers accommodation, camping, meals, fuel, tyres and minor repairs, as well as a breakdown service and a cold beer.

The only other designated camping grounds are at Dalhousie Springs and Purni Bore where you can find toilets and water. Elsewhere you can camp close to the track on any one of the designated routes across the desert.

Desert Parks Pass

To enter or travel this reserved land in the state's north, you need a Desert Parks Pass. For an economical fee, the pass includes a good range of maps and booklets and is valid for a year.

Left: *Sand dunes in the Simpson Desert. Witjira National Park, one of the gateways to the Simpson Desert, is jointly managed by the Irrwanyere Aboriginal Corporation and National Parks and Wildlife, South Australia.*

The shingleback or stumpy-tailed lizard (Trachydosaurus rugosus) is found throughout arid parts of Australia. Unlike many reptiles, these lizards give birth to very large, live young which weigh about 35 per cent of the mother's weight.

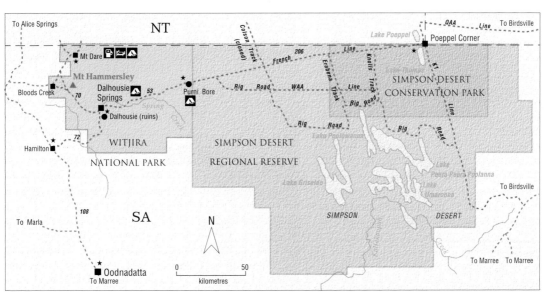

Canunda National Park

The south-eastern coast of South Australia has one of the wildest, most untouched coastlines on the continent. Canunda National Park takes up 9358 hectares of coast that is dominated by large sand dunes and, in the north of the park, rugged limestone cliffs.

Southern right whale (Eubalaena australis) *and calf. These whales and the minke whale pass along this coast on their annual migrations.*

Walking, Fishing and Wildlife

There are a number of walking trails, giving travellers an opportunity to experience this park first-hand. Some trails lead along the edge of the cliffs while others take you to good vantage points or historic places of interest.

For the keen angler this part of South Australia's coast can provide good catches of salmon, mulloway, flathead and the occasional shark.

Nature watchers may sight some of the world's rarest birds, including the orange-bellied parrot and the hooded plover, as well as having the chance to see penguins and seals which are regular visitors along this coast.

Access and Camping

Access by conventional vehicles is limited to Cape Buffon and Boozy Gully in the north of the park, and to Oil Rig Square in the central section of the park.

For those with a 4WD, the complete park is accessible by following the orange marker posts that lead through the park from Southend to Carpenter Rocks. Excellent sand driving techniques are required and

you must stick to the marked track. This route can be challenging.

You can camp near Southend, Oil Rig Square and Number Two Rocks. A permit from the ranger is required to camp in the park. There are caravan parks in Millicent and Carpenter Rocks.

Right: Huge sand dunes dominate the southern part of Canunda National Park. Much of the park is accessible only by 4WD.

Coorong National Park

The Coorong is a series of shallow lagoons that provide a rich habitat for hundreds of thousands of waterbirds. It is protected from the rolling surf of the Southern Ocean by a narrow strip of sand dunes known as the Younghusband Peninsula.

A surf angler on the Younghusband Peninsula. Ninety Mile Beach on the ocean side of the peninsula is quite remote and relatively lightly fished.

Fishing and Birdwatching

There is excellent surf fishing for mulloway, whiting, flathead, salmon and shark. In the lagoon, mullet, bream and flounder abound.

The whole area is one of Australia's most important wetlands and it is a birdwatcher's paradise, with over 200 species of birds being recorded. The lakes regularly support over 120 000 waders, a large number of black swans, and an abundant population of Cape Barren geese, as well as being the largest pelican breeding area in Australia.

Access, Camping and Accommodation

The mainland side of the park is accessible to conventional vehicles while the ocean beaches are strictly 4WD territory. All vehicles must stay on the marked routes. Access tracks across the dunes to the beach are well marked.

The route north along the beach from Tea Tree Crossing is closed from late October to late December each year to protect the endangered hooded plover during its breeding season.

There are plenty of places to camp that can be accessed by car, 4WD or boat. These include Mark Point, Long Point, and Tea Tree Crossing. A camping permit is needed.

Noonameena House, in the heart of the park, offers accommodation for up to eight people.

SA

Murray River National Park

The Murray River National Park is made up of three distinct sections of floodplain spread along the Murray River from above Renmark to just north of Loxton in the heart of the Riverland of eastern South Australia. The park protects not only the natural wonders and rich wildlife, but also preserves ancient Australian Aboriginal middens, canoe trees, ceremonial rings of stone, and burial sites found throughout the park.

Fishing on the Murray River. Golden perch and Murray cod remain popular target species, but catfish and silver perch are now quite rare.

fact file

WHERE: 180 to 240 km east of Adelaide, via the Sturt Highway
Map: SA 4 N2

WHEN: September to April

WHY: Camping, magnificent river scenery, fishing, birdwatching

SIZE: 13 250 ha

RANGER: Berri
(08) 8585 2111

Activities

Fishing, camping, birdwatching, canoeing and cruising on a houseboat are popular pastimes, while bushwalks can be enjoyed throughout the park.

Canoeing here is very pleasant and trips of up to 4 days can be done in the Bulyong Island area, incorporating Ral Ral Creek and the Murray, while 1 or 2 day trips can be planned in the Katarapko section of the park. Both the Bulyong Island and the Katarapko sections are very popular with canoeists.

There are boat launching facilities in a number of places, except in the Lyrup Flats section.

Access and Camping

Access to the Katarapko section is off the Sturt Highway, west of the township of Berri. Dirt roads lead to numerous camping sites along Katarapko Creek and the Murray River.

Lyrup Flats is located upstream from Berri with the Sturt Highway giving good access to an all-weather dirt road that leads to a number of large camping areas and to tracks that head to smaller individual camps along the river.

Bulyong Island, not far upstream from Renmark, is a popular spot and while it doesn't have any designated camping areas, it is possible to camp at many points along the river.

Camping permits, available from the ranger, are required for camping anywhere in the park.

The Murray River National Park offers pleasant places for houseboats to pull up and enjoy a bit of fishing. All three sections of the national park are popular for houseboat cruising.

More National Parks of Importance

Belair National Park

SIZE: 840 ha
MAP: SA 4 J3

In 1891, Belair National Park, just 13 km south of Adelaide, became the first national park in South Australia. The park protects one of the few remaining areas of native bushland in the Adelaide Hills and includes a range of facilities which visitors can enjoy. The Old Government House situated within the park is now a museum.

A number of sealed roads head off through the park giving good access to much of it and the park's facilities. Barbecue facilities abound and walks radiate to all corners of the park.

Playford Lake, close to the developed area, supports good numbers of waterbirds and a 1 km walk around the lake is a pleasant way to view the birdlife.

The park is open to day visitors only and an entrance fee is charged. For further information, phone the ranger on (08) 8278 5477.

Gammon Ranges National Park

SIZE: 128 228 ha
MAP: SA 3 K2

The Gammon Ranges, a maze of twisted landforms, steep-sided gorges and rugged, weather-worn bluffs, make up the most northern extension of the Flinders Ranges.

A couple of 4WD tracks cut through the park but the heart of the area, around the Plateau and Mainwater Pound, is really the realm of the adventurous and experienced bushwalker. For the not so adventurous there are a couple of shorter walks available.

Access is via reasonable dirt roads for the last 115 km from Copley, which is 570 km from Adelaide.

There are a number of designated bush camps such as Italowie Gorge, Weetootla Gorge and Grindells Hut (the homestead near the hut can be rented).

For details contact the ranger at Balcanoona on (08) 8648 4829 or at Hawker on (08) 8648 4244.

Contrary to its name, the Port Lincoln parrot (Barnardius zonarius) has a wider distribution and is seen across much of southern Western Australia, into South Australia, and can be seen in Belair National Park.

The white cypress pine (Callitris glaucophylla) grows clinging to a cliff face in the inhospitable terrain of the Gammon Ranges National Park. Under better conditions these trees can grow to 30 metres high.

SA

Cooper Creek, Inna-mincka Regional Reserve. In drought years, the creek dries up and only some waterholes, such as Cullyamurra Waterhole which is the largest in Central Australia, remain.

Innamincka Regional Reserve

SIZE: 13 800 sq km
MAP: SA 2 N4

The Cooper Creek and the Coongie Lakes complex of northern South Australia make up one of the great wetland areas of outback Australia. Surrounded by harsh gibber plain and the sand ridges of the Strzelecki Desert, Cooper Creek brings life to this arid region. In good years water fills the Congie Lakes creating an oasis that teems with life.

All the roads leading to Innamincka are dirt for some distance. They can be closed after heavy rain.

All tracks in the reserve require a South Australian Desert Parks Pass (this can be purchased for an economical fee), which is also necessary for camping. Along Cooper Creek or out at Coongie Lakes you will find some of the best camping spots in Central Australia.

Accommodation is available at the Innamincka pub, phone (08) 8675 9901, or at the Innamincka Trading Post, phone (08) 8675 9900, where all fuels and supplies are also available.

For more information contact the Desert Parks Hotline on 1800 816 078.

Innes National Park

SIZE: 9141 ha
MAP: SA 4 F4

The outstanding coastal scenery, the top surfing, the magical diving and the great fishing bring people back time and again to the southern toe of Yorke Peninsula and Innes National Park.

This wild coast is protected in most places by sheer high cliffs and probably the best spot to experience such a dramatic scene is at the Gap, near Reef Heads. Further north is the protected waters of delightful Pondalowie Bay.

There are a number of small camping spots dotted around the coast, including Gym Beach and Shell Beach, but the most popular is Pondalowie Bay itself.

Entrance and camping fees are payable. Accommodation is also available—contact the ranger on (08) 8854 3200, for details.

The Stenhouse Bay Trading Post, phone (08) 8854 4066, offers basic supplies and fuel.

Lake Eyre National Park

SIZE: 1 225 000 ha
MAP: SA 2 F6

At over 8000 sq km, Lake Eyre is the largest salt lake in Australia, the largest saltpan in the world, and also the lowest point in Australia. In the last 100 years the lake has only had a significant amount of water in it six times, the most spectacular being in 1974, when it filled to capacity with about 34 cubic km of water.

Lake Eyre South, just off the Oodnadatta Track, 90 km west of Marree, is the easiest access. A 4WD track via Muloorina homestead and another south of William Creek lead to the lake's shore.

A South Australian Desert Parks Pass (available for an economical fee) is required for access and camping. For more information contact the National Parks and Wildlife Service at Hawker on (08) 8648 4244 or the Desert Parks Hotline on 1 800 816 078.

Lincoln National Park

SIZE: 29 000 ha
MAP: SA 4 D3

Great camping, good fishing, diving, surfing and four wheel driving plus a variety of coastal scenery and plentiful wildlife make this region an ideal summer destination although dangerous freak waves can occur in rough weather.

A 4WD track from Sleaford Mere heads west behind the dunes to Wanna and leads to many popular surf fishing spots. Another 4WD track leads east to West Point and Memory Cove. A permit and key are required to drive this route.

A sealed road leads south from Port Lincoln. Entry and camping permits are available at the park entrance. A good dirt road heads into the park.

Camping is allowed at a number of spots in the park. At Taylors Landing you can also launch small boats. Donington Cottage is available to rent, while an Eyre Park Pass will save you money. Contact National Parks and Wildlife Service in Port Lincoln on (08) 8688 3111.

The Australian sea lion (Neophoca cinerea) is one the most endangered of the world's seals and sea lions. They can be seen off the coast of Lincoln National Park.

don't miss

In the north of Lincoln National Park take the 1.1 km walk uphill to the Flinders Monument which commemorates Matthew Flinders' visit in 1802. There are stunning views of Port Lincoln and the nearby islands.

SA

Gym Beach in the north of Innes National Park. There are some great walks in the park, including the 3-hour walk from Browns Beach to Gym Beach.

Giant gum tree in Mount Remarkable National Park. The area has a relatively high rainfall of up to 600 mm per year, allowing large areas of quite dense woodland to develop.

Mount Remarkable National Park

SIZE: 15 632 ha
MAP: SA 3 H7

This park in the southern Flinders Ranges takes in the area around Alligator Gorge, Mambray Creek and the high peak of Mount Remarkable. The area is rich in wildflowers and birds, as well as red kangaroos, euros and the delightful, but rarer, yellow-footed rock wallaby.

There are plenty of great walks in the park such as the walk through Alligator Gorge and from Alligator Gorge to Mambray Creek. Longer walks are also possible.

Access to Alligator Gorge is via a good dirt road from Wilmington, while Mount Remarkable itself is accessible from Melrose.

The Mambray Creek camping area is reached off Highway 1. You'll need to book in advance and obtain a camping permit. There are a number of back-packing camp sites, some with water.

Campfires are banned in the park from 1 November to 30 April.

For more information contact the ranger at Mambray Creek, on (08) 8634 7068.

Naracoorte Caves National Park

SIZE: 70 ha
MAP: SA 4 N8

This small park, 370 km south-east of Adelaide, is on the World Heritage List because of the discovery of rich fossil beds in Victoria Cave, which include the remains of marsupials and other extinct animals. Provision has been made for visitors to view the 'dig'.

A number of other caves are open to tourists, including Blanche Cave, Wet Cave and Alexandra Cave. There are tours conducted daily.

Between November and February, thousands of common bentwing bats make a spectacular sight at dusk as they leave the caves in search of food.

The camping ground in the park is well set up and a permit is required before you can camp.

For further information, contact the ranger at Naracoorte, on (08) 8762 2340, or Mount Gambier, on (08) 8735 1177.

The little red flying fox (Pteropus scapulatus) is common in much of southern Australia, and can be seen with bentwing bats near Naracoorte.

Popular Parks at a Glance

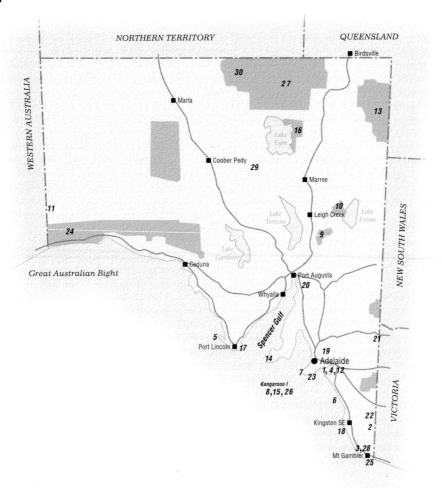

	Campi	Carava	Disable	4WD	Picnic	Toilets	Walkin	Kiosk	Inform
1 Belair NP	●	●	●		●	●	●	●	●
2 Bool Lagoon NP	●	●			●	●	●		
3 Canunda NP	●			●	●	●	●		
4 Cleland WP & CP			●		●	●	●	●	●
5 Coffin Bay NP	●	●		●	●	●	●		●
6 Coorong NP	●	●		●	●	●	●		
7 Deep Creek CP	●			●	●	●	●		●
8 Flinders Chase NP	●	●	●		●	●	●		
9 Flinders Ranges NP	●	●			●	●	●	●	●
10 Gammon Ranges NP	●			●		●	●		
11 Gawler Ranges NP			●		●		●		
12 Granite Island RP					●	●	●	●	●
13 Innamincka RR	●			●		●	●		●
14 Innes NP	●	●			●	●	●	●	●
15 Kelly Hill CP			●		●	●	●	●	●

	Campi	Carava	Disable	4WD	Picnic	Toilets	Walkin	Kiosk	Inform
16 Lake Eyre NP	●			●					
17 Lincoln NP	●	●		●	●	●	●		
18 Little Dip NP	●	●		●	●	●	●		
19 Morialta CP					●		●	●	●
20 Mount Remarkable NP	●	●			●	●	●		●
21 Murray River NP	●	●		●	●	●	●		
22 Naracoorte Caves NP	●	●			●	●	●		●
23 Newland Head CR	●					●	●		
24 Nullarbor NP	●	●		●					
25 Piccaninnie Ponds CP	●						●	●	
26 Seal Bay CP	●		●				●	●	●
27 Simpson Desert CP & RR	●			●					
28 Tantanoola Caves CP			●		●	●	●	●	●
29 Wabma Kadarbu Mound Springs CP	●			●			●		
30 Witjira NP	●			●		●	●	●	

Map 1

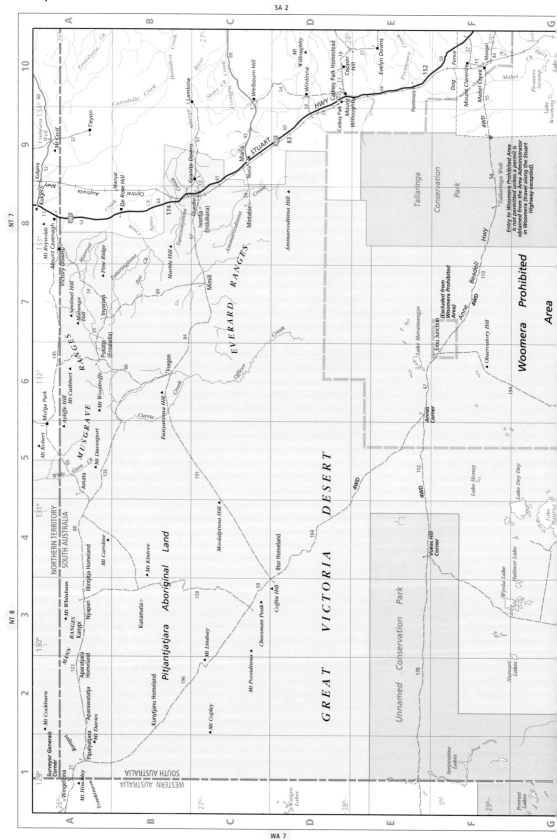

Entry to Woomera Prohibited Area is not permitted unless a permit is obtained from the Area Administrator in Woomera (travel along the Stuart Highway excepted).

©Global Book Publishing Pty Ltd & Universal Press Pty Ltd

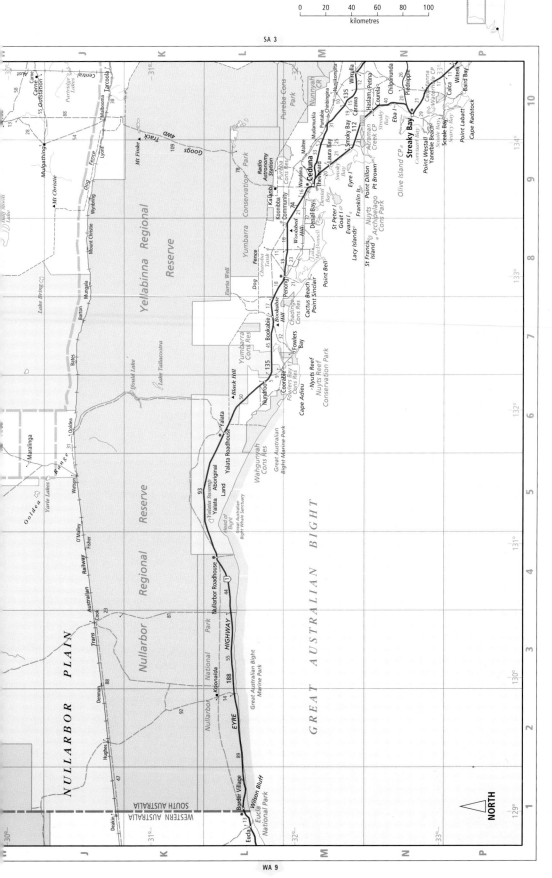

0 20 40 60 80 100
kilometres

NORTH

NULLARBOR PLAIN

NULLARBOR

Nullarbor Regional Reserve

Yellabinna Regional Reserve

Yumbarra Conservation Park

GREAT AUSTRALIAN BIGHT

Great Australian Bight Marine Park

Nullarbor National Park

Great Australian Bight Marine Park

WESTERN AUSTRALIA
SOUTH AUSTRALIA

EYRE HIGHWAY

Eucla
Eucla National Park
Wilson Bluff

Border Village

Nullarbor Roadhouse

Koonalda

Yalata Roadhouse
Yalata
Yalata Aboriginal Land
Yalata Swamp
Wahgunyah Cons Res
Head of Bight
Great Australian Bight Whale Sanctuary

Black Hill
Nundroo
Coorabie
Fowlers Bay Cons Res
Fowlers Bay
Cape Adieu
Nuyts Reef
Nuyts Reef Conservation Park

Bookabie
Bookabie Hill
Chadinga Cons Res
Cactus Beach
Point Sinclair
Penong
Dog Fence
Charcubi Tank
Barton
Bates
Mungala
Barrie Well

Wookshed Hill
Denial Bay
Goat I
Evans I
St Peter I
Point Bell
Lacy Islands
St Francis Island
Nuyts Archipelago Cons Park
Point Dillon
Pt Brown
Franklin Is

Wandana
Maltee
Mudamuckla
Thevenard
Ceduna
Kalanbi
Koonibba Community
Radio Astronomy Station
Pureba Cons Park

Laura Bay
Smoky Bay
Eyre I
Denial Bay
Acraman Creek CP

Olive Island CP
Point Westall
Yanerbie Beach
Smooth Pool
Sceale Bay
Searcy Bay
Streaky Bay
Corrisant Bay
Eba I

Nunjikompita
Chinbingina
Puntabie
Haslam
Petina
Courela
Cungena
Waddikee CP
Calca
Witera
Point Labatt
Cape Radstock
Baird Bay
Piednippie
Chilpinunda

Wirrulla
Carawa
Nunyah CR

Mt Christie
Mulgathing
Mt Finke
Googs Track
4WD Track
Dog Fence
Lyons
Malbooma
Wynbring
Mount Christie
O'Malley
Fisher
Watson
Ooldea
Yarle Lakes
Maralinga
Ooldea Range
Lake Tallacootra
Ifould Lake
Denman
Hughes
Deakin
Cook
Trans Australian Railway

Carne
Tarcoola
Partridge Lakes
Central
Lake Bring
Emu Moon Lakes

WA 9

SA

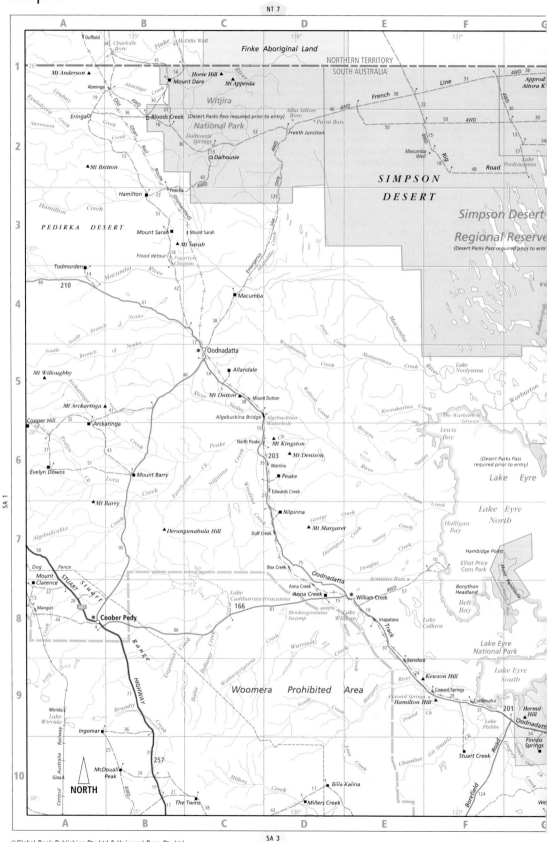

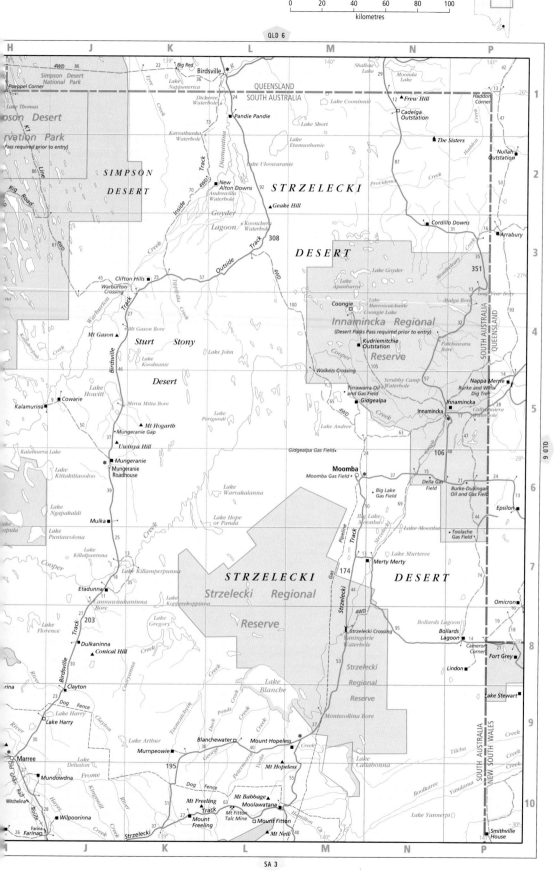

kilometres

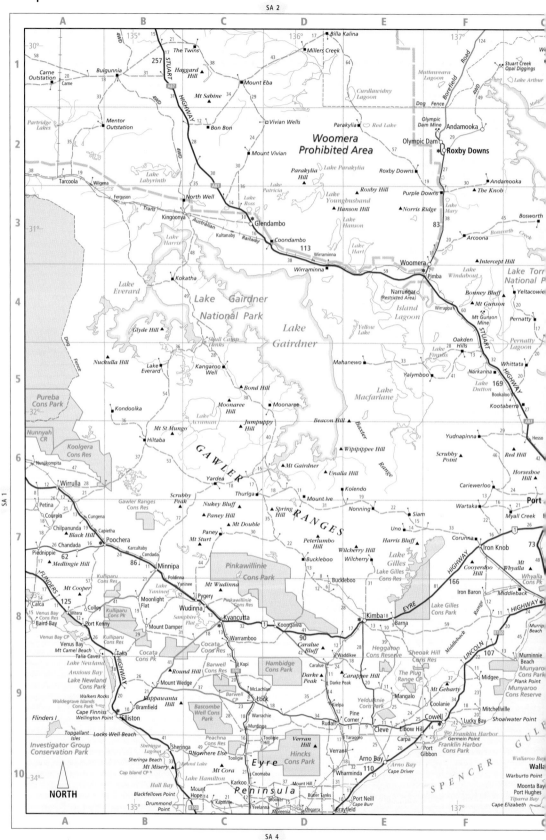

SA 2

SA 1

NORTH

SA 4

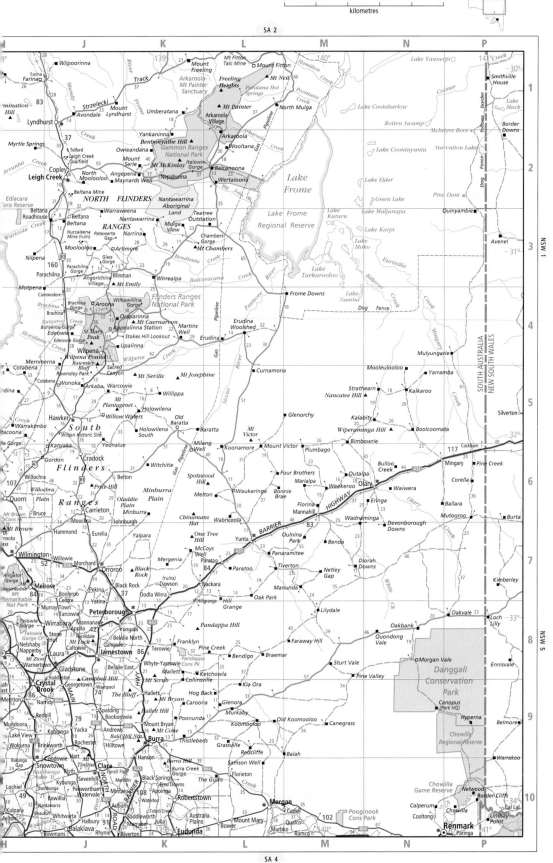

SA

Map 4

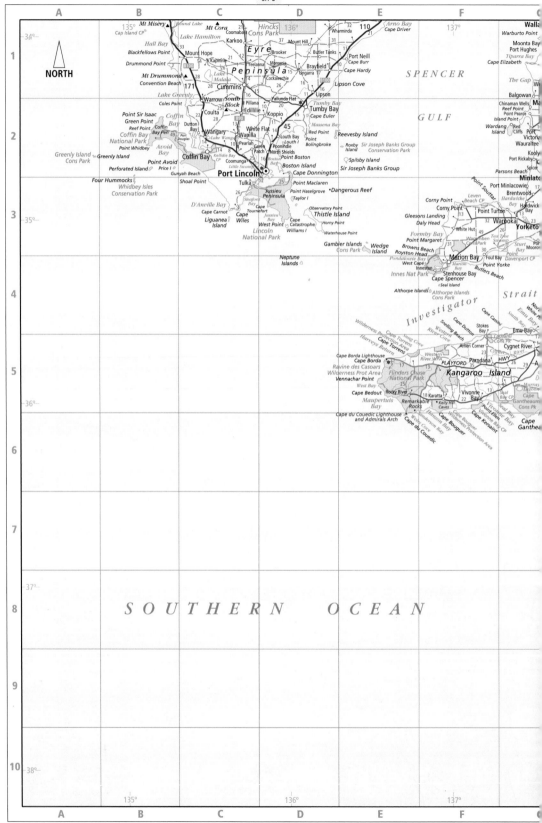

SA 3

NORTH

SPENCER

GULF

Eyre Peninsula

Port Lincoln

Investigator

Strait

Kangaroo Island

SOUTHERN   OCEAN

Western Australia

One of the first things visitors to Western Australia notice is space—and with a total area of over 2.5 million sq km taking up about one third of the Australian continent, it's really not surprising. The scenery in the west is full of amazing variety and contrasts, with many of its landscapes like no other place in the country. The state's national parks and reserves, which are all managed by the Conservation and Land Management (CALM) department, are found throughout the whole length and breadth of the state. From the temperate south-west regions and for over 3000 km to the tropical north—even out into the desert heartland of the state—the parks cover a wide range of climates, terrain, wildlife and, importantly for visitors, a vast choice of things to see, do and experience.

Leeuwin–Naturaliste National Park

Here at Cape Leeuwin, which is located on the south-westernmost tip of Western Australia, the balmy waters of the Indian Ocean meet the cooler waters of the wild Southern Ocean. Stretching north from this low cape and its historic lighthouse is a series of rocky headlands, cliff-lined beaches and sweeping bays dotted with reefs and islands, topped at the northern end by Cape Naturaliste and another historic lighthouse.

On land a disjointed, convoluted but near continuous strip of land is reserved as national park between these two great capes, with the park taking its name from these two rugged bluffs.

In the Past

Australian Aboriginal occupation of the area dates back to around 40 000 years ago, while the earliest European account of the area was recorded in the log of the Dutch East India Company ship, the *Leeuwin*, in 1622.

Many explorers followed, including England's Matthew Flinders, who named Cape Leeuwin in 1801, and the French navigator, Nicolas Baudin, from whom Hamelin Bay, Cape Naturaliste and Geographe Bay got their names.

Over the past 150 years, the region has been known at different times for its sealing and whaling, grazing and pastoral leases, fishing and timber industry and, more recently, for its world-class vineyards.

Today the park is a popular holiday destination for West Australians, who are attracted by the sheltered bays and beaches, good fishing, dramatic windswept coastal scenery, limestone caves, jarrah and karri forests, excellent surfing and wineries.

Right: The collared sparrowhawk (Accipiter cirrhocephalus) hunts from the cover of open forests and woodlands; the male will return to the nest with food for the female and chicks.

Cape Naturaliste

Sealed roads lead to the lighthouse built in 1903 and to Bunker Bay, a picturesque spot which is good for a picnic, swim, or for snorkelling and fishing. The West Coast road takes you to Naturaliste Lookout and to Gull Rock, while another sealed road, 3 km south of the lighthouse, takes you to Sugarloaf Rock.

A number of good walking trails, ranging from easy to moderate and taking from 30 minutes to 2 hours to complete, connect these access points.

The Cape to Cape Track starts at the Naturaliste lighthouse and ends 120 km south at the Leeuwin lighthouse; it takes about five to seven days. Cape Naturaliste Lighthouse tours are available Thursday to Tuesday, 9.30 a.m. to 4.00 p.m.

Yallingup and Smiths Beach

These holiday destinations are just a few kilometres apart and both are popular with surfers keen to tackle the huge rolling swells. Fishing from the rocks and along the beach at Smiths Beach is also a favourite sport. There is a choice of caravan parks and other accommodation at both places.

Canal Rocks to Prevelly Park

At Canal Rocks, a series of rocks extends into the ocean making a natural canal. This is a good fishing spot, but dangerous for swimming. Both the walkway and bridge give good views of the canal and the power of the surging ocean. There is also a protected boat ramp here.

Gracetown is situated on the lovely and scenic Cowaramup Bay, which has a good lookout on the right before you reach the town. Fishing is a popular pastime and when the swells are right, there's some surfing. There are picnic facilities, toilets and a caravan park at the Caves Road turn-off.

Located at the mouth of the Margaret River and just outside the national park, Prevelly Park is famous for its magnificent surfing with the annual 'Margaret River Classic' attracting top surfers from around the world. Canoeing on the pristine waters of the Margaret River, with its myriad birdlife, is also popular.

Left: Towering jarrah trees (Eucalyptus marginata) form almost pure forests, with few other tree species. The column-like trunks are widely spaced, allowing light to reach smaller shrubs.

Quininup Falls flows freely after winter rains but dries up between mid-spring and late autumn. It can be reached by 4WD track from Quininup Road or on foot from the Moses Road car park.

WA

Right: *The tranquil Lefroy Brook flows through a lush tangle of regrowth karri. Ferns and mosses grow among the thick leaf litter and birds are prolific in the dense understorey.*

It is worth visiting the old Ellensbrook Homestead, situated near the mouth of the Margaret River. Alfred Bussell built Ellensbrook in 1857 for himself and his young wife, Ellen. The building has now been restored by the National Trust and is open to the public.

Hamelin Bay and Cosy Corner
Set in a protected bay behind Hamelin Island, this pretty bay is especially popular with families, anglers and divers. A boat ramp is available for launching small craft, while the long beach is ideal for walking and swimming. There is a caravan park beside the beach.

Cosy Corner, which is situated just a few kilometres south, is a reef- and island-studded bay that stretches south to Cape Hamelin. It's a magical dive spot and offers great fishing.

don't miss

A walking track from the Ellensbrook Homestead leads to the appealing Meekadarabee Falls. The name comes from the language of the local Aboriginal people, and means 'the bathing place of the moon'.

Cape Leeuwin
The impressive Leeuwin Lighthouse dominates the Cape and offers startling views of the surrounding coast. Tours of the lighthouse are conducted by the Augusta–Margaret River Tourist Bureau and the lighthouse is generally open between 9.00 a.m. and 4.00 p.m. each day.

Whale Watching
The annual whale migration to and from Antarctica can be seen close up along the Leeuwin–Naturaliste coastline. Humpback and southern right whales swim past on their way to northern breeding grounds during early winter and return south in late spring.

The best vantage points to see the whales are Cape Leeuwin, Cape Naturaliste, Gracetown Lookout at Cowaramup Bay, and Sugarloaf Rock. It is estimated that 3000 to 4000 humpbacks make their way along this coast each year.

Once the haunt of busy whalers, the coastline is now popular with avid whalewatchers. There are regular sightings from July to November.

Fishing, Diving and Sailing
The fishing along this stretch of coastline is excellent all year round, with good catches of skippy, dhufish, snapper, whiting and flathead on offer to keen anglers. During late summer and early autumn Australian salmon make their migratory run up the coast to around Perth and back again, and the fishing can be electric!

Abalone and crayfish are also found in the area. Don't forget that you need a Recreational Fishing Licence to take abalone, rock lobster, marron, and for net fishing or freshwater angling. Contact the Fisheries Department, Perth on (08) 9482 7333 or check out the web at www.wa.gov.au/westfish/index.html.

There is a multitude of great diving spots in the many protected bays around the islands and reefs. Fourteen ships are known to have sunk during storms and

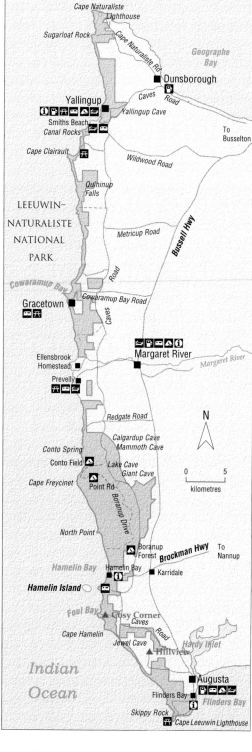

Below: *With the warm Leeuwin Current running offshore, fishing from the beach, off rocks, and from small boats is excellent all year.*

after hitting reefs around Hamelin Bay. A great dive trail has been established which takes in four of those wrecks that are still visible.

The excellent wind conditions along this part of the coastline make both sailing and windsurfing popular summertime attractions here too.

Boranup Forest

Boranup Forest is the largest known karri forest growing in limestone sands and covers 3200 hectares. By 1913, most timber from the area had been cleared and the last mill closed. Remnants of the old mills destroyed by fire some years ago can still be seen at Karridale.

The karri (Eucalyptus diversicolor) *has adapted to regular fires. Seeds ripen in the heat and fall into the ash beds, to germinate in winter rains.*

The karri forest has since regenerated, with most trees (some up to 60 metres in height) now less than 100 years old.

Grass-trees (balgas) also grow quite prolifically in this region.

There is a pleasant, tall-timber drive through the forest, and the Boranup camping area, set in the bush, is quite basic with barbecues, tables and toilet facilities, but no water.

Caves

Beneath the sweeping landscape of the park an extraordinary 360 caves have been discovered. Fossils of long-extinct marsupial lions, Tasmanian tigers, a shark, koalas, and even the remains of a gigantic wombat-like creature that was the size of a modern-day horse (dated around 37 000 years ago) have been found here. This cave system is among the oldest and most valuable archaeological sites in Australia.

While most caves are accessible only to experienced speleologists, four of the most spectacular—featuring some shawl and helictite formations—are open to the public with regular guided tours. These are Yallingup Cave, to the north of the park, Mammoth and Lake Caves in Boranup Forest, and Jewel Cave in the south near Augusta.

In addition, there are two adventure caves in Boranup Forest: Giants and Calgardup Caves. Take a torch and wear strong footwear and old protective clothing—the caves are a lot of fun, but care must be taken.

Experienced cavers should contact the ranger for access to other caves in the area.

The Western Australian Christmas tree (Nuytsia floribunda), *named for its December blooms, is actually a member of the parasitic mistletoe family.*

Wildlife and Wildflowers

Native animals that inhabit the national park include western grey kangaroos, brush-tail possums, honey possums and fat-tail dunnarts. There is also a wide range of seabirds, as well as wedge-tailed eagles, kites and the red-tailed tropic bird. In all, around 200 species of birds have been recorded.

The colourful wildflowers are particularly plentiful around headlands and in low heath areas in spring and early summer. Acacias, tiny orchids, coastal daisy bushes, wattles, banksias, cocky's tongue and one-sided bottlebrushes are all found throughout the park.

Other Attractions

While travelling between various sections of the park, you will encounter other notable features: numerous wineries, cheese factories, craft shops, galleries and studios making anything from gumnut ornaments to jewellery, pottery and furniture.

Most wineries open their cellar doors for both tasting and bottle sales. The art galleries, craft studios and factories often have demonstrations of their craft and samples for sale.

Access and Camping

Roads to all of the main areas in the park are either sealed or good gravel. In addition, there are several 4WD tracks to remote coastal areas, where the fishing, diving and surfing can be excellent.

You can contact the Boranup camping area and Conto camping area (located off Caves Road, south of Prevelly Park), by

Right: *Cattle egrets* (Ardea ibis) *forage for insects in wet pastures. In the breeding season their white plumage is tinged with orange.*

Left: *The slow-moving, mostly herbivorous shingleback, or stumpy-tailed, lizard* (Trachydosaurus rugosus) *favours grassland and scrubland.*

Below right: *The array of flowering shrubs on the coastal plain includes the beautiful chenille honey myrtle* (Melaleuca huegelii) *shown here.*

phoning CALM at Margaret River, (08) 9757 2322.

There are caravan parks at Yallingup (08) 9755 2164, Augusta (08) 9758 1593, and Hamelin Bay (08) 9758 5540. For Canal Rocks Beach Resort phone (08) 9755 2116.

There are also a number of caravan parks in the surrounding area, including Dunsborough and Margaret River township—all of these make good bases from which to explore nearby sections of the park.

Fuel, water and general supplies are available at Dunsborough, Margaret River township and Augusta.

Cape Range National Park and Ningaloo Marine Park

The Cape Range is the backbone of Cape Range National Park, and its many spectacular gorges are the park's greatest attraction. There are also long stretches of sandy beaches linking the park to Ningaloo Marine Park, which protects the beautiful coral of Ningaloo Reef.

Sheer walls of limestone edge the blue waters of Yardie Creek; black-footed rock wallabies are sometimes spied on the ledges of the southern cliffs.

Cape Range National Park

Established in 1969, Cape Range National Park takes up much of the west coast and the spine of land known as North West Cape. The most famous gorge here is Yardie Creek Gorge, at the southern end of the park. This rugged country is home to the rare, black-footed rock wallaby.

Exploring the Park

There are some excellent walks in the park, along long stretches of beaches and across rugged range country.

Over on the eastern side of the range from the Thomas Carter Lookout there are a couple of walks up to 8 km in length, while at the Shothole Canyon car park a steep walk will take you to the top of the canyon rim.

On the western side of Cape Range there's the Mandu Mandu Creek walk, while at Yardie Creek, you have a choice of a walk along the creek, another along the northern side of the gorge, or the bird hide and the fauna hide walk.

If you have a canoe you can enjoy a pleasant paddle on Yardie Creek. It's a great way to experience the gorge and see the wildlife. Yardie Creek Tours have boat tours on the creek and operate most days of the tourist season.

Ningaloo Reef and Marine Park

The Ningaloo Marine Park adjoining Cape Range National Park takes in the water from the eastern tip of North West Cape south to Amherst Point. Ningaloo Reef, just offshore, is a truly magnificent coral reef—the fishing is great and the diving superb. The waters provide a home for a great variety of fish, as well as dugongs, turtles, manta rays and whale sharks.

The marine park protecting this coral reef has been divided up into a number of zones and you need to be aware of

the regulations, bag limits and what you are allowed to do and not do in each area of the park. Even with such intensive management though, the choices are endless and you won't be disappointed.

Access and Camping

The national park is easily accessible via a bitumen road off the Great Northern Highway. This leads to the small town of Exmouth, or to the holiday hamlet of Coral Bay. Both have a range of accommodation, camping, supplies, tours and other necessities.

From Exmouth the bitumen road heads north, hugging the coast, and then south all the way to Yardie Creek. Inside the park is the Milyering Information Centre, and obtaining a camping permit here opens up the possibility of a number of excellent camp sites dotted along the coast, including the most popular one at Yardie Creek.

South of Yardie Creek and north of Coral Bay is real 4WD territory. Camping is allowed on the Ningaloo Homestead property for a small fee. Phone the owners on (08) 9942 5936.

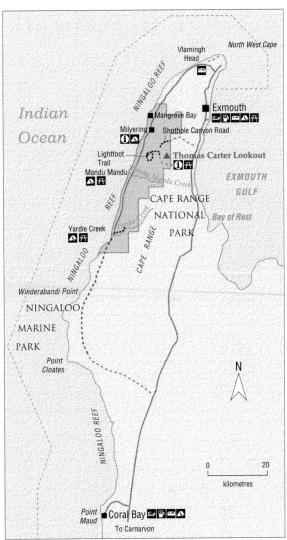

tourist info

Exmouth Tourist Bureau
(08) 9949 1176

Dive Shops: Coral Bay
(08) 9942 5940,
Exmouth (08) 9949 1201

Milyering Information
Centre (CALM)
(08) 9949 2808

Yardie Creek Tours
(08) 9949 2659

WA

Above: *Ningaloo Reef has more than 180 species of coral—some of which is just 100 metres from shore—and is home to a multitude of colourful tropical fish. Non-divers can view the scene from the comfort of a glass-bottom boat.*

Purnululu National Park

Scientists tell us that this place is a geological master-piece, with the unique Bungle Bungle Range rising from the flat, surrounding plain as a great bulk of weather-worn sandstone. Around the range's southern ramparts the beehive-shaped domes, for which the Bungles are renowned, dominate the landscape.

fact file

WHERE: 3000 km north of Perth via Broome, 110 km north of Halls Creek and 250 km south of Kununurra—4WD only
Map: WA 2 F8

WHEN: May to September; the park is closed 1 January to 31 March

WHY: Spectacular ranges, beehive-shaped domes and magnificent gorges

SIZE: 209 000 ha

RANGER: Visitor Information Centre (dry season only) (08) 9168 7300, or CALM Kununurra (08) 9168 0200

Australian Aboriginals know the area as Purnululu and have lived in the region and used its resources for generations.

The surrounding country was first opened up to European graziers in the late 1800s, while the national park was proclaimed in March 1987. It is managed by the Department of Conservation and Land Management (CALM) together with the local Australian Aboriginals, a number of whom are employed as rangers within the park.

Taking up a triangular-shaped piece of countryside, the national park and its adjoining conservation park covers 319 000 hectares.

Cathedral Gorge and Piccaninny Gorge

Located about 10 km east of the Walardi Camp is the car park and access track to Cathedral and Piccaninny Gorges. If there is any one gorge to go to while in Purnululu, it is Cathedral Gorge—it is a spectacular place, so take your time and enjoy it. You should allow about 2 hours for the return walk.

The walk to Piccaninny Gorge continues along Piccaninny Creek but is really an overnight walk of 30 km return. Make sure you let the ranger know before setting out on this one.

Right: Keen eyes may spot the frill-necked lizard (Chlamydosaurus kingii) in the national park. The spectacular frill, sometimes as large as a dinner plate, is spread to intimidate predators.

Echidna Chasm, Froghole and Mini Palms

The car park and access trails for these gorges are located

about 15 km to the north of Kurrajong Camp. Echidna Chasm is an easy to moderate 2 km walk through a very narrow chasm with the walls towering upwards for over 100 metres. Froghole is an easy walk of 1.5 km but you should still allow about 1 hour, while the walk to Mini Palms is a harder 3-km jaunt, which could take 3 hours or more.

From the Air

To fully appreciate the stunning beauty of the unusual Bungles you really need to see the range from the air. Scenic flights are available in helicopters from either Turkey Creek, phone Heliwork on (08) 9168 1811, or from the airstrip located to the south of Walardi Camp, phone (08) 9168 7335.

Light aircraft fly over the range from Halls Creek and Kununurra. While the flight is cheaper from

Distinctively striped, the Bungle Bungles are the eroded remnants of an ancient plateau. The orange bands are silica, while the darker bands are lichen; beneath is a core of white sandstone.

Halls Creek, you miss out on flying over delightful Lake Argyle and the amazing Argyle Diamond Mine.

Access and Camping

About 110 km north of Halls Creek, a rough 4WD route leads 53 km from the Northern Highway into the park and to the visitor centre and ranger station. The visitor centre has a public phone, soft drinks and souvenirs.

From this point it is just 5 km north to Kurrajong Camp or 16 km south to Walardi Camp. Both camps have facilities such as toilets, water and fireplaces with wood provided. There is a separate area for campers with their own generators. An entry fee and a camping fee per night is payable.

A number of tour operators based in either Kununurra or Halls Creek take visitors on a flight over the range and into the national park where camping

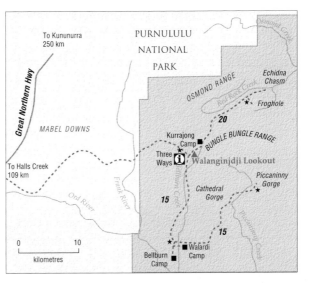

accommodation, transport and other amenities can be provided. Phone East Kimberley Tours on (08) 9168 2213, Oasis Air on (08) 9168 6462 or Alligator Airways on (08) 9168 1333.

Stirling Range National Park

The blue, many-peaked outline of the Stirling Range, when seen from a distance, stands tall, mysterious and alone. This truly dominant and intriguing landmark in the south-west corner of Western Australia looks for all the world like islands rising from a flat sea floor.

fact file

WHERE: 330 km south-east of Perth, and 75 km north of Albany
Map: WA 8 G9

WHEN: October and November for wildflowers, spring and autumn for bushwalking

WHY: Wildflowers, bush-walking, photography

SIZE: 115 920 ha

RANGER: Albany Regional Office (08) 9842 4500

The Stirling Range is known for the concentration, diversity and beauty of its wildflowers.

Australian Aboriginals have lived around the Stirling Range for over 40 000 years.

Matthew Flinders had given the name of Mount Rugged to the eastern massif in 1802, but the real value of the Stirling was not realised until 1843, when botanist James Drummond began a study of the botanical riches that have lured visitors here ever since.

As early as the 1920s the recreational potential of the range was recognised, and today this area is one of Western Australia's premier national parks; its scenic and botanical attractions draw visitors in their thousands.

Surrounded by rolling farm land, the abrupt form of the Stirling Range has over a dozen summits reaching up over 750 metres, with Bluff Knoll standing supreme in the east at 1073 metres.

The general vegetation and terrain around the mountain range is thick, often

Above: There are more than 13 species of banksias found in the Stirling Range. The flowers are rich in nectar and attract a variety of native birds.

The bright red bracts (leaf-like parts) of mountain bells (Darwinia oxylepis) give the impression of a single large flower, but they actually surround a cluster of smaller flowers.

prickly, with scrub covering much of the lower slopes. This gives way to rough stony sections with sparse growth in the higher parts.

Activities

The 42-km Stirling Range Drive runs through the centre of the park and is one of the best mountain drives to be found anywhere in Australia.

For those interested in wildflowers, the park and the Stirling Range Drive is magnificent with over 1500 species, 60 of which are endemic to the range.

The whole of the Stirling Range is a mecca for bush-walkers, with a variety of marked trails and harder routes ideal for exploring different sections of the park. Some of the formal walking trails include interesting routes to the crest of Mount Magog, Mount Talyuberlup, Mount Toolbrunup and Bluff Knoll. The Ridge Trail is a difficult and demanding route which climbs up to Ellen

Peak in the east and winds along the top of the ridge to Bluff Knoll.

There are also quite a number of much easier wildflower and scenic walks ranging from a few hundred metres to over 5 km.

Other activities in the park include abseiling, as well as photography and viewing the region's bountiful wildlife. Over 130 different species of birds have been recorded, while mammals include the often-seen western grey kangaroo.

Access and Camping

All roads leading into the park, and the main tracks within, are either sealed or quite good gravel, suitable for conventional vehicles and caravans.

Throughout the park a number of picnic areas have been set up with barbecues, tables and toilet facilities. Camping is only allowed at the Moingup Springs camping area. A permit is required.

Overnight walkers should ensure they record their intended route and estimated time of return in the park's log books which are located at the Moingup Springs camp site and at the Bluff Knoll picnic site.

The Stirling Range Retreat Caravan Park, phone (08) 9827 9229, is found on the northern edge of the park on Chester Pass Road.

The summit of Bluff Knoll, the highest peak in the park, is the only place in Western Australia where snow is likely to fall in winter.

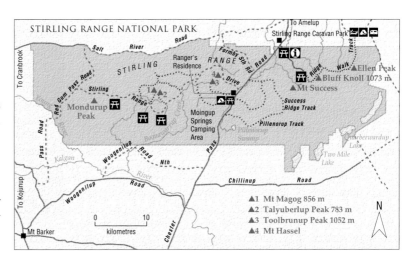

Cape Le Grand National Park

Long stretches of pristine, white, sandy beaches, clear aquamarine water and massive rocky outcrops are the outstanding features of this 32 000-hectare park just west of Esperance. An impressive chain of granite peaks, including Mount Le Grand and Frenchman Peak, rise above the surrounding undulating heath-covered sandplains.

fact file

WHERE: 50 km east of Esperance on the south coast of Western Australia
Map: WA 9 D10

WHEN: September to May

WHY: Coastal and granite outcrop scenery, 4WD, swimming, bushwalking, fishing

SIZE: 32 000 ha

RANGER: (08) 9075 9022

The plains support a wide variety of plant life, with wildflowers in spring making a colourful show. Almost tame kangaroos are another special attraction, as are the Australian sea lions and New Zealand fur seals that laze on the rocky foreshores or in the bays. In deeper water, southern right whales are often spotted.

Activities

Bushwalking is one of the national park's most popular activities. Numerous walking trails range from just a few hundred metres to a scenic 15-km coastal track from Le Grand Beach in the west to Rossiter Bay in the east.

Fishing is also popular. Salmon, blue groper and whiting are among the regular catches. Small boats can be launched off Le Grand Beach and at Lucky Bay.

New Zealand fur seals (Arctocephalus forsteri) *are found on the park's coast. They are smaller and have a more pointed snout than Australian seals.*

Swimming and snorkelling are a highlight of a visit here in summer.

Access and Camping

Access into the park is by sealed road from Esperance. Within the park most main roads are sealed or good gravel.

For those with 4WD vehicles there is a beach access route into the park from Esperance which leads from Wylie Bay to Le Grand Beach.

There are camping areas at Lucky Bay and at Le Grand Beach. Gas stoves should be used, as no wood fires are permitted. A camping fee applies.

Above: *The showy* Banksia speciosa, *notable for its long, serrated leaves, flowers through most of the year. It is one of many species found in the park.*

Left: *Heath-covered sandplains interspersed with swamps and freshwater pools are an ideal habitat for emus. They forage for fruits and insects.*

Kalbarri National Park

The Murchison River and the 80-km gorge it has cut, together with the spectacular coastal cliffs near the river's mouth, combine to form the magnificent centrepieces of Kalbarri National Park. The 186 000-hectare park has immense appeal to bushwalkers, photographers, anglers, canoeists and wildflower enthusiasts.

fact file

WHERE: 167 km north of Geraldton, 1 km from Kalbarri town
Map: WA 6 D5

WHEN: All year, although it can be hot in summer—the cool months are best for walking

WHY: Scenic gorges, bushwalking, photography, water sports

SIZE: 186 000 ha

RANGER: (08) 9937 1140

Top right: *The rich fishing grounds of the tidal Murchison River yield mulloway, tailor, sand whiting and the prized black bream. There is good fishing from both shore and dinghy.*

Above right: *Now compacted and weathered, the multicoloured layered sandstone of Kalbarri's cliffs and gorges began as sediment laid down on tidal flats more than 400 million years ago.*

The Coast and Gorge Country

Red Bluff, a rocky headland at the end of a surfing and swimming beach, is the beginning of a picturesque section of coastline. A sealed road leads along the clifftop with pull-ins to main points of interest, while a 12-km clifftop walking trail also leads south to Natural Bridge.

There's a beautiful beach at the foot of Eagle Gorge and colourful layered sands at Rainbow Valley; from Eagle Gorge an 8-km trek leads to Natural Bridge.

The Murchison River has carved some spectacular gorges and escarpments into the countryside. At each of the main vantage points of the Loop, Hawks Head, Z Bend and the Ross Graham Lookout there are stunning views as well as picnic facilities and walking trails.

Rafting and canoeing—for the experienced only—are popular, especially after heavy rains when the river is navigable.

Access and Camping

Access to the park is along gravel roads leading off the sealed road into Kalbarri.

As there are no formal camp sites in the park, most visitors use the thriving fishing and tourist township of nearby Kalbarri as a base.

WA

More National Parks of Importance

Right: The beach at Point Ann, in Fitzgerald River National Park, was the southern end of the rabbit-proof fence built in 1904 and stretching as far north as Meekatharra.

Royal hakea (Hakea victoria) is a feature of Fitzgerald River National Park's coastal heathland. The large, variegated and leathery leaves are long-lasting, with the colour becoming deeper each year.

With the removal of feral animals, Francois Peron National Park is now a sanctuary for the rare bandicoots and bettongs that once thrived along this arid coast.

Fitzgerald River National Park

SIZE: 329 039 ha
MAP: WA 8 J8

This is one of Australia's most significant national parks and has been gazetted as a World Biosphere Reserve. It is rich in flora with 1784 different plant species recorded, of which 75 are endemic. A number of rare animals, including the dibbler—a small, speckled, marsupial mouse—live in the park. The birdlife is prolific, with 184 recorded species.

Fishing along the coast and in the rivers is popular, while keen photographers will appreciate the rugged coastline, which is also a good viewing place for southern right whales.

There are also a number of walking trails within the park. Conventional vehicle access is available to many of the main attractions. A 4WD vehicle will give access to Fitzgerald Inlet, Trigelow Beach, Quoin Head and Whalebone Beach.

There are basic camping facilities at 4-Mile Beach, Quoin Head, Fitzgerald Inlet and Hamersley Inlet.

For more information contact the ranger on (08) 9835 5043.

Francois Peron National Park

SIZE: 52 529 ha
MAP: WA 6 B1

This park takes up the northern half of the Peron Peninsula that juts into the protected waters of Shark Bay. The park and the surrounding area, including the waters of Monkey Mia (where bottlenosed dolphins mingle with people), are part of the Shark Bay World Heritage Area.

The old Peron homestead and outbuildings in the park have been restored and opened up to the public with a visitor centre in the old overseer's quarters.

Project Eden has seen the reintroduction of many native mammals previously extinct on the mainland, and the waters around the park are home to thousands of dugongs, turtles, dolphins and manta rays. There is good fishing by boat or from the beach all year round.

Access to the old homestead is along a well-maintained dirt road, while travelling further is 4WD only.

Camping is permitted in the park at Big Lagoon, Gregories, Bottle Bay, Cattle

park, and special trails have been established for horse riders.

Throughout the park there are a number of pleasant picnic spots, with barbecues, tables, and toilets, including disabled access.

Access to the park is by a good sealed road 10 km from the Perth suburb of Midland.

Bush camping is permitted within the park, but an application must be made to the park ranger, phone (08) 9298 8344.

Karijini National Park

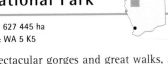

SIZE: 627 445 ha
MAP: WA 5 K5

Spectacular gorges and great walks, all set in the heart of the red raw rock of the Pilbara, make the extensive Karijini National Park one of the most impressive parks in the state. It was originally called Hamersley Range National Park, after the range on which it is centred.

Some of the most enjoyable walks in the park include Oxers Lookout, Joffre Falls, the Gorge Rim Walk as well as the Fortescue Falls and the nearby Fern Pool walk, the latter spot perfect for a swim. There are more extensive walking trails that range from just an hour or two to full-day ventures.

All the roads in the national park are either bitumen or gravel and are suitable for conventional vehicles.

The only camp sites located in the national park are Joffre, Weano and Fortescue. Entry and camping fees apply. A visitor centre is located not far from the Fortescue camping area. Phone (08) 9189 8121.

To contact a ranger (at Tom Price), phone (08) 9189 8157.

Well, Herald Bight and South Gregories. Campers must be fully self-sufficient. Wood fires are banned. Camping and entry fees apply.

Contact the ranger in Denham on (08) 9948 1208, or at Monkey Mia on (08) 9948 1366.

John Forrest National Park

SIZE: 2676 hectares
MAP: WA 8 C4

Sheltered in the Darling Range Escarpment, this is the state's second-oldest park (established as a reserve in 1898), set in a jarrah forest that is still largely in its natural state. In the spring, thousands of tourists come just for the wide variety of wildflowers.

Another major feature of the park is the walking trails, which range in length from 200 metres to several kilometres, with most of the park's scenic attractions found along them. A favourite walk is the extensive John Forrest Heritage Trail.

Bike riding, particularly mountain biking, is also extremely popular in the

Cycads, grass trees and a range of wildflowers— from orchids and kangaroo paws to wattles and banksias—form the lush understorey of the jarrah forest in John Forrest National Park.

Waterways have carved spectacular gorges into the ancient plateau of Karijini National Park. The banded rock exposed here was laid down as sediment on the seafloor 2500 million years ago.

WA

Covered with scattered shrubby trees, grasses and spinifex, Mount Augustus rises 717 metres above the stony sandplain. Springs and waterholes around its base make it an oasis for wildlife.

Millstream–Chichester National Park

SIZE: 199 736 ha
MAP: WA 5 J3

This park, straddling the Fortescue River, has natural freshwater springs fed from deep underground. Ivory-coloured water-lilies and clear pools surrounded by tall palms add to the beauty of this oasis.

In the northern section of the park is Python Pool, a perma-nent waterhole at the base of a tall cliff in the Chichester escarpment. There are a number of popu-lar walking trails, while the two drives around the park take in Deep Reach Pool, Crossing Pool and the Cliff Lookout. Swimming, boating, canoeing and windsurfing are great ways to enjoy the waterways.

All roads are gravel and suitable for conventional vehicles. Camping areas are provided at Crossing Pool, Deep Reach Pool, and in the north at Snake Creek near Python Pool. The Millstream Home-stead Visitor Centre is the best spot for more information, phone (08) 9184 5144. Entry and camping fees are charged.

Right: Variegated fairy-wrens (Malurus lamberti) thrive in the vegetation fringing waterholes in Millstream-Chichester National Park.

don't miss

The Homestead Walk, which starts at the visitor centre in Millstream–Chichester National Park, is a delightful trail through an ancient eco-system of tall palms and paperbarks, winding past Chinderwarriner Pool.

Mount Augustus National Park

SIZE: 9168 ha
MAP: WA 5 H8

Located some 450 km east of Carnarvon, Mount Augustus is the world's largest rock. It is more than twice as big as Uluru (Ayers Rock) and millions of years older.

One of the main attractions at Burrin-gurrah, as the peak is called by the local Wadjari people, is the climb to the top of the mount. Be warned, however, that this is a strenuous walk of 6 km each way. Other walking trails lead to Edneys Lookout, several Australian Aboriginal art sites and waterfalls.

A delightful picnic spot is found at nearby Cattle Pool—a permanent water-hole on the Lyons River lined by large, white river gums. Access to and around the park is by gravel roads. Camp-ing is not allowed, but a full range of accommodation is available at the Mount Augustus Outback Tourist Resort which is located just outside the park, phone (08) 9943 0527.

Rangers are based here from April to October, or phone CALM, Denham, on (08) 9948 1208.

Torndirrup National Park

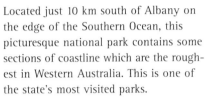

SIZE: 973 ha
MAP: WA 8 F10

Located just 10 km south of Albany on the edge of the Southern Ocean, this picturesque national park contains some sections of coastline which are the roughest in Western Australia. This is one of the state's most visited parks.

The area is a delight for bushwalking, both cross-country and around the park's many spectacular bays and headlands. There are both short and long walks with well laid-out trails available. Places not to be missed by visitors include the Gap, Natural Bridge, the Blowholes, Stony Hill and Salmon Holes—all are extremely dramatic and very scenic places.

Other activities include fishing, rock climbing (in designated areas), whale-watching in winter and wildflower viewing in spring.

With sealed roads leading to all main areas, access is suitable for conventional vehicles. There is no camping in this park, but there are numerous locations to enjoy a picnic.

Contact the CALM office at Albany on (08) 9842 4500 for more information.

Walpole–Nornalup National Park

SIZE: 18 000 ha
MAP: WA 8 D10

This park, situated 430 km south of Perth, is well known for its magnificent tall-timber country, featuring huge karri and tingle trees. Other superb scenic attractions include pristine rivers, waterfalls and long expanses of unspoilt coastline.

Popular activities include bushwalking, scenic drives, beach fishing, canoeing and sailing. The Valley of the Giants, featuring huge karri and red tingle trees, some several hundred years old, is the park's most popular attraction. It is also known for its wildflowers.

A conventional vehicle will get you around the park. There is also a 4WD

access track that heads west from pretty Peaceful Bay, and to Bellanger Beach and the Blue Holes.

There are well-organised camping areas with toilets, barbecues and tables. Bush camping is allowed in designated areas. There are also four caravan parks, at Coalmine Beach, Rest Point, Peaceful Bay and on the South Coast Highway.

For more information contact CALM, Walpole, on (08) 9840 1027.

Below: *The massive, granite span known as Natural Bridge, located in Torndirrup National Park, was carved out by the pounding action of powerful Southern Ocean swells.*

Below: *The wheelchair-accessible Tree Top Walk spans a 40-metre gully in Walpole-Nornalup's Valley of the Giants. Visitors can stroll through a canopy of red tingle.*

WA

Popular Parks at a Glance

Map labels:

- Wyndham
- Kununurra — 16
- Derby
- Broome
- Halls Creek — 20, 8
- Port Hedland
- Karratha — 15
- Exmouth — 4
- 13
- Newman
- Lake Mackay
- Lake Disappointment
- Carnarvon
- 2
- Denham — 7, 10, 17
- 12
- Mt Magnet
- Lake Barlee
- Geraldton
- Lake Moore
- 18
- Kalgoorlie
- Northam
- Norseman
- Perth — 11, 30
- 21, 29, 26
- Bunbury — 14
- 22, 19
- 6
- Esperance — 3
- Augusta — 1, 5, 9, 24, 25
- 23, 27, 28
- Albany
- Great Australian Bight
- NORTHERN TERRITORY
- SOUTH AUSTRALIA

	Camping	Caravan Access	Disabled Access	4WD Access	Picnic Areas	Toilets	Walking Tracks	Kiosk	Information
1 Beedelup NP					●	●	●		
2 Burringurrah (Mount Augustus) NP					●	●	●		●
3 Cape Le Grand NP	●	●			●	●	●		●
4 Cape Range NP	●	●	●		●	●	●	●	●
5 D'Entrecasteaux NP	●			●					
6 Fitzgerald River NP	●			●		●	●		●
7 Francois Peron NP	●			●	●				●
8 Geikie Gorge NP				●	●	●			
9 Gloucester NP				●	●	●			
10 Hamelin Pool Marine NR				●		●			●
11 John Forrest NP				●	●	●	●	●	●
12 Kalbarri NP				●	●	●	●		●
13 Karijini NP	●	●	●		●	●			●
14 Leeuwin–Naturaliste NP	●	●	●		●	●			
15 Millstream–Chichester NP	●	●			●	●	●		●

	Camping	Caravan Access	Disabled Access	4WD Access	Picnic Areas	Toilets	Walking Tracks	Kiosk	Information
16 Mirima NP					●	●	●		
17 Monkey Mia Reserve					●	●	●		●
18 Nambung NP				●	●	●			●
19 Porongurup NP					●	●	●		
20 Purnululu NP	●			●	●	●	●		●
21 Serpentine NP					●	●	●		
22 Stirling Range NP	●	●			●	●	●		
23 Torndirrup NP							●		
24 Walpole–Nornalup NP	●	●			●	●	●		●
25 Warren NP	●				●	●	●		
26 Wellington Forest NP	●				●	●	●		●
27 West Cape Howe NP	●								
28 William Bay NP							●		
29 Yalgorup NP	●				●	●	●		
30 Yanchep NP					●	●	●	●	●

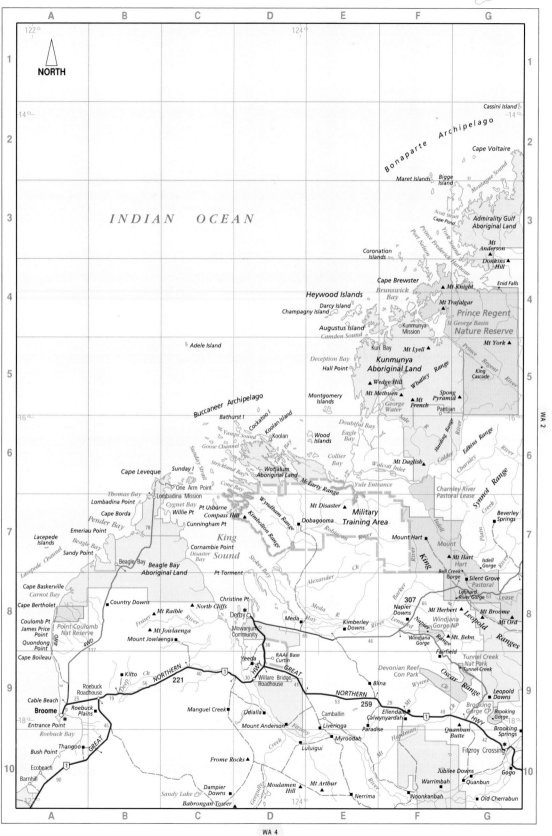

0   20   40   60   80   100
kilometres

NORTH

INDIAN   OCEAN

Bonaparte   Archipelago

Cassini Island

Cape Voltaire

Maret Islands   Bigge Island   *Montague Sound*

Scott Strait   Cape Pond   Admiralty Gulf Aboriginal Land

Coronation Islands   *Prince Frederick Harbour*   *Port Nelson*   Mt Anderson

Cape Brewster   Brunswick Bay   ▲ Mt Knight   Enid Falls   Donkins Hill

Heywood Islands   ▲ Mt Trafalgar   Prince Regent

Darcy Island   St George Basin   Nature Reserve

Champagny Island   Kunmunya Mission

Augustus Island   *Camden Sound*   Mt York ▲

Adele Island   Kuri Bay   Mt Lyell ▲   *Prince*   *Regent*   King Cascade

Deception Bay   Kunmunya Aboriginal Land   *River*

Hall Point   Whatley Range   *King*

Montgomery Islands   ▲ Wedge Hill   ▲ Mt Methuen   Mt French ▲   Spong Pyramid ▲

George Water   Pantijan

Buccaneer   Archipelago

Bathurst I   *Harding Range*   *Edkins Range*   *River*

Cockatoo I   Koolan Island   *Doubtful Bay*   Eagle Bay   Calder   *Charnley*   *Synnott*   *Range*

Yampi Sound   Koolan   Wood Islands   R.

Goose Channel   Collier Bay   *Walcott Inlet*   Mt Daglish ▲

Strickland Bay   Cape Leveque   Sunday I   *Yule Entrance*   Charnley River Pastoral Lease

Thomas Bay   One Arm Point   *McLarty Range*   *Isdell*   Beverley Springs

Lombadina Point   Lombadina Mission   Cone Bay   *Wyndham Range*   Mount Hart ■   Mount ■

Cape Borda   Cygnet Bay   Pt Usborne   Compass Hill   Mt Disaster ▲   Military Training Area   Mt Hart ▲

Emeriau Point   Willie Pt   Cunningham Pt   Oobagooma ■   *King*   Isdell Gorge

Lacepede Islands   *Beagle Bay*   Sandy Point   Cornambie Point   *Disaster Bay*   King Sound   *Robinson   River*   ■ Mt Hart   Bell Creek Gorge

Lacepede Channel   Beagle Bay   Beagle Bay Aboriginal Land   Pt Torment   *Barker*   Silent Grove Pastoral

Cape Baskerville   *Carnot Bay*   *Alexander*   *Meda*   Lennard River Gorge   Lease

Cape Bertholet   ■ Country Downs   ▲ Mt Raible   ★ North Cliffs   Christine Pt   Hay R.   307   Napier Downs   65   Mt Herbert ▲   ▲ Mt Broome

Coulomb Pt   James Price Point   *Point Coulomb Nat Reserve*   Derby ★   *Fraser*   Meda ■   Kimberley Downs   *Lennard*   Napier   Windjana Gorge NP   ▲ Mt Bebn   Mt Ord ▲

Quondong Point   Mt Jowlaenga ▲   Mowanjum Community   46   Windjana Gorge   *Range*   Leopold

Cape Boileau   Mount Jowlaenga ■   Yeeda ■   RAAF Base Curtin   Fairfield   Tunnel Creek Nat Park   Ranges

■ Kilto   *Deep Ck*   Willare Bridge Roadhouse   *Great*   Blina ■   *Oscar*   Tunnel Creek   Leopold Downs

Cable Beach   Roebuck Roadhouse   Northern   221   36   30   41   Northern   53   259   29   Ellendale   49   Brooking Gorge CP   Brooking Gorge

Broome ★   Roebuck Plains   19   40   Camballin ■   Calwynyardah   Quanbun Butte   Brooking Springs

Entrance Point   Manguel Creek ■   Udialla ■   Liveringa ■   Paradise ■   *Hawkman*   Fitzroy Crossing ★

Roebuck Bay   45   Mount Anderson ■   *Fitzroy*   Myroodah ■   Gogo

Bush Point   *Great*   Frome Rocks ▲   *Creek*   Luluigui ■   Jubilee Downs ■   Quanbun ■

Thangoo ■   Warrimbah ■   Old Cherrabun

Ecobeach   Dampier Downs ■   Moulamen Hill ■   Mt Arthur ▲   Noonkanbah ■

Barnhill   90   *Sandy Lake*   Babrongan Tower ▲   *Geegully*   Nerrima ■   *River*

122°   124°   124°

© Global Book Publishing Pty Ltd & Universal Press Pty Ltd

WA 2

W A

WA 4

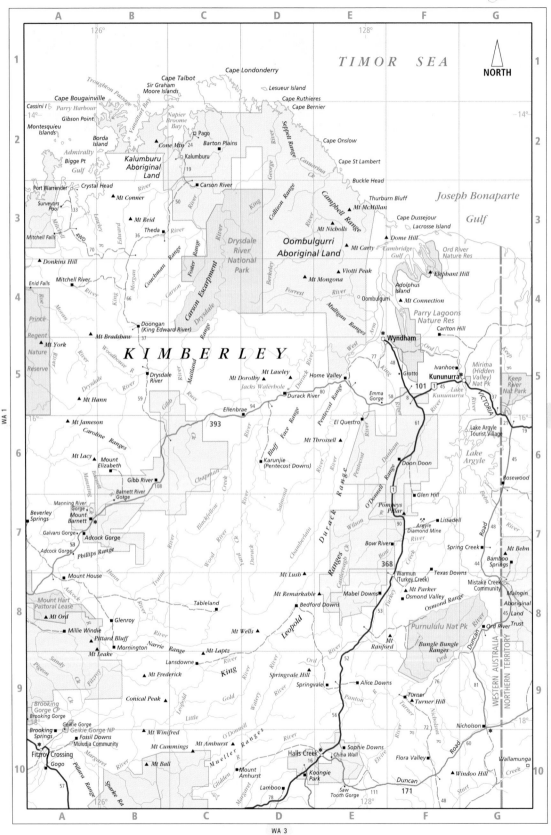

0 20 40 60 80 100
kilometres

NORTH

WA 1

WA 3

TIMOR SEA

Joseph Bonaparte
Gulf

KIMBERLEY

WESTERN AUSTRALIA / NORTHERN TERRITORY

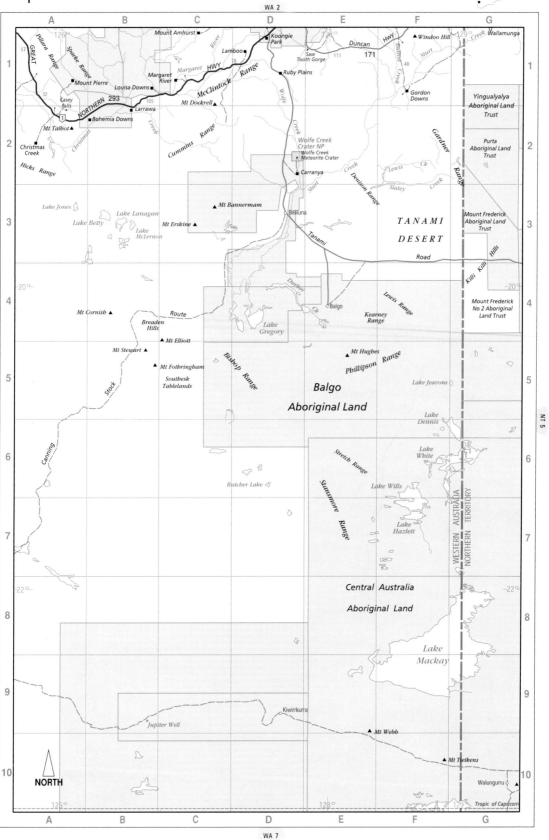

kilometres

WA 2

Map 4

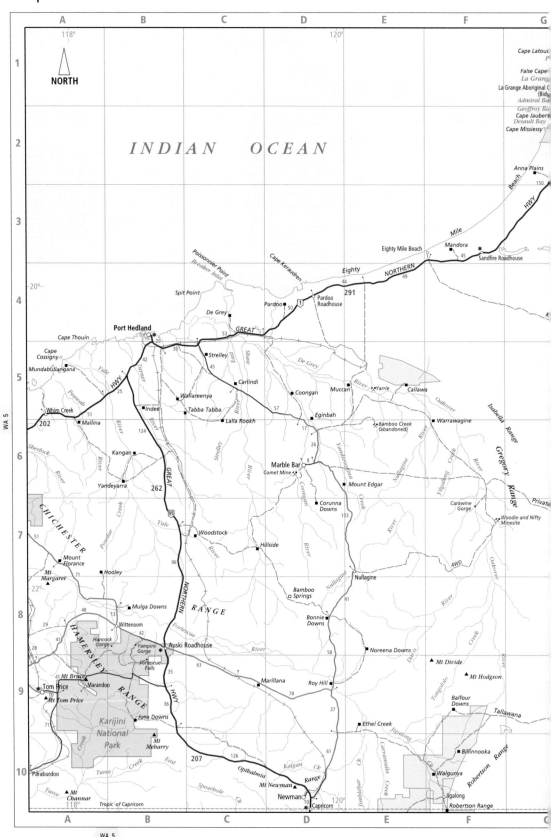

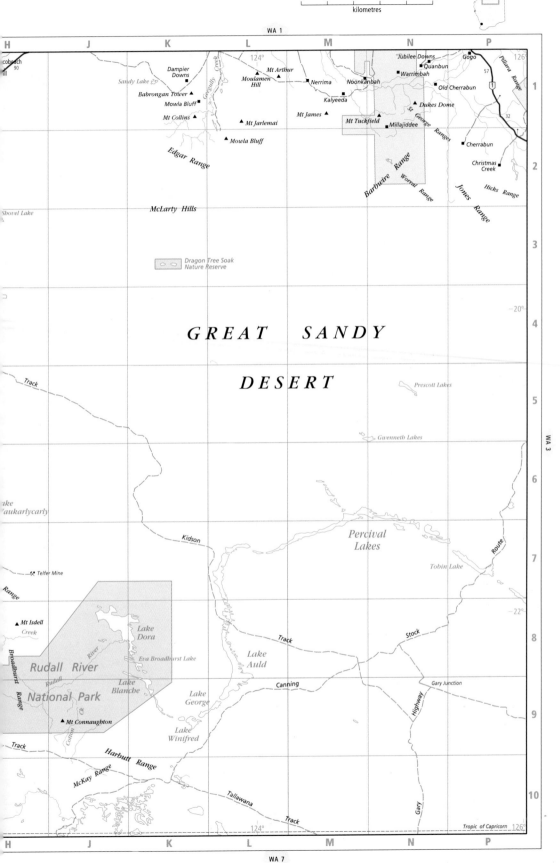

0   20   40   60   80   100
kilometres

H   J   K   L   M   N   P

GREAT   SANDY

DESERT

cobeach
90

Sandy Lake

Dampier
Downs

Babrongan Tower
Mowla Bluff
Mt Collins

Edgar Range

McLarty Hills

Shovel Lake

Dragon Tree Soak
Nature Reserve

ake
aukarlycarly

Track

Range
Mt Isdell
Creek

Broadburst Range

Rudall   River

National Park

Rudall
River

Mt Connaughton

Track

McKay Range

Harbutt Range

124°

Moulamen
Hill

Mt Jarlemai

Mowla Bluff

Mt Arthur
Nerrima
Kalyeeda

Mt James

Mt Tuckfield

Barbwire

Range

Worral Range

Noonkanbah

Jubilee Downs
Quanbun
Warrimbah

Old Cherrabun

Dukes Dome
St George Ranges

Millajiddee

Gogo
57

Pilbara Range

126°

32

Cherrabun

Christmas
Creek

Hicks Range

Jones Range

Prescott Lakes

Gwenneth Lakes

Kidson

Telfer Mine

Lake
Dora

Eva Broadhurst Lake

Lake
Blanche

Lake
George

Lake
Winifred

Percival
Lakes

Tobin Lake

Lake
Auld

Canning

Track

Stock

Route

Gary Junction

Highway

Tallawana

Track

Gary

−20°

−22°

Tropic of Capricorn

124°   126°

WA 3

WA

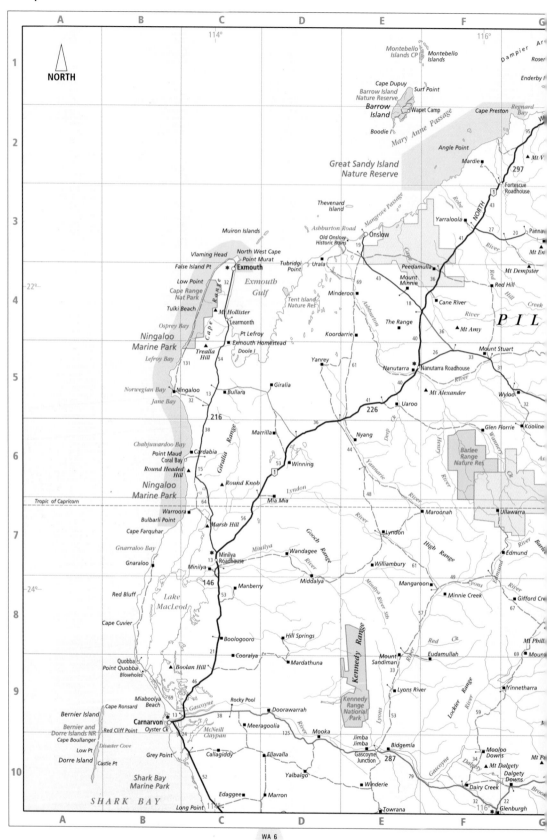

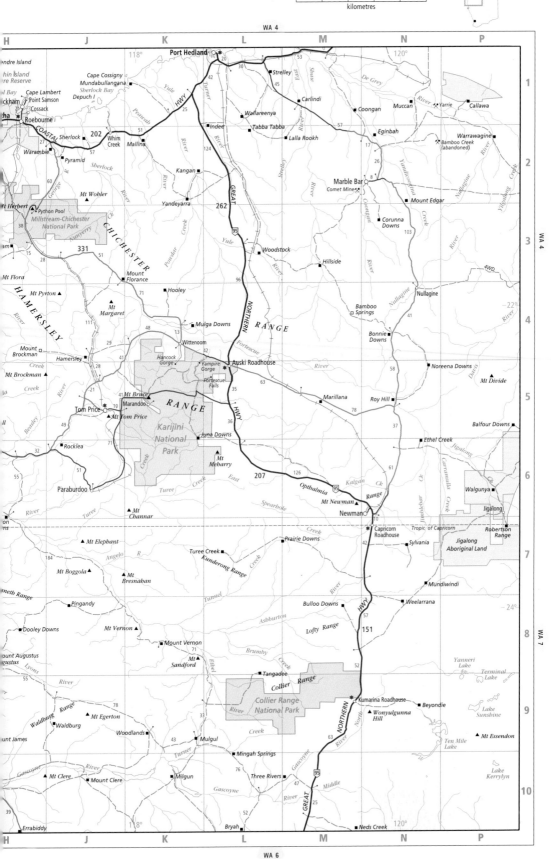

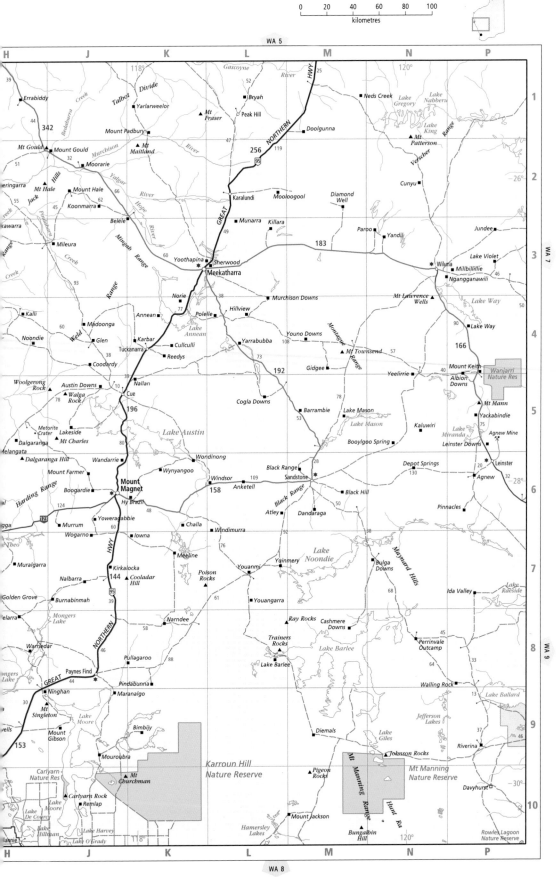

0 20 40 60 80 100
kilometres

WA

H   J   K   L   M   N   P

Errabiddy
Talbot Divide
Gascoyne River
NORTHERN HWY
120°

52
Bryah
Mt Fraser
Peak Hill
Neds Creek
Lake Gregory
Lake Nabberu

Yarlarweelor
Doolgunna
Lake King Range

44
342
Mount Padbury
47
256
119
Mt Patterson
Verlacher

Mt Gould
Mount Gould
Murchison River
Mt Maitland
95

51
32
Moorarie
Yalgar River
Cunyu
−26°

eringarra
Mt Hale
Mount Hale
66
GREAT
Karalundi
Mooloogool
Diamond Well

55
Jack
45
Koonmarra
62
Hope River
Munarra
Killara
Paroo
Yandil
Jundee

kawarra
Belele
49
183
Wiluna
Lake Violet

Mileura
Mingah Range
60
Yoothapina
Sherwood
Millbillillie
Nganganawili
46

Creek
93
Meekatharra
Mt Lawrence Wells
Lake Way
50

Kalli
Norie
38
Murchison Downs
90
Lake Way

60
Madoonga
Annean
77
Polelle
Hillview
Montague Range
166
4

Noondie
Weld
Glen
Karbar
Lake Annean
Youno Downs
108
Mt Townsend
57

Woolgerong Rock
Tuckanarra
Cullculli
Yarrabubba
73
192
Gidgee
Yeelirrie
40
Mount Keith
Wanjarri Nature Res

Coodardy
Reedys
78
Albion Downs

Austin Downs
39
10
Nallan
Cogla Downs
Mt Mann

Walga Rock
Cue
Barrambie
Lake Mason
75
Yackabindie

Metorite Crater
Lakeside
196
Lake Austin
53
Lake Mason
Kaluwiri
Agnew Mine

Dalgaranga
Mt Charles
80
Booylgoo Spring
Lake Miranda
Leinster Downs

Melangata
Dalgaranga Hill
Wandarrie
Wondinong
Black Range
28
Depot Springs
20
Leinster

Mount Farmer
Wynyangoo
Windsor
109
Sandstone
130
Agnew
32
−28°

Boogardie
Mount Magnet
Anketell
158
Black Hill
Pinnacles

124
Hy Brazil
48
50

Murrum
Yoweragabbie
60
Challa
Windimurra
Atley
Dandaraga
Maynard Hills

Wogarno
Iowna
76
92
Lake Noondie
Bulga Downs
Ida Valley
Lake Raeside

Muralgarra
Meeline
Youanmi
Yuinmery
68

Kirkalocka
144
Cooladar Hill
Poison Rocks
61
Youangarra
Ray Rocks
Cashmere Downs
45
Perrinvale Outcamp

Nalbarra
95
Trainers Rocks
Lake Barlee
64
33

Golden Grove
Burnabinmah
39
Narndee
Lake Barlee
Walling Rock
13
Lake Ballard

elarra
Mongers Lake
58
88
Diemals
Jefferson Lakes
37
Riverina
46

Warriedar
Pullagaroo
Lake Giles
9

ongers Lake
Paynes Find
Pindabunna
Mt Manning Nature Reserve
Davyhurst
−30°

Ninghan
44
Maranalgo
Pigeon Rocks
Johnson Rocks

30
Mt Singleton
Lake Moore
Bimbijy
Karroun Hill Nature Reserve
Mt Manning Range
Hunt Ra

Mount Gibson
Carlyarn Nature Res
Mouroubra
Mt Churchman
Bungalbin Hill
Rowles Lagoon Nature Reserve
10

153
Carlyarn Rock
Remlap
Lake De Courcy
Lake Moore
Mount Jackson
Hamersley Lakes
120°

Iannie
Lake Hillman
Lake Harvey
Lake O'Grady
118°

H   J   K   L   M   N   P

0 20 40 60 80 100
kilometres

NORTH

Tropic of Capricorn

Walungurru

Lake
MacDonald

Highway

Windy Corner

Lake Anec

Ryan Buttes

Gary

126°

128°

129°

—24°

NT 8

GIBSON DESERT

Lake
Cobb

ke Jones

Lake Hopkins

oben

McPhersons Pillar

Gibson Desert
Nature Reserve

Lake Blair

Mt Cox

Alfred and Marie Range

Lake
Newell

Lake
Farnham

Christopher
Lake

Rawlinson Range

Mt Destruction

Carnegie Range

Robert

Walter
James Range

Range

Docker

Creek

Kaltukatjara
(Docker River)

Mt Colin

Tsakalos Hills

Lake
Gruszka

Hwy
(abandoned)

Mt Buttfield

Gill Pinnacle

26

Giles

Mt Gordon

Giles Meteorological
Station

Mt Russell

Mt Deering

49

28

16

Lassetters
Cave

Gunbarrel

Jamieson Range

215

Central Australia
Aboriginal Land

Dean

Creek

River

River

Hill

WESTERN AUSTRALIA

NORTHERN TERRITORY

Lake
Sprenger

Mt Beadell

Hwy

Notabilis
Hill

Todd Range

Mt Charles

Barrow Range

Bentley
Hill

106

Mt Daisy
Bates

Mt Fanny

Amy Giles
Rocks

Mt Gosse

Mt Cockburn

Surveyor Generals
Corner

Sutherland Range

Lake
Breaden

Heather Range

Mt Harvest

248

Mt Rawlinson

Mt Chiantbus

Ranges

26°

Boyd Lagoon

85

Warburton Range

Mt Talbot

Mt Eveline

Mt Squires

Cavenagh Range

Mt Jane

Bell Rock

Mt Hinckley

Wingellina

44

21

Aparawatatja

Pipalyatjara

Mt Davies

Warburton

40

Road

Central

Rowe Hills

215

Townsend Ridges

Baker
Lake

Point Read

Lake Kadgo

Central Australia
Aboriginal Land

Kunytjanu
Homeland

Tomkinson Ranges

WESTERN AUSTRALIA

SOUTH AUSTRALIA

The Hann
Breakaways

Hanns Tabletop
Hill

Mt Irving

Lennis Hills

Mt Copley

Ryans Bluff

GREAT VICTORIA

SA 1

Point Lilian

Saunders Range

Saunders Point

DESERT

Waigen Lakes

—28°

Lake Thistle

Neale Junction

Neale Junction
Nature Reserve

Unnamed
Conservation
Park

Wanna Lakes

Serpentine
Lakes

126°

128°

129°

WA

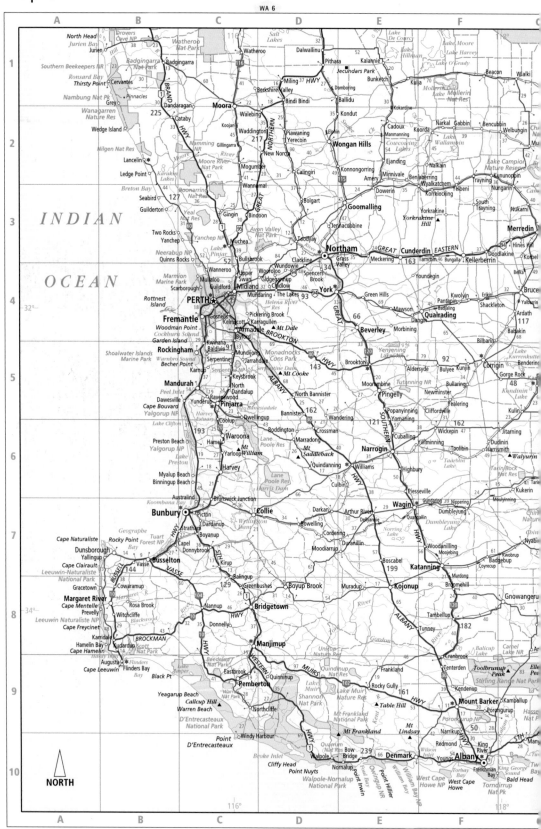

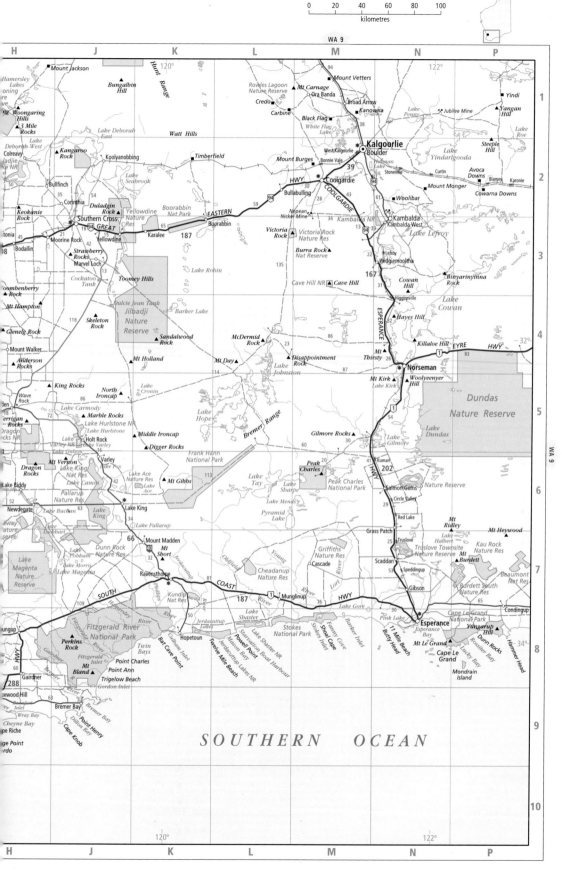

0 20 40 60 80 100
kilometres

H   **J**   **K**   **L**   **M**   **N**   **P**

120°

Mount Jackson

Hamersley
Lakes
oning
ve

Bungalbin
Hill

Rowles Lagoon
Nature Reserve

Mt Carnage
Ora Banda

Mount Vetters

94

Yindi

1

Woongaring
Hills
3 Mile
Rocks

Kangaroo
Rock

Credo
Carbine

Broad Arrow
Kanowna

Lake
Penny

Jubilee Mine

Yangan
Hill

Lake
Roe

Steeple
Hill

Colreavy
ladjie
de NR
50

Bullfinch
35

Koolyanobbing

Timberfield

Black Flag
White Flag
Lake

West Kalgoorlie

Kalgoorlie
Boulder

Stoneville
Curtin

Lake
Yindarlgooda

Avoca
Downs
Blamey
Karonie

Steeple
Hill

2

Corinthia

Duladgin
Rock

Yellowdine
Nature
Res

Mount Burges
Bonnie Vale

HWY
Bullabulling
30

Coolgardie
28

39

94

Mount Monger

Cowarna Downs

Keokanie
Rock

Southern Cross
Yellowdine

Karalee

187

EASTERN
Boorabbin

59

43

Nepean
Nickel Mine
34

61

Woolibar

Kambalda
Kambalda West

Bodallin

Moorine Rock
Strawberry
Rocks
Marvel Loch

13

Toomey Hills

Lake Robin

Victoria
Rock

Victoria Rock
Nature Res
Burra Rock
Nat Reserve

135

31

Lefroy
Widgiemooltha

Lake Lefroy

3

umbenberry
Rock

Mt Hampton

Skeleton
Rock

Dulcie Jean Tank
Jilbadji
Nature
Reserve

Barker Lake

Sandalwood
Rock

118

Cave Hill NR

Cave Hill

167

Cowan
Hill

Higginsville

Binyarinyinna
Rock

Lake
Cowan

4

Glenelg Rock

Mount Walker
Anderson
Rocks

Mt Holland

McDermid
Rock
23

Mt Day

14

Disappointment
Rock

Lake
Johnston

86

87

Hayes Hill

Mt
Thirsty
26

Killaloe Hill

Norseman

EYRE
83

HWY
32°

5

Wave
Rock
den
rrigan
Rocks
ragon
ks NR

King Rocks
72

North
Ironcap
86

Marble Rocks
Lake Hurlstone NR
Lake Hurlstone

Middle Ironcap

Lake
Cronin

Lake
Hope

Bremer Range

Gilmore Rocks
30

60

Mt Kirk
Lake Kirk

Woolyeenyer
Hill

54

Lake
Gilmore

Lake
Dundas

Dundas
Nature Reserve

6

Mt Vernon
Dragon
Rocks
Lake Biddy
52

Holt Rock
Varley

Digger Rocks

Lake
Varley NR
Lake Varley
Lake King
Nat Res
Lake Camm
42
Pallarup
Nature Res

Frank Hann
National Park

Lake Ace
Nature Res
Lake
Ace

Mt Gibbs
113

Lake
Tay

Lake
Sharpe

Peak
Charles
20

Peak Charles
National Park

41
Kumarl
23

202

HWY

Salmon Gums
Circle Valley

Nature Reserve

29

7

Newdegate

away
ature
serve

Lake Magenta
Nature
Reserve

Lake Buchan
63

Lake
King
34

Lake
Lockhart

Dunn Rock
Nature Res

Lake
Cobham
Lake Morris
Lake Magenta

Lake Pallarup

Mount Madden
Mt
Short
32

66

Ravensthorpe

SOUTH

Jerdacuttup

Oldfield

Young

COAST
187

Cheadanup
Nature Res

Griffiths
Nature Res
Cascade

River

Lort

River

Munglinup
26

Lake Gore

HWY

Red Lake

Grass Patch

Truslove
25

Scaddan

Speddingup
53

Gibson

Mt
Ridley

Mt Heywood

Mt
Halbert
Truslove Townsite
Nature Reserve

Kau Rock
Nature Res
Mt
Burdett

Beaumont
Nat Res

Condingup
65

8

ungup

HWY
60

Gairdner

288

oxwood Hill

63

Perkins
Rock

Mt
Bland

Kundip
Nat Res

Fitzgerald River
National Park

Fitzgerald
Inlet
Point Charles
Point Ann
Trigelow Beach
Gordon Inlet

Bart Cove Point

Twin
Bays

Culham Inlet

Jerdacuttup
Lakes

Hopetoun

Jerdacuttup
Lakes NR
Twelve Mile Beach
Mason Bay

River

50

81

Lake
Shaster

Starvation Boat Harbour

Lake Shaster NR
Stokes
National Park
Fanny Cove
Stokes Inlet
Shoal Cape
Powell Point

Barker Inlet

Pink Lake
Esperance Bay
11 Mile Beach
Butty Head

Esperance

Cape Le Grand
National Park
Mt Le Grand
Cape Le
Grand
Mondrain
Island

Yungarup
Hill
Dunn Rocks
Lucky Bay
Rossiter Bay

Hammer Head

34°

8

Bremer Bay
Point Henry
Bremer Bay
Dillon Bay

Wray Inlet

Cheyne Bay
pe Riche

ge Point
rdo

Cape Knob

9

SOUTHERN OCEAN

10

120°

122°

H   **J**   **K**   **L**   **M**   **N**   **P**

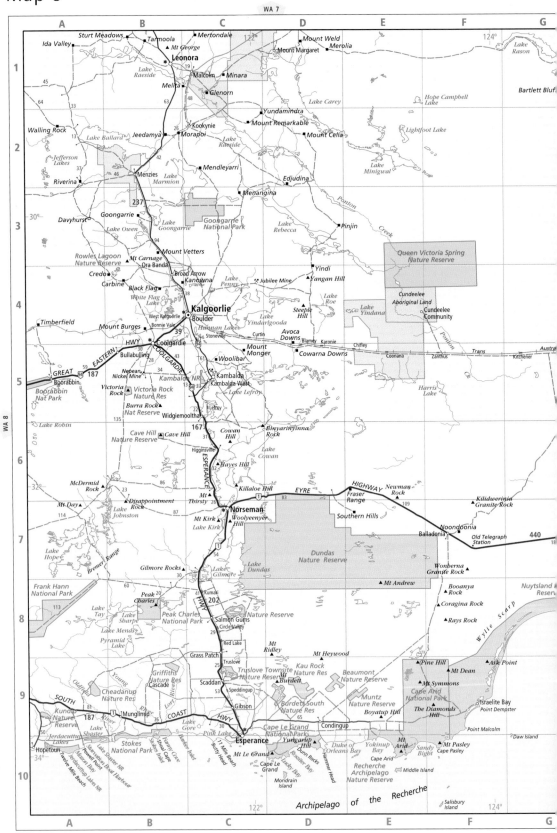

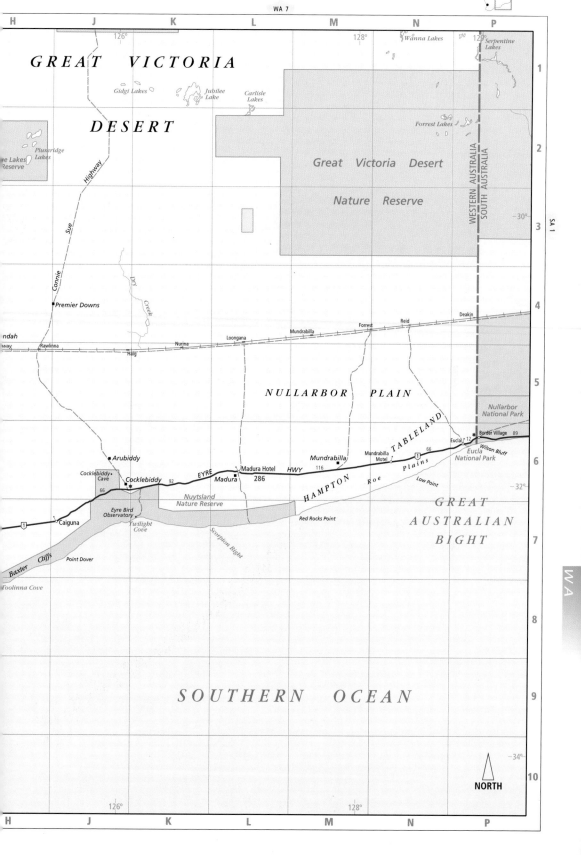

0 20 40 60 80 100
kilometres

GREAT VICTORIA

DESERT

Gidgi Lakes
Jubilee Lake
Carlisle Lakes
Plumridge Lakes
e Lakes Reserve

Wanna Lakes
Serpentine Lakes

Forrest Lakes

Great Victoria Desert

Nature Reserve

WESTERN AUSTRALIA
SOUTH AUSTRALIA

—30°

SA 1

WA

Sue Highway
Connie
Dry Creek
Premier Downs

ndah
way
Rawlinna
Haig
Nurina
Loongana
Mundrabilla
Forrest
Reid
Deakin

NULLARBOR   PLAIN

Nullarbor
National Park

Arubiddy
Cocklebiddy Cave
Cocklebiddy
92
EYRE
Madura Hotel
Madura   286
HWY   116
Mundrabilla
Mundrabilla Motel
66
TABLELAND
Plains
Eucla   12
Border Village 89
Wilson Bluff
Eucla
National Park

Nuytsland
Nature Reserve
Eyre Bird Observatory
Twilight Cove
Red Rocks Point
Scorpion Bight
HAMPTON
Roe
Low Point

GREAT
AUSTRALIAN
BIGHT

—32°

Caiguna
66
1
Baxter Cliffs
Point Dover
oolinna Cove

SOUTHERN   OCEAN

—34°

NORTH

Northern Territory

The Northern Territory, big and sparsely populated, is a region of many unique natural wonders, equally as spectacular as the world's best scenic locations. Still, barely 2 per cent of land within the 1 346 200 sq km of the Northern Territory is reserved as national parks. These protected areas reflect a vibrant diversity of landscape. There are the verdant wetlands of the far north, the semi-arid woodland forests and grassy plains of the Barkly Tableland and the dry arid zone of the south where the red sand dunes are interspersed with mountain ranges and rocky outcrops. Take time to explore and enjoy this ancient land. It will be impossible to see it all on one holiday, so choose your destinations carefully and make the most of your time in the magnificent north.

Kakadu National Park

One of this country's finest national and natural treasures is Kakadu National Park, which is also Australia's biggest national park. Towering over the park's wetlands is the huge 500-km long Arnhem Land escarpment, and everywhere you look in this ancient landscape you are left with a feeling of majesty and awe. Its natural geological features include interesting rock formations, huge waterways, quiet and peaceful streams, towering cliffs, spectacular waterfalls and cool lagoons.

The sacred lotus (Nelumbo nucifera) *raises its umbrella-like leaves above the surface of billabongs and creeks in northern Australia. Its large flowers are various shades of pink.*

As well as Kakadu's unique geology, its diverse wildlife and extensive plant life all add up to a truly magnificent area. Kakadu also boasts some of the country's best Aboriginal rock art.

Proclaimed in 1979, the value of Kakadu's treasures is also reflected in the park's World Heritage listing, which occurred in 1981. The park was subsequently extended in various stages and now occupies 19 804 sq km.

A large portion of this wonderful park is owned by Australian Aboriginals (the Gagudju Association) who have maintained strong personal and spiritual links with these traditional lands for at least 60 000 years. The park is leased back to the Commonwealth and is managed by a specially selected board of management where the traditional owners are represented. Within the park boundaries are a couple of mineral leases and these have been the cause of quite a lot of controversy over recent times.

Today Kakadu National Park is drawing visitors from around Australia and, indeed, from all over the world, at a rate of well over 220 000 people every year, and the number is continually growing. Most come in the Top End's dry season, from April to October, when the climate is almost perfect for exploring and taking in all of the park's attractions.

For those few who come during the wet season, some of the rewards on offer are even more spectacular—the waterfalls

are flowing at full strength, the many billabongs are full, and the area is lush and green everywhere. Roads to some of the more remote attractions may, however, be flooded and impassable during this time of year.

In contrast, by late in the dry season much of the bushland is tinder dry; grass fires, lit in the park as part of its management control system, have blackened much of the bushland area.

Activities

There are some splendid bushwalks leading off from car parks (as well as other cross-country treks) usually incorporating one of the park's many attractions, such as rock art, waterfalls, billabongs, fishing spots and swimming holes, to name a few.

The many indigenous art sites found in the park on cliffs, rock faces and in large natural rock shelters record Aboriginal history, culture and

Right: *The waterways in Kakadu, like this one near Jabiru, are lush and full during the wet season, when up to 1300 mm of rain falls on the region.*

beliefs. They also record the visits of Macassans who arrived from the north to fish, gather trepangs (sea cucumbers) and search for pearls. Visits by the Dutch, and later the British, are shown, and their ships, axes and firearms all feature in Kakadu's ochre art galleries.

Kakadu's Aboriginal rock art is of world significance and Ubirr Rock has been added in its own right to the World Heritage listing for its cultural, anthropological and archaeological value. Ubirr Rock, together with the other important rock art sites in the park at Nourlangie, Nanguluwur and Anbangbang, give the whole area a feeling of the ancestral power of the land unmatched anywhere else in the country.

Nature lovers will be enthralled by the 300 or more species of birds, including egrets, jabirus and brolgas, as well as many grass and bushland species. Wallabies, euros, wild black pigs, and even the occasional wild Timor pony

are also found in the park, as are crocodiles.

To see and enjoy the park properly, allow at least 4 or 5 days (even more, depending on your personal interests). Insect repellent for flies and mosquitoes, a hat and good comfortable walking gear, fishing lines and lures are needed for your camping stay. The following are some of the park's most interesting and truly picturesque areas.

Some Aboriginal rock art sites in the Northern Territory are thought to be over 18 000 years old, and it is estimated that there are some 7000 art sites in Kakadu National Park alone.

Jabiru

This centre is Kakadu's residential hub. Fuel, supplies, a post office, supermarket, a wide range of services and accommodation, including the famous Gagudju Crocodile Hotel are all found here.

Scenic flights over Kakadu can also be arranged in Jabiru.

Bowali Visitor Centre and Park Headquarters

Located on the edge of town on the Kakadu Highway, this is certainly worth a visit. Everything you need to know about the park is here, making this an ideal starting place for your Kakadu visit.

Ubirr

Ubirr is just 3 km north of the Border Store (which sells fuel and supplies) and some 40 km from Jabiru. This is one of the main accessible rock art sites in the park. A 1-km, easy walking circuit trail leads from the car park, while the main art site is also accessible by wheelchair.

There are various art styles, including the stick-like Mimi figures, some of which are estimated to be up to 20 000 years old, but the more recent, dramatic, x-ray style is the most striking.

Climb to the top of the rocky escarpment for splendid views over the Kakadu countryside, the nearby billabongs of the Arnhem wetlands and the huge Arnhem Land. The view from here, particularly around sunset, is quite stunning.

Nourlangie Rock

About 19 km south of the visitor centre is Nourlangie Rock, which is an art site of great significance to the traditional

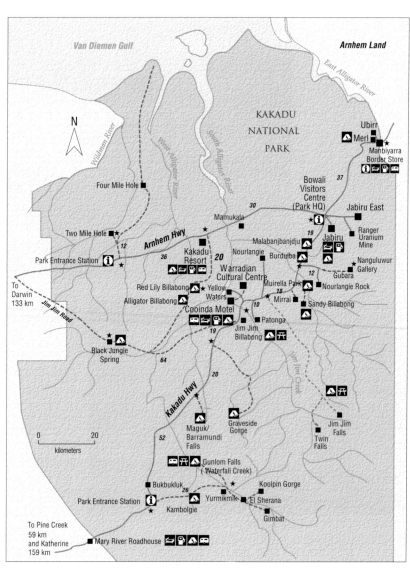

owners. The main circuit trail of 1.5 km is a relatively easy stroll lasting about 1 hour—and most of it is accessible by wheelchair. The main galleries here include some excellent artwork, with signboards explaining the figures and the stories behind them. Namarrgon, the Lightning Man, is one of the gallery's most impressive figures.

Nanguluwur Gallery Walk

This relatively easy, 3.4-km return walk (allow 2 hours) passes through flat and open woodlands on the western side of Nourlangie Rock and leads to one of the most interesting rock art sites in Kakadu.

Its walls are like pages in a living history book, illustrating aspects of the lives of local Australian Aboriginal people from ancient times to the modern era.

Jim Jim Falls and Twin Falls

These falls are spectacular in the wet season when water thunders over the top of the Arnhem escarpment and plummets 200 m to the creek below. The falls are usually reduced to not much more than a trickle as the dry season progresses. Camping is allowed at Jim Jim where toilets, barbecues and tables are provided.

There are 300-plus native bird species that inhabit Kakadu National Park, including the coastal-dwelling rufous-banded honeyeater (Conopophila albogularis).

NT

Commercial boat tours operate year-round on Yellow Waters; fishing and crocodile spotting are also popular in this wetland region.

Below: *Kakadu has about 6000 crocodiles. The salt-water or estuarine croco-dile (Crocodylus porosus) is the largest living reptile in the world.*

Camping is not allowed here, but situated just 1 km away is the Gagudju Cooinda Lodge which has a motel, caravan sites and camping facilities. Also located here is the Warradjan Aboriginal Cultural Centre, which provides a good insight into the local culture.

Barramundi Falls (Maguk)

Further south in Kakadu National Park, Barramundi Falls is reached by a 12-km 4WD track leading to a small waterfall, which tumbles down through the sandstone escarpment into a large, clear pool at the bottom. There are some beautiful swimming spots with sandy beaches along the walking track to the falls.

Gunlom Falls

Previously known as the UDP Falls, the Gunlom Falls are in the southern section of the park, 37 km off the main Kakadu Highway. The access road leads to a grassed picnic area, with the falls and the large, sandy-bottomed plunge pool only around 100 m away. The walking trail to the falls is suitable for wheelchair access. The Gunlom Falls are at their best when they are in flood.

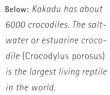

warning

Dangerous estuarine, or saltwater, crocodiles inhabit a number of the Kakadu waterways. Do not go into, and be very careful near, the water in these areas—look out for the crocodile warning signs. Many of the most popular swimming holes in the park are safe, but if in doubt, check with the local rangers.

For a great day trip only (as there is no camping allowed), a visit to the nearby Twin Falls is thoroughly recommended. On reaching the end of the trail at one of the creek's white sandy beaches, it's then into the water—take your inflatable mattress for a great paddle (about 1 km) towards the falls.

Yellow Waters

Located virtually in the centre of the park, Yellow Waters is a magnificent billabong on the South Alligator River. A boardwalk along the edge of this picturesque waterway is a must for birdwatchers, while boat cruises, especially at sunrise and sunset, are always popular. Crocodile spotting and fishing for prize barramundi are also highlights.

Park Access

There's good access to Kakadu National Park, both from Darwin and from the south at Pine Creek. Both of the access routes are good, sealed, all-year-round roads which will only be closed in the most extreme weather conditions. An entry fee applies and your permit is valid for 14 days (or multiple entries to the park within the 14-day period).

Check with the rangers about road conditions within the park—some are accessible by 4WD only.

Camping

Kakadu offers some really superb camping experiences—often near waterfalls, billabongs, or with rocky escarpment outlooks. They range from caravan parks (including those at Jabiru, Cooinda and Kakadu Holiday Village), to several formal camping areas at Merl (near Ubirr), Muirella Park (between Jabiru and Yellow Waters), Mardugal (near Yellow Waters) and at Gunlom Falls. These areas are all equipped with showers, flushing toilets and water, and have adequate facilities for the disabled. Note that a camping fee is charged at these spots.

Throughout the park there are a number of other, less developed, tent camping areas, most with toilets and barbecues, but not showers. There are some in more remote locations with no facilities at all.

In addition to camp sites there are picnic areas located near many of the main attractions. Hotel or motel accommodation is available at Jabiru, Cooinda and at the Kakadu Holiday Village near the South Alligator River.

tourist info

Jabiru Tourist Centre
(08) 8979 2548 for tours

Kakadu Resort
(08) 8979 0166 for tours
to all parts of the park

Twisted brown trunk of the tree Allosyncarpia ternata. *This tree occupies a variety of habitats including monsoon rainforest, upland savannah and rocky areas of the Arnhem Land Plateau.*

Below: *Great egrets (*Ardea alba) *were once hunted for the long plumes they develop in the breeding season, which were used to decorate ladies' hats.*

Gregory National Park

Measuring 1 050 000 ha, Gregory National Park is the Northern Territory's second-largest park after Kakadu. The Territory's largest waterway, the mighty Victoria River has, over millions of years, created a sweeping vista of towering red escarpments, majestic cliffs and hidden gorges with most of it protected within the park. The explorer Augustus Charles Gregory was the first European to explore the area during 1855 and his reports brought pioneer cattlemen into the Victoria River region.

fact file

WHERE: 160 km south-west of Katherine on the Victoria Highway
Map: NT 4 D5

WHEN: May to September

WHY: Rugged scenery, history, excellent bush-walks and camping, remote 4WD tracks

SIZE: 1 050 000 ha

RANGER: Timber Creek (08) 8975 0888, Bullita (08) 8975 0833 or Wickham River (08) 8975 0600

Activities

Some of the best gorges and escarpments can be found off the main road near the Victoria River Crossing. The Escarpment Walk, and Joe's Creek Walk, the latter with hundreds of tall *Livistona* palms along the way, are particularly appealing. Australian Aboriginal art is also found on cliff faces along the trail. This is an easy to moderate walk, and you should allow 1 hour for the return trip.

The Kuwang Lookout, 57 km west of the crossing, is also worth visiting, and overlooks the surrounding countryside and Stokes Range.

An excellent boat ramp is easily accessible at Big Horse Creek and the river offers great fishing for barramundi. A well-established camping area with pit toilets is also located here.

Access further into the park to the old Bullita Homestead, which is 41 km off the highway from the turn-off 15 km from Timber Creek, is along a gravel track which, with care, can be covered in a conventional vehicle. The homestead has been restored and opened to visitors and is worth seeing.

Livistona humilis is a small, single-trunked fan palm tree that grows to 4–6 metres tall. It is found only in the far north of the Northern Territory.

Along the way a turn-off to the right leads to Limestone Gorge—an area of strange, grey dolomite towers and many fine examples of odd-looking boab trees. From the car park, there's an interesting 2-km circuit walk, the Limestone Ridge Trail, which leads through the limestone outcrops and flat savannah grasslands.

Camping areas with barbecues and toilets are located at Limestone Gorge and near the homestead.

Further into Gregory National Park is strictly 4WD country. There are three old stock routes—Bullita, Humbert and Wickham Tracks—that have an excellent set of trek notes and historic information available at the beginning of the tracks. It is necessary to sign an 'intentions book' detailing your vehicle, occupants and travel plans, and you also need to sign off at the end of the track. These old trails are particularly remote and

tourist info

Fishing and crocodile-
spotting trips on the
Victoria River are avail-
able by phoning:
Barra Fishing Safaris
(08) 8975 0688
Victoria River Roadhouse
(08) 8975 0744

quite rough and challenging in parts. For
the adventurous they offer some great
4WD experiences, splendid scenery and
lovely, remote camp sites beside rivers
and waterholes along the way. There are
no facilities at all along any of these
4WD tracks, so it is important to make
sure you carry enough water and vehicle
spares on these tracks.

Access

The best access to Gregory National
Park is via the Victoria Highway from
Katherine in the east or Kununurra in
the west. A dirt road route from Top
Springs and Victoria River Downs is a
spectacular and little-used route that
takes in Jasper Gorge.

All roads in the area, including the
Victoria Highway, may be closed after
heavy rains, particularly during the
summer wet season.

*Victoria River in Gregory National
Park is the Northern Territory's
largest waterway, and can easily
be explored on a boat tour.*

The nutwood tree (Terminalia arostrata) *is
found only in the Top End. The Northern
Territory national parks system nurtures
many species of plants not seen elsewhere.*

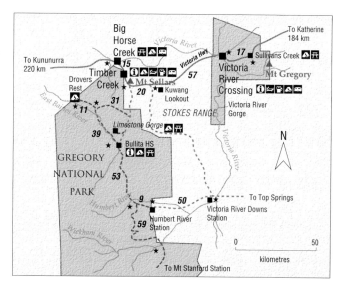

Uluru–Kata Tjuta National Park

Uluru (Ayers Rock) and Kata Tjuta (the Olgas) are mystical, mysterious symbols in the heart of the Australian continent and are revered by both the Australian Aboriginal and European Australian cultures. While Uluru stands majestically some 340 metres above the surrounding plain, Kata Tjuta rises to 600 metres; both these land forms are remnants of a 100-million-year-old landscape.

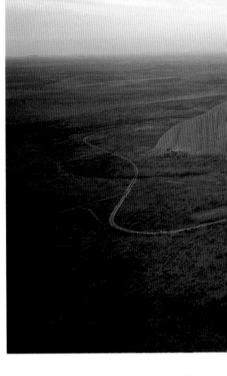

fact file

WHERE: 465 km south-west of Alice Springs along the Stuart Highway and Lasseter Highway Map: NT 8 F8

WHEN: Beginning of April to end of October

WHY: Uluru (Ayers Rock): second largest monolith in the world, Australian Aboriginal culture, Kata Tjuta (the Olgas), stunning views, walking trails

SIZE: 132 566 ha

RANGER: National Park headquarters: (08) 8956 2299

In the Past

The Australian Aboriginal people of this region, who have lived here for many generations, call themselves by the collective name of Anangu ('we people') and are made up of three main groups: the Yankunytjatjara, the Pitjantjatjara and the Ngaanyatjara.

The first European explorer to visit this area was Ernest Giles, who in 1872 named Mount Olga; W. E. Gosse arrived in 1873 and named Ayers Rock.

During the early part of the 1930s pastoral activity and mining exploration commenced, with tourism starting in the late 1940s. By the middle of the 1970s over 50 000 visitors a year were tramping over and around Uluru.

In 1985, after a long legal battle, the Anangu and the Uluru–Kata Tjuta Land Trust accepted the freehold title to their lands, which was then leased back to the Commonwealth Government as a national park. The park is now carefully managed on a co-operative basis with the traditional owners having a majority representation on the board.

In 1987 the United Nations inscribed Uluru–Kata Tjuta National Park onto the World Heritage List and it is now one of 12 Australian Biosphere Reserves.

Activities

It is important to note that both Uluru and Kata Tjuta are areas of special significance to Australian Aboriginal people and a number of sacred sites exist. When walking around both places the visitor will see signs which clearly mark where access is closed to the public.

For safety and cultural reasons the Anangu prefer that visitors do not climb up the rock, but those that do should remember that it is very steep and they should only climb along the route with the safety chain. The journey is 1.6 km return and should take about 2 hours.

Ernest Giles described Kata Tjuta's domes as 'round stones ... mixed as plums in a pudding and set in vast and rounded shapes upon the ground'.

Left: *Uluru is Australia's second-largest monolith and has long carried the status of a national icon. The Aboriginal people of this area prefer that visitors do not climb Uluru due to cultural reasons.*

business out of Alice Springs, so you should find something to suit you.

While the opportunity for photography is great, especially at sunrise and at sunset, the Anangu people do not like to be photographed. They ask that visitors do not film them or take photographs of their important spiritual areas.

Desert grevillea (Grevillea eriostachya) has a wide geographic range across central and western Australia. Also known as yellow flame grevillea, it is in flower here, at the base of Uluru.

Access and Accommodation

Major airlines offer flights to Yulara.

The 465-km drive from Alice Springs is along the sealed Stuart and Lasseter Highways and all the roads within the park are sealed.

There are no camping facilities or other accommodation within Uluru–Kata Tjuta National Park itself. The resort at Yulara has a range of accommodation from luxury to budget, as well as camping and supply facilities.

Many of the geographic features of Uluru mark the ancient beliefs of the Australian Aboriginal people and these features may be seen by the visitor while walking along the circular path around Uluru. This walk is about 9-km long and should take around 4 hours. At Kata Tjuta, the Valley of the Winds Walk is 6 km (allow 3 hours return), while the Olga Gorge Walk is shorter, about 2 km and 1 hour return.

Over 400 species of plant life, 22 species of mammals, 150 different bird groups and many reptiles and frogs have been recorded, but visitors are likely to see only a fraction of these.

There are many tours departing from the Ayers Rock Resort. For more information contact the Visitor Centre. There are also more than 50 tour operators conducting

tourist info

Uluru–Kata Tjuta
Cultural Centre
(08) 8956 3138

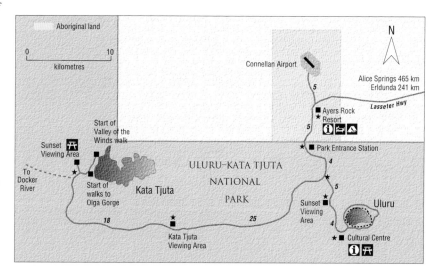

Litchfield National Park

Situated in the Top End, Litchfield National Park is thought by some people to be more spectacular than Kakadu! The park offers some of the most magnificent and diverse landscapes anywhere in the Northern Territory.

Dry woodlands and forests dominate the huge sandstone plateau which forms the heart of the park. Close to the plateau escarpment, springs give rise to creeks which tumble through rapids before cascading as waterfalls into deep pools in the rainforest valleys below. The most spectacular of these are Wangi, Florence, Tjaynera and Tolmer Falls.

Wangi Falls is a favourite of many visitors, as it allows camping within a 100-m stroll of a lovely, sandy pool set at the foot of the falls.

One of the most popular activities in Litchfield National Park is bushwalking. These walks range from flat and easy to some quite strenuous trails which often lead to crystal clear pools in which to cool off, refresh and relax.

Evidence of early pastoralist activity is found at the historic remains of the old

Some of the interesting features of Litchfield National Park include these intriguing magnetic termite mounds, as well as pockets of rainforest.

Blyth Homestead, while the Lost City is a spectacular collection of free-standing sandstone formations.

For nature-lovers, brush-tailed possums and wallabies are regularly seen, along with blue-winged kookaburras and red-tailed black cockatoos.

Access and Camping

Today, most of the main sections of the park can be reached by sealed road. It is an easy 2-hour drive of 130 km from Darwin, via Batchelor. A 4WD track leads through the southern portion of the park to the Daly River Road.

Within the national park the main camping areas are at Wangi, Buley Rockholes and Florence Falls. There are several other bush camping areas scattered throughout the park. A camping fee applies at each of the main camping areas.

Sealed road access and short walking tracks in Litchfield National Park lead to refreshing swimming sites such as Buley Rockholes.

West MacDonnell National Park

The magnificent MacDonnell Ranges in central Australia reach heights of over 1500 metres above sea level and span some 400 km east to west across vibrant desert country not far from the town of Alice Springs.

Commercial tour operators offer many different scenic trips throughout West MacDonnell National Park; some of the best views are seen from the air.

fact file

WHERE: This park stretches from the fringe of Alice Springs township westwards for 220 km
Map: NT 7 D4

WHEN: April to September (Larapinta Trail may be closed between October and April)

WHY: Numerous scenic gorges and waterholes, walking trails, swimming, hiking, camping, cycling, scenic drives, Australian Aboriginal culture

SIZE: 206 973 ha

RANGER: Parks and Wildlife Commission, Park Visitor Information, Alice Springs
(08) 8951 8211

Early Aboriginal Australians lived and travelled throughout these lands pursuing their nomadic way of life until European explorers passed through the region in the 1860s. Then came the pastoralists, the telegraph line and the modern township we call Alice Springs.

The West MacDonnell National Park was established in 1994. The major natural features of the park are linked by the Larapinta Trail, a world-class bushwalking trail which follows the backbone of the ranges for about 220 km. This marvellous walking trail starts at the Alice Springs Telegraph Station and continues to Simpsons Gap. It then winds west via all the major attractions in the park— Standley Chasm, Serpentine Gorge, Glen Helen Gorge, Ormiston Gorge, Mount Sonder, Mount Giles, Redbank Gorge— to Mount Zeil.

All walkers must register with the nearest ranger station before setting off on a major walk. Most of the waterholes are extremely cold and will provide a very refreshing swim.

All these features are accessible by conventional vehicle and a short walk, with the exception of the mountain peaks and Roma Gorge which is 4WD access only. Namatjira Drive, which services the park, is sealed as far as Glen Helen Gorge, 130 km from Alice Springs. Beyond that point a formed gravel road runs west.

The variety to be found here is fantastic. There's early European history, rare wildlife, magnificent scenery, cool enjoyable swimming and walking trails, while the area is also an important refuge for a number of rare plant species and home to a special species of Central Australian fish.

Right: *Glen Helen Gorge is accessible and well worth visiting. The brilliant colours of this gorge are due to the dramatic red quartzite rock.*

tourist info

Commercial tour operators service the park from Alice Springs—for details contact the Visitor Information Centre (08) 8952 5800

NT

More National Parks of Importance

Devils Marbles Conservation Reserve

SIZE: 1829 ha
MAP: NT 6 G6

The Devils Marbles are situated on either side of the Stuart Highway, 120 km south of Tennant Creek. These fascinating spherical and egg-shaped granite boulders, some balanced precariously on others, are a spectacular natural phenomenon that are well worth exploring, especially in the early morning or late evening light.

There are many informal walking tracks where the visitor may wander through the boulders and find great photo opportunities.

Bush camping facilities are provided which include shaded picnic tables, as well as fireplaces and toilets. A nominal camping fee applies.

The Devils Marbles is a registered Aboriginal sacred site and visitors are asked to respect the cultural heritage of the area.

For more details, phone the Parks Office, Tennant Creek (08) 8962 4599.

Right: The historic lighthouse at Cape Don on the Cobourg Peninsula overlooks the remote and pristine beaches for which this area is famous.

The rounded rocks that make up the unusual Devils Marbles formation are the eroded remains of a 1.5-billion-year-old granite intrusion.

Gurig National Park and Cobourg Marine Park

SIZE: Gurig: 226 484 ha;
      Cobourg: 223 667 ha
MAP: NT 2 C2

The Cobourg Peninsula protrudes out into the Arafura Sea. This small peninsula contains Gurig National Park and the surrounding Cobourg Marine Park.

The park is home to four main groups of Australian Aboriginals who now own and help manage the area.

During the 1500s, Macassans came from the north—collecting trepang, fishing and looking for pearls. In 1838 the British founded the Victoria Settlement in the seemingly idyllic setting of Port Essington, but it was abandoned little more than a decade later in 1849.

Gurig's main attractions are its remoteness, its pristine white sandy beaches and the superb fishing from the nearby coral reefs and offshore islands. The old Victoria Settlement, with its eerie crumbling ruins, is well worth a visit.

The park is 570 km by road from Darwin. Currently only 15 vehicles at any one time are allowed, and an access permit from the Parks Permits Officer is required, phone (08) 8999 4555. It is advisable to book well in advance.

Camping is allowed at Smith Point. Accommodation is also available in well set-up beach huts. The Gurig Store at Black Point, phone (08) 8979 0263, can organise the accommodation, as well as supplying fuel and limited supplies. You can phone the Black Point Ranger Station on (08) 8979 0244.

Nitmiluk (Katherine Gorge) National Park

SIZE: 292 099 ha
MAP: NT 2 C8

Katherine Gorge, with its high cliffs of grey and orange sandstone towering over deep waterholes and lush pockets of rainforest, is one of the Territory's major natural attractions.

Now set within Nitmiluk National Park, much of the area included within the park is the traditional home of the

The distinctive red, rocky escarpment in Watarrka (Kings Canyon) National Park looks all the more spectacular against the stark white trunk of this eucalyptus tree.

Jawoyn people who help manage the park. The park has two main sections: the Katherine Gorge section in the south, and the Edith Falls section in the northwest. Both parts have sealed road access available all year round.

Wildlife found in the park includes kingfishers, butcherbirds and bowerbirds, wallabies, bandicoots and freshwater crocodiles.

Tour boat cruises operate from a base near the entrance to the majestic Katherine Gorge, where canoes are also available for hire. Barramundi fishing is a popular pastime on the river as well.

Bushwalking is another favourite activity, with both short and long walks available. Another way to see the gorge is by helicopter, which offers an exhilarating ride through the gorge system.

To contact rangers at Katherine Gorge, phone (08) 8972 1886, or at Edith Falls, phone (08) 8975 4852.

Watarrka (Kings Canyon) National Park

SIZE: 105 717 ha
MAP: NT 8 F6

Set in the George Gill Range and forming part of the Watarrka National Park, the geological masterpiece known as Kings Canyon has evolved over millions of years. The moist crevices of the canyon act as a refuge for many different animals as well as more than 600 plant species, of which over 60 are rare or relicts from a bygone era.

The national park was declared in 1983 and the land was handed back to the local Luritja people who are now involved in its management.

There are some magnificent walks in the area including the Kings Creek Walk and the longer Kings Canyon Walk, both of which should not be missed.

The shortest route to the national park from Alice Springs is along the Stuart and Ernest Giles Highways, while the Mereenie Loop Road via Hermannsburg is a slightly longer route of 327 km and will soon be sealed all the way. Access from Uluru is 279 km on a sealed road.

Kings Canyon Resort (08 8956 7422), located 7 km from the canyon and within the national park, has hotel rooms, serviced caravan sites and grassed camping grounds. You can phone the ranger on (08) 8956 7488.

Canoeing is a popular adventure activity and a great way to get close to the huge sandstone cliffs of Katherine Gorge in Nitmiluk National Park.

Popular Parks at a Glance

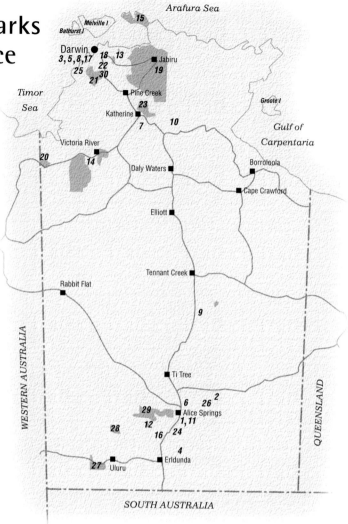

	Camping	Caravan Access	Disabled Access	4WD Access	Picnic Areas	Toilets	Walking Tracks	Kiosk	Information
1 Alice Springs DP			●		●	●	●	●	●
2 Arltunga HR			●		●	●	●		●
3 Casuarina CR			●		●	●	●		
4 Chambers Pillar HR	●			●	●	●	●		
5 Charles Darwin NP			●		●	●	●		
6 Corroboree Rock CR					●	●	●		
7 Cutta Cutta Caves NP					●	●	●		●
8 Darwin Botanic Gardens			●		●	●	●		●
9 Devils Marbles CR	●	●			●	●			
10 Elsey NP	●	●		●	●	●			
11 Emily and Jessie Gaps NP					●	●	●		
12 Finke Gorge NP	●			●	●	●	●		
13 Fogg Dam CR				●			●		●
14 Gregory NP	●	●		●	●	●	●		
15 Gurig NP & Cobourg MP	●			●	●	●	●	●	●
16 Henbury Meteorite Craters CR	●			●	●	●	●		
17 Holmes Jungle NP				●			●		
18 Howard Springs NP				●	●	●	●	●	●
19 Kakadu NP	●	●	●	●	●	●	●	●	●
20 Keep River NP	●	●		●	●	●	●		●
21 Litchfield NP	●			●	●	●	●	●	●
22 Manton Dam RA				●			●		
23 Nitmiluk NP	●	●		●	●	●	●	●	●
24 Rainbow Valley CR	●			●		●			
25 Territory Wildlife Park			●		●	●	●	●	●
26 Trephina Gorge Nature Park	●	●		●	●	●	●		●
27 Uluru–Kata Tjuta NP			●		●	●	●	●	●
28 Watarrka (Kings Canyon) NP	●			●	●	●	●		●
29 West Macdonnell NP	●	●	●	●	●	●	●	●	●
30 Window on the Wetlands VC			●		●	●			●

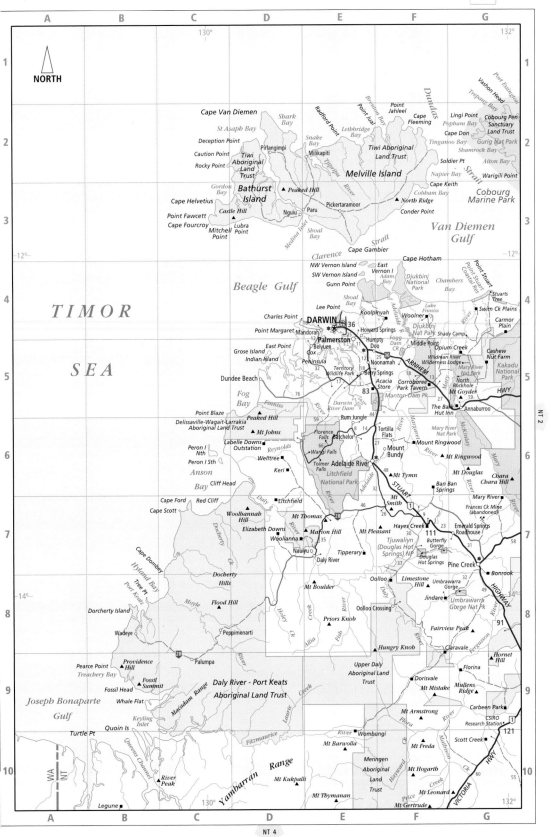

0   20   40   60   80
kilometres

NORTH

Map 2

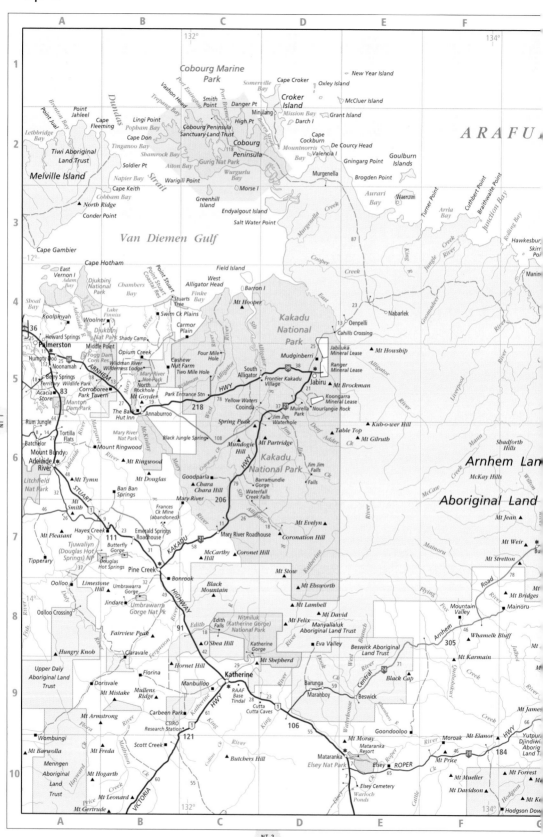

0 20 40 60 80
kilometres

NORTH

136°
138°

1

Rimbija I
Cape Wessel

Wessel
Islands

Marchinbar Island

2

Cumberland Strait

Stevens Island
Guluwuru Island

Nth West
Crocodile Island

Drysdale Island
Raragala Island
Truant Island

Brown Strait

Cunningham
Islands
The English Companys Islands

3

Mooroongga
Island
Elcho Island
Alger I
Bromby Islands

Malay Road

Stewart
Galiwinku
Point Napier
Inglis
Island
Cape Wilberforce

Rabuma I
Howard
Island
Flinders Pt
Boney Point
Bremer Island

−12°

Castlereagh
Bay
Buckingham
Bay
Probable I
Melville
Bay
Nhulunbuy

Ramingining
Mallison
Island
Yirrkala

4

Woolen
Arnhem
Bay
Gove
Cape Arnhem

Arafura
Swamp
Gapuwiyak
Peninsula

Goyder
River
Port Bradshaw

Gulbuwangay
Road

HEM LAND
416
Arnhem
Frederick
Hills
191
Mt Alexander
Wanyanmera Point

5

Central
109
MITCHELL RANGE
Maidjunga
Camburinga Village
Point Alexander

Caledon Bay

Goyder
Durabudboi
Mt Caledon
Cape Grey

Trial Bay
Bald Point

6

River
Koolatong
River
Myaoola Bay
Wardarlea Bay
Point Arrowsmith

Parsons
Range
Mt Fleming
Jalma
Bay
Grindall Bay
Cape Shield

Mt
Ramsay
Isle Woodah
Nicol Island

7

Range
Walker
Mt Ranken
River
Morgan I
Blue Mud
Bay
Burney I
Bartalumba
Bay
North Point
Island

Zamia Ck
Cape Barrow
Chasm I
Port Langdon
North East Isles
Hawk Island

Galdu
Batb
Winchelsea
Island
Thompson Bay
Bacchus Hill

Milyakburra
Warwick Channel

Bickerton
Island
Alyangula
Umbakumba

Leane
Groote
Angurugu
Bluff Hill

Rose
River
Snowden Peak
Arnhem Land
Aboriginal
Land Trust
Eylandt
Ilyungmadja Point
Dalumbu Bay

−14°

8

Phelp
River
Tasman Point
Sandy Hill
Ungwariba Point

erang Hill
157
Rantyirrity
Point
South Point
Numbulwar
Cape Beatrice

Marangala Bay
Marangala Point

Nyinpinti Point
Inamalamandja Point

Range
Edward Island

9

Warrakunta Point

GULF OF

St Vidgeon
Port Roper
Limmen
Bight
18
Roper
44
Port Roper
Maria Island

River
Marra Aboriginal
Land Trust
CARPENTARIA

10

Towns
107

136°
138°

NT

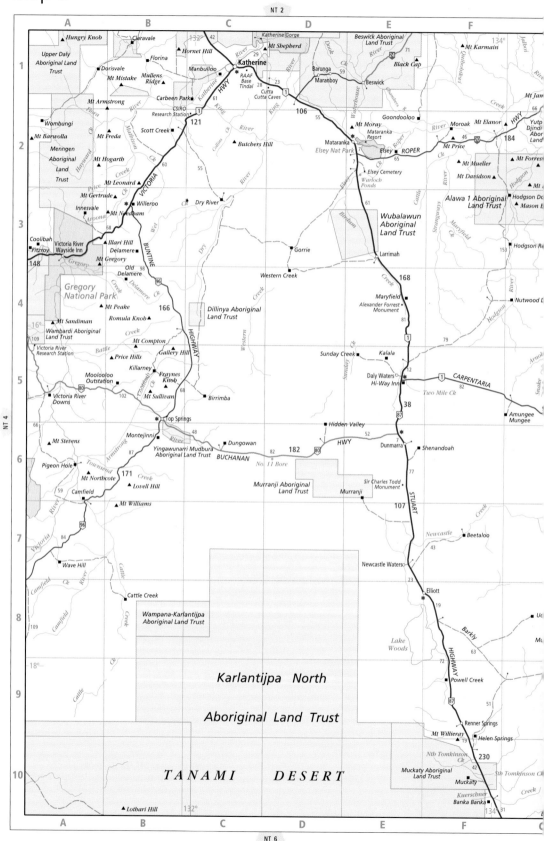

0   20   40   60   80
kilometres

NORTH

NT

J   K   L   M   N   P

136°   138°

1
2
3
4
5
6
7
8
9
10

-16°

-18°

GULF   OF

CARPENTARIA

Sir Edward
Pellew Group

Somerang
Hill
157
Numbulwar
Nyinpinti Point
Edward Island
Warrakunta Point
St Vidgeon
18
Roper
44
Port Roper
Limmen
Bight
Maria Island
Marra Aboriginal
Land Trust
Towns
107
River
Nathan R.
River
Rosie
The Four Archers
Nathan River
Bing
Bong
Creek
West
Island
Wurralibi Aboriginal
Land Trust
Watson I
North Island
Cape Vanderlin
Vanderlin
Island
Sth West
Island
Centre I
Wurralibi Aboriginal
Land Trust
Bing Bong
34
Batten Point
Port
McArthur
King Ash
Bay
McArthur
Jandanku
Aboriginal
Land Trust
103
Batten
Tirwallah Range
Borroloola
21
20
Mt Featbertop
43
The Fletcher
McArthur R.
Manangoora
Narwinbi
Aboriginal Land Trust
Tawallah
51
Greenbank
Bauhinia Downs
Billengarrah
75
26
Seven Emu
River
Calvert
Creek
River
Broadmere
Ck
45
McArthur
River Mine
110
Eight Mile Waterhole
255
Foelsche
River
Robinson
River
Kanggoo River
Sandy
Creek
Running
Creek
Gold
OT Downs
58
Cape Crawford
14
McArthur River
Cape Crawford
Balbirini
37
McArthur River
Spring Creek
Bukalara   Range
55
Robinson River
Garawa Aboriginal
Land Trust
Creek
Pungalina
48
Calvert
Creek
TABLELANDS
Mambaliya Rrumburriya
Wuyaliya Aboriginal
Land Trust
Mallapunyah
River
Creek
Surprise
Bluey
Little
Calvert
R.
Redbank
Mine
57
30
Calvert Hills
Wollogorang
109
Kiana
Puzzle
Creek
Road
93
HWY
Settlement
Creek
River
Branco
China   Wall
Waanyi-Garawa
Aboriginal Land Trust
Walhallow
45
Creek
Nicholson
Route
73
Anthony
Lagoon
19
Cresswell
Downs
134
16
Calvert
Benmara
Creek
Benmara
Ck
Baubinia
Ck
River
Nicholson
Buddycurrawa
Creek
Eva Downs
Creek
Creswell
TABLELANDS
377
75
Creek
Fish
Hole
Ck
Cleanskin
Ck
Sth Nicholson
Tarrabool
Lake
Corella
Lake
Brunette Downs
HWY
Creek
Mittebah
Ck
Bluff   Range
Corella
101
Lake
Sylvester
Brunette
77
103
Connells Lagoon
Conservation
Reserve
Carrara   Range
Little   Range
Lawn
Hill   Ck
136°
Mittebah
Carrara
Creek
138°

Map 4

0 20 40 60 80
kilometres

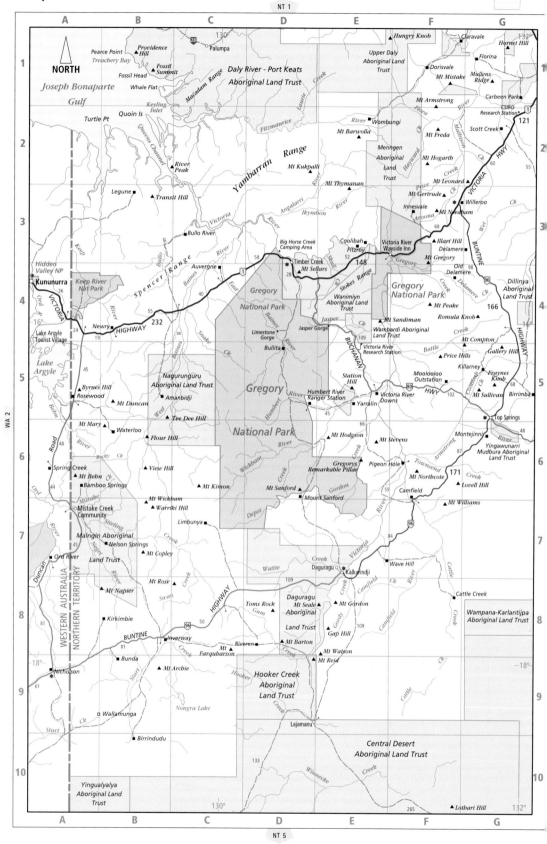

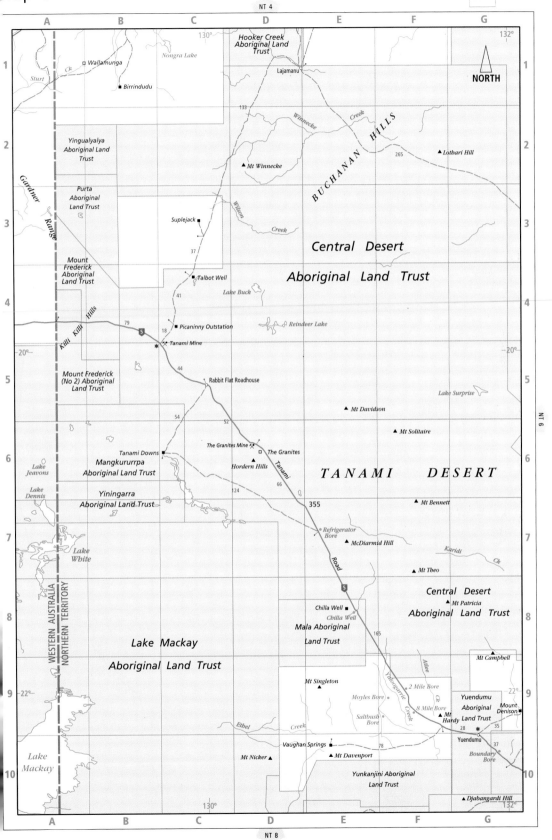

Map 6

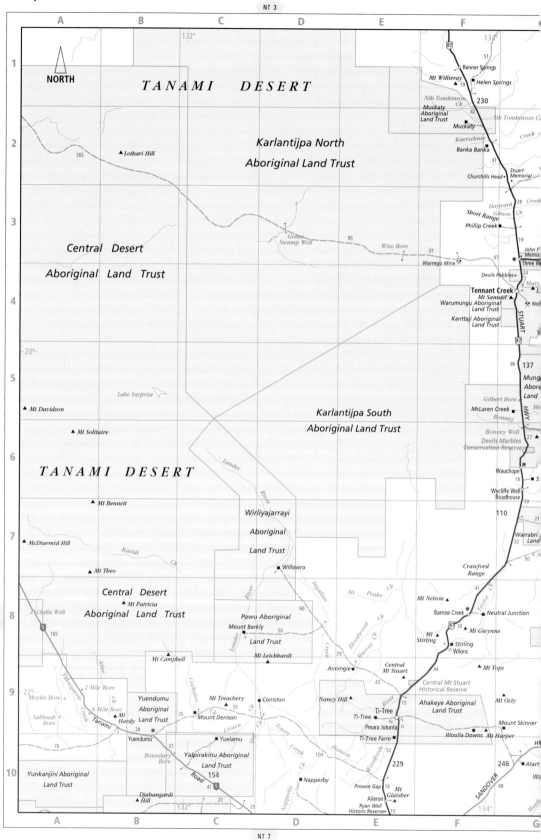

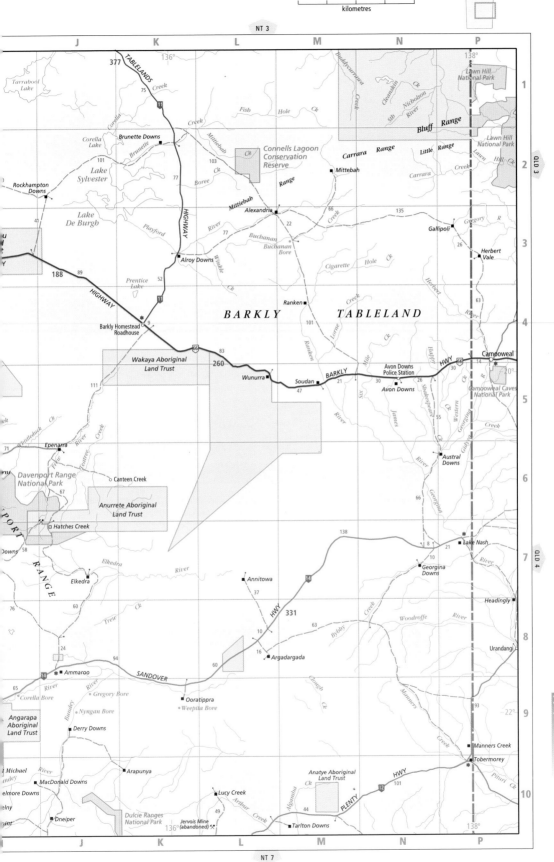

0   20   40   60   80
kilometres

1

OLD 3

2

3

4

5

6

OLD 4

7

8

9

NT

10

377 TABLELANDS
75
Tarrabool Lake
Corella
Corella Lake
Brunette Downs
Brunette
101
Lake Sylvester
Rockhampton Downs
Lake De Burgh
41
Playford
188   89
HIGHWAY
Prentice Lake
52
Barkly Homestead Roadhouse
9
Wakaya Aboriginal Land Trust
260
83
Wunurra
111
Epenarra
71
Davenport Range National Park
67
Canteen Creek
Anurrete Aboriginal Land Trust
Hatches Creek
Downs 58
Elkedra River
Elkedra
60
76
24
94
Ammaroo
65
Corella Bore
River
Gregory Bore
Nyngan Bore
Angarapa Aboriginal Land Trust
Derry Downs
Michael
MacDonald Downs
elmore Downs
elny
Dneiper
Dulcie Ranges National Park
136°

Creek
136°
Fish   Hole   Ck
Connells Lagoon Conservation Reserve
103
Mittiebah
77
Boree   Ck
Range
Mittiebah
Alexandria
22
River
77
Buchanan
Buchanan Bore
Alroy Downs
89
Ranken
101
BARKLY   TABLELAND
Soudan
47
21
River
138
331
Annitowa
37
HWY
10
16   Argadargada
60
SANDOVER
Ooratippra
Weepita Bore
Arapunya
Lucy Creek
49
Jervois Mine (abandoned)
136°

Buddyewurraga Creek
Cleanskin
Nicholson River
Sth
Lawn Hill National Park
Bluff   Range
Carrara   Range
Little   Range
Mittebah
Carrara
Cigarette   Hole   Ck
Lorne   Creek
Ranken
Ck
Mile   Ck
James   River
River
66
Georgina
Lake Nash
10   21
8
Georgina Downs
Woodroffe   River
Bybby
Creek
Clough   Ck
Manners
Anatye Aboriginal Land Trust
Algamba   Ck
PLENTY   HWY
Arthur   Creek
44
Tarlton Downs

138°
Lawn Hill National Park
135
Gregory   R
Gallipoli
26
Herbert Vale
63
Herbert   River
Camooweal
HWY   66
14
30
Avon Downs Police Station
30   26
Avon Downs
Camooweal Caves National Park
Austral Downs
Western   Ck
Shakespeare   Ck
55
Georgina
66
River
Gidyea   Ck
Headingly
Urandangi
93
Manners Creek
Tobermorey
101
Piluri   Ck

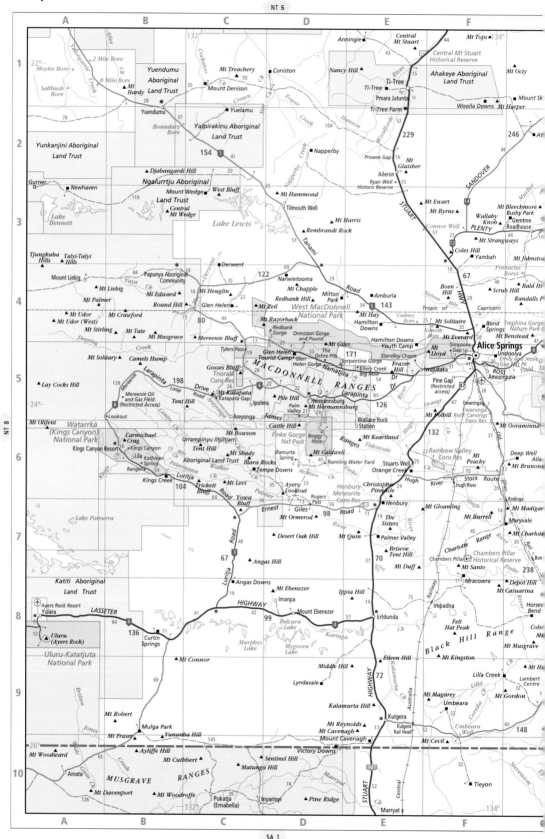

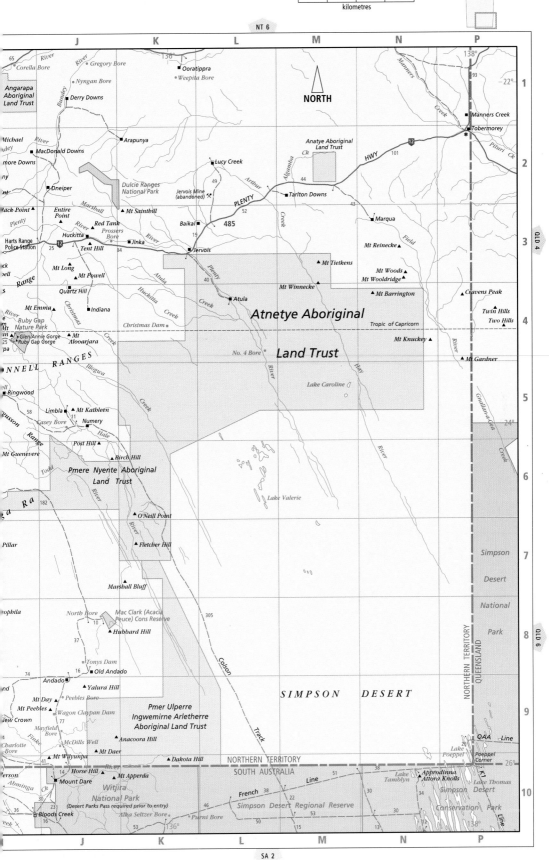

Map 8

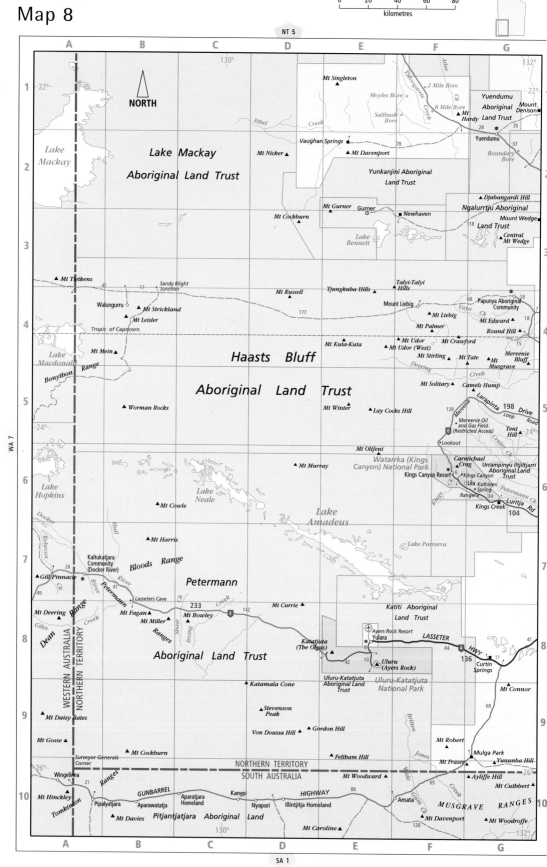

0 20 40 60 80
kilometres

NORTH

Index and Gazetteer

Text entries for National Parks are shown in **bold**. Map references appear in the form of map title and grid reference, eg. WA 6 F2.

Acknowledgements

The Publisher believes that permission for use of all images has been obtained from the copyright owners, however, if any errors or omissions have occurred Global Book Publishing would be pleased to hear from copyright owners.

pp. 8–9, centre top: Image courtesy of Tourism Queensland Image Library
p. 17, right: Image courtesy of Tourism Queensland Image Library
pp. 18–19, bottom: Image courtesy of P&O Australian Resorts

p. 19, top: Image courtesy of Tourism Queensland Image Library
p. 23, top: Image courtesy of Tourism Queensland Image Library
p. 25: Image courtesy of Tourism Queensland Image Library
pp. 30–31: Image courtesy of Tourism Queensland Image Library
p. 32: Image courtesy of Tourism Queensland Image Library
p. 34, bottom: Image courtesy of Tourism Queensland Image Library
p. 37, centre: Image courtesy of Tourism Queensland Image Library
p. 38, top: Image courtesy of Tourism Queensland Image Library
p. 39, bottom: Image courtesy of Tourism Queensland

p. 51: Table information reproduced with permission of Queensland EPA
p. 55, bottom left: Image courtesy of Tourism New South Wales
p. 60, top: Image courtesy of Tourism New South Wales
p. 74, bottom: Image courtesy of John Hancock
p. 76, top: Image courtesy of Tourism New South Wales
p. 78: Image courtesy of Tourism New South Wales
p. 79, bottom: Image courtesy of Tourism New South Wales
p. 100, top: Image courtesy of Tourism Victoria
p. 103, centre: Image courtesy of Tourism Victoria

p. 106, top right: Image courtesy of Tourism Victoria
p. 108: Image courtesy of Tourism Victoria
p. 144, bottom left: Image courtesy of P&O Australian Resorts
p. 146, bottom left: Image courtesy of P&O Australian Resorts
p. 234, top: Image courtesy of Northern Territory Tourist Commission
p. 238, bottom: Image courtesy of Northern Territory Tourist Commission
p. 243, bottom: Image courtesy of Northern Territory Tourist Commission.